Native Americans
in Comic Books

Native Americans in Comic Books

A Critical Study

MICHAEL A. SHEYAHSHE

McFarland & Company, Inc., Publishers

Jefferson, North Carolina, and London

LIBRARY OF CONGRESS CATALOGUING-IN-PUBLICATION DATA

Sheyahshe, Michael A., 1975–
Native Americans in comic books : a critical study / Michael A. Sheyahshe.
p.   cm.
Includes bibliographical references and index.

ISBN 978-0-7864-3565-4
illustrated case binding : 50# alkaline paper ∞

1. Indians of North America — Humor.   2. Indians of North
America — Caricatures and cartoons.   3. Indians in popular culture.
4. Indians in mass media.   I. Title.
E99.H77S54   2008   305.897 — dc22   2008013201

British Library cataloguing data are available

Cover illustration ©2008 Pictures Now

Manufactured in the United States of America

*McFarland & Company, Inc., Publishers
Box 611, Jefferson, North Carolina 28640
www.mcfarlandpub.com*

For Mary, Hannah, and Jack —
without you, none of my work
would be possible or even worthwhile.
I love you.

Table of Contents

Preface

You have shown me the path which I must walk. Neither am I white man nor red. I am a man — a brother and protector to all peoples. — *Red Wolf,* Marvel Comics

Despite the fact that mainstream society sometimes views comic books as a juvenile pastime, I will be the first to admit that comics are a (not-so-secret) guilty pleasure of mine. Comic books — and their colorful characters — have delighted me for too many years to count. The stories, and the idea of the mythic hero, continue to hold a special meaning for me.

My identification with the mythic heroism of the comic book genre developed long before my ability to read. Popular culture being what it is, I was lucky enough to be bombarded with the mythic heroes of comic books in several media forms before ever thumbing through any comic pages. In the mid to late 1970s, a heroic renaissance of sorts occurred on television. At least for me, it did.

Many of my earliest memories consist of images of watching the Incredible Hulk transform before my eyes. I remember marveling at how beautiful and strong Wonder Woman seemed. Monochromatic images of both the Lone Ranger and Tonto galloped through my mind from those thrilling days of yesteryear. Superman protected Metropolis in the television serial from the 1940s, and Ultra-Man battled monsters larger than Mount Fuji — all for my enjoyment. Television served well the comic book heroes that I loved so much.

Given my relative isolation as a youth, television in many ways served as a surrogate medium to comic books. I grew up on a farm that was far removed from the urban convenience of a local comic book shop. Yet, thanks to the few infrequent trips "into town" a friend and I made, a genuine comic book collection blossomed betwixt us two. Over the years, we endlessly passed these rich spoils back and forth: comics, conversations, ideas, sketches, and jokes.

This rustic isolation carried over into my cultural identity. I am a member of the Caddo Nation (*Hasinai* in our own tongue), an Indigenous culture in Oklahoma. Because I had few other Indigenous people in my life, I relished those heroes that shared my ethnic identity. Being far removed from urban life made me hold on to whatever I could identify with, especially a Native American super hero found in a comic book or even on television. Growing up, knowledge of being Indigenous made seeing a Native hero that much more exciting for me. I was always rooting for the "red" hero as a kid and was always thrilled and anxious to see a hero with whom I could culturally identify.

The realization that there are far too few of these heroes saddens me more now than it might have back then. Ignorance might not have been bliss, but it was a calming salve that kept me looking for the next identifiable Native hero.

From the world of Marvel Comics, *X-Force*'s Warpath (aka, James Proudstar) seemed larger than life. To me, Dani Moonstar seemed to exemplify the strength and beauty inherent in Native women. All the comic book evidence indicated to my little kid self that the Indigenous hero served as an integral part in saving the day. Take the most easily recognizable Indigenous hero, Tonto, for example. I knew that the Lone Ranger would have never lived through so many adventures had Tonto not saved him at the last possible second so many times. These are the heroes of color that sparked the imagination of my young Indigenous mind.

As an adult I've come to understand that there is more to comic book color than just a choice in spandex. While I may have realized this subconsciously as an adolescent, it was not until later in life that many of the major themes and ideals that serve as the foundations of comic book stories became more lucid to me.

Certain patterns started reoccurring to me as a comic book reader. The esteemed Indigenous heroes I held so dear seemed to more readily fall into certain categories. Some of these heroes had no real cultural ties to Indigenous people, but faked it with only a bit of war paint and buckskin. Others had biological ties, but they were ostracized for this (adding to the dramatic air, I suppose). It became evident that many of the powers and abilities my Native heroes possessed seemed to pale in comparison to other mainstream heroes. The clothing used to depict my heroes was predictable and sub-par compared with many other comic book heroes. Given all this, it took very little time to understand that the Native hero, along with his clothing, powers, and even culture, was treated differently.

In many ways, knowing these hidden and underlying themes makes reading comics even more enjoyable: being able to identify common cultural themes and types sometimes becomes like a game of "I Spy." I could even make a game out of which particular stereotypes an individual comic book character might embody — "I bet this one talks like Tonto"; "You think this one will have Pan-Indian clothing?"; or "Here it comes: now he's suddenly a mysterious Indian shaman!" Yet, becoming aware of cultural disparagements in comic books has the potential to drain the fun out of reading them. Even so, such examination is necessary for both Native American and non–Native comic book readers. What is the popular phrase, something like "we murder to dissect"?

In his chapter on Native American superheroes, Pewewardy asserts,

> America cannot truly understand the real issues of contemporary American Indian
> lifestyles and worldview without understanding the popular Indian images of the
> past, present, and future. Understanding the contemporary images and perceptions of
> American Indians in comic books is extremely important, not only for Indian people
> but also for the mainstream culture [198].

While his statement makes a case for the need for cultural examination of comic books, the question remains: what makes this particular statement true? Why would we need to know about comic books and how they represent Indigenous people?

Comic books can reveal more about popular society and culture than just the black-and-white idea of good versus evil. Each panel and page has the power to illustrate much more than the mere ideas and thoughts of heroes and villains. A comic book can inspire and teach. More importantly, comics can provide their audiences with a clearer view of ingrained societal and cultural attitudes. Each edition can illustrate action-packed snapshots of popular society, and in these snapshots, one can study a minute and pristine microcosmic universe. And as with our own universe, a comic book universe can at times be troubled by misrepresentation.

While many may maintain that such cultural misrepresentations are merely relics from the days of yesteryear or that stereotypes do not occur in modern times, evidence suggests otherwise. Reports of comic books misrepresenting Indigenous people made their way into the headlines in 1992. The author of an article in *Native Nevadan* reported that Marvel Comics distorted the view of Hopi people in their comic, *NFL Superpro* in the issue "The Kachinas Sing of Doom." The article described the comic's depiction of Hopi people in the clothing of their traditional enemies, the Navajo (Dine). The article further described the tribe's outrage by imagery where the supposedly troublesome "Kachina — a doll-like carved figure — is hit in the head and a mask and costume fall off, revealing a muscular white body" ("Marvel Comics Apologize to Hopi," *Native Nevadan* [Reno], April 30, 1992, 17).

I admit I have some personal interest vested in this research, as I am Indigenous. My ethnicity does not, however, make the research of comic books any less viable or less necessary. The fact that investigation of comic books can be called research, despite the belief among the general population for many years that they were for children only, speaks to how comic books have progressed into the respectable realms of criticism and critique formerly reserved for the upper echelons of academia and literature. Perhaps Horn states it best in *The World Encyclopedia of Comics*: "Now that they are no longer dismissed as grubby purveyors of mindless entertainment, the cartoonists and their employers must expect to be called into account on aesthetic and ethical grounds (just as novelists, book publishers, playwrights and filmmakers are)" (62).

Despite this cultural interest, I feel that this particular work — an examination of Native Americans and their representation in comic books — is singularly important, because it is the first of its kind. While there are numerous critiques and studies of comic books in general, including the specific genres within, there is a serious neglect in all these studies of an extensive and intensive examination about how Indigenous people are represented in this medium. Pewewardy, quoted above, offers a single and highly enlightening chapter on this subject, yet no other textual resource containing extensive research on the topic seems to exist. Numerous resources briefly mention Native Americans in comics, but none explore the subject with any great length or depth.

It is therefore the purpose of this book to distill, synthesize, and clarify this massive blur of information and find the truth that will serve as a reference for people seeking guidance about the representation — both good and bad — of Indigenous peoples in comics.

I use the term *Indigenous* for a particular reason. In the past, outsiders working in various media have provided many different names for Native Americans: Indian, savage, redskin, and so forth. Here, I shall stick to my own descriptive preference: Indigenous. When I use this term, it will be used mainly in reference to Native American people located in North America. It is not my intention to confuse the term's meaning or to overlook those Indigenous peoples from around the world, such as those in New Zealand, South America, or even Iceland. While these are Indigenous people in their own right, this work's focus will be on representations of Native North American peoples who may be described as Indigenous.

This work highlights the numerous ways that Indigenous people have been stereotyped in the pages of American comic books. I shall examine this topic both as a reader of comic books and as a member of an Indigenous community (Hasinai). I can do nothing else but see things from the particular point of view my life experience affords me, and this allows me to explain in explicit terms misrepresentation when it occurs.

This book is not only the first of its kind, but also it has become a wonderful personal journey for me. What began as a typical term paper in my college undergraduate years evolved to become more than just a brief treatment of the subject. The investigation of many fascinating comic book titles in search of some inner truth has led me to some vastly rewarding personal treasures.

During my work on this book I have been honored to correspond with some of the very artists who create comic books with Native American characters. *Scout* creator and artist and *Turok* writer Tim Truman has proven to be a friendly and inexhaustible source of information about not only all things comic book-related, but also environmental issues. He has given me some insight into video game creation as well. His approachable manner encouraged me to contact others in the business.

Albert Schwartz recalled his experience working on comic books, such as the original *Tomahawk*, in the 1940s. Schwartz's explanation of how he was assigned to comics like *Tomahawk* allows for much speculation on how the lax attitude affected cultural sensitivity in that time. The writer also discusses his view on minorities in comic books, especially during his time writing in the 1940s.

Rachel Pollack was good enough to share her thoughts on the newer adaptation of *Tomahawk* from Vertigo comics. Pollack also related her ability to gather information for her comic book, giving readers a preview into the Wampanoag worldview — an Indigenous culture displayed in *Tomahawk*. Pollack also took time to compare and contrast the spiritual ideas found in her book.

Steve Englehart, who seems to have worked on everything imaginable in the comic book world (and beyond!) divulged the "inside track" about the creation of his character Coyote for Epic. Englehart talked about his concern not only to provide a good story but also to conduct research on his own so as to present an accurate account of Native American mythology. He also discussed the importance of comic book writers stepping outside of their own worlds and transcending their own cultural limitations.

My thanks to Terry LaBan, who took time out of his busy schedule to share intimate secrets of how he developed the innovative *Muktuk* character. LaBan also offered frank commentary about his experience in the comic book industry and he expressed his views on Native American character in general.

Legend Mike Grell talked in depth about the humanity behind his character in the *Shaman's Tears* series from Image Comics. Grell tells all, allowing a unique glimpse into his reasons for creating a multiethnic hero. He also gave an educational look at how the comic book industry changes original concepts to make them more commercially viable.

John Ostrander shared some insight about the revival of the Red Wolf character during his work on the *Blaze of Glory* series from Marvel. Ostrander takes us through the natural emotional evolution of Red Wolf, continuing from where the original character left off in the 1970s. He also provided a candid look at the idea of artistic control between writer and artist and how the results are interesting at best.

Jon Proudstar traced a journey to a place where characters like the ones found in his *Tribal Force* can exist. Besides providing insight into his own comic book, Proudstar offers parallels of past Native American outlooks and those of modern Americans, especially in light of recent terrorist events. Proudstar also directly addresses the need of Indigenous youth for Native American heroes. This need for something to connect with is a position I greatly identify with.

Rob Schmidt, though he does not share the same cultural identity as the main characters in his *Peace Party* comic book, provided vast information about Native American representation in all popular media. His website and subsequent blog are great places to begin researching information on Indigenous comic characters.

After hearing about the sheer "awesomeness" (is that really a word?) of *Kabuki* for years, and after reading the *Echo — Vision Quest* graphic novel, it was a supreme honor to communicate with artist David Mack about his work with the Native American female character. His work seems earnest in its attempts at human accuracy, honest with emotional subjects, and down to earth in its communication. In addition to the artistry and craftsmanship evident in the *Vision Quest* graphic novel, Mack himself proved to be an invaluable resource to understanding the creative process behind characters like Echo.

Like Jon Proudstar (creator of *Tribal Force*), Jay Odjick is an Indigenous creative talent working to make his dream a reality. He is the creator of *The Raven*, a smaller, independent comic book featuring a Native American main character. Odjick works hard to avoid many of the stereotypes that will be explored in this book. In a commercially based business like the comic book industry, this seems impossible at times. However, Odjick shares his experiences and successes at making this a reality. He represents what this popular medium needs more of: Indigenous people creating Indigenous characters.

Jeff Mariotte is a prolific author and all around good guy. His insight into the *Gen13* character Sarah Rainmaker offers frank commentary about her and her relation to other characters on the *Gen13* team. Mariotte wrote many of the *Gen13* graphic novels and also has many other books under his belt.

Authors Jacquelyn Kilpatrick and Bradford W. Wright provided additional insight not only into Indigenous comic book characters but also into the entire creative process. I feel enriched by simply meeting these individuals and my research directly benefited from their input.

While reading comic books with Indigenous characters can be simultaneously frustrating and exciting, it was exhilarating to be afforded the opportunity to discuss the themes, ideas, and aesthetics with some of the creators themselves. Had I not taken on this study, I might never have had such a wonderful opportunity to pick the brains of some fascinating comic book artists and creators.

The reader may notice that I have yet to mention research done on comic strips, the pioneering predecessor to comic books. While this is true, I feel there is a distinct difference between comic books and comic strips. One can look to several authorities to understand these subtle differences, but this discourse focuses on comic books and comic strips are a different format entirely. While I must briefly touch on this topic to give a historical examination of comic books, fully looking at representation of Indigenous people in comic strips is a subject for a different book.

This is not an examination of every Native American character ever found in comic books. Instead, the focus centers on identifying particular stereotypes, generalizations, and misrepresentations that dominate the specific genre of comic books. In many cases, this focus centers primarily on the Indigenous main character in a comic, while in other instances the Indigenous character is secondary.

This book also deals with the misrepresentations found predominantly in American comic books and serves to illuminate a topic in the literature of comic books that seems poorly documented until now. The text provides both a catalog of various titles starring Indigenous people and an evaluation of them for positive or negative representation. Questions that are addressed include those posed by Raymond William Stedman in his *Shadows of the Indian: Stereotypes in American Culture*:

> Is the descriptive language debasing towards Native American culture? Do the Indigenous people talk like Tonto? Do they appear to be one pan-Indian tribe? Are there attempts at humor that stem from the notion of stupid or drunk Indians? Are they portrayed solely as an historical or extinct people? Are Indigenous people portrayed as either noble or savage? Is the overall attitude condescending towards Native Americans? Is there a sense of humanity within the Indigenous characters? [240–251].

This investigation does not gauge whether comic books are good or bad, generally speaking. Instead, it aims to create a specific awareness of how the medium portrays Indigenous people and their respective cultures and heritages.

This work involves more than just a critical survey. It serves as a tool and a source of information to assist Indigenous people in evaluating their own creative process to uncover misrepresentation and so avoid major pitfalls into which so many artists and writers seem to fall. In short, this review may assist those Indigenous individuals who are interested in creating stories and comic books with Native American imagery. Put simply, as Indigenous people, we must tell our own stories and begin to represent ourselves more truthfully, especially in popular media such as comic books. It is the aim of this analysis to arm us with the knowledge to accomplish this goal. Despite all this studious exploration, I still enjoy comics as much as I did as a boy — possibly even more so now. These days, I am able to run down to the local comic book shop much more easily than when I was a boy on the farm. I can even opt to increase my collection of comic books with Indigenous characters by purchasing them on an online auction — a luxury that did not exist for me in childhood. No matter how I decide to obtain my comics, I continue to collect and read them as an adult. It is my hope that this work might bring about some small change in the way Native Americans are portrayed. Maybe some future Native American child (maybe on some distant future farm) will be able to look up to Native heroes of a higher caliber and cultivate a sense of pride about his or her own ethnicity.

Introduction

As White America progressed technologically and economically, and as the idea of romanticizing western expansion became more popular, stories reflecting the noble savage theme became extremely popular. The very first dime-store novel contains elements of cultural misrepresentation. True to their James Fenimore Cooper legacy, these "penny dreadfuls" more often than not assigned Indigenous people the role of the unthinking barbarian who impeded progress and threatened the American way of life. Dime-store novels impressed upon young readers how important white heroes, such as Buffalo Bill Cody, were in maintaining the status quo by subduing the bloodthirsty Indians.

With the idea of young readership in mind, a collection of newspaper comic strips became the first comic books. "Comic books first emerged as a distinct entertainment medium in the 1930s.... Although they are often grouped together with comic strips, the two mediums are the not the same. The key difference lies in marketing" [Wright *xv*]. Comic strips come with the purchase of a newspaper; comic books are an all-inclusive package. Of course, the Western was one of the first pioneers within this new medium. With the Western came all the same stereotypes about Native Americans that had previously pervaded the dime-store novel. For the most part, Indigenous people became plot devices to move the story along and make the central character (most always a white man) more heroic.

Of course, as comic books progressed so did the Native American character within — but only marginally. Indigenous characters evolved slowly from the despised faceless nemesis of the hero to the simple-minded helper. Some Native characters even became popular enough to warrant their own comic book title, but always under the guise of their dutiful subservience to the white man.

It was not until several decades later that a Native American character would serve as the central protagonist of a comic book, *sans* paternal white hero. Yet, even with these cultural advances, Indigenous characters were not without their stereotypic flaws. Indispensable to picturesque or pastoral illustrations of historical times, Indigenous characters nevertheless continued to be flat, two-dimensional characters who were mere caricatures of real Native people.

It would be nice to say that all this is now behind us; that comic books of today are as substantially different from their predecessors as "New" Coke is from "Original" Coke.

Bradford W. Wright, author of *Comic Book Nation*, offers a further insight into the notion of the Native American comic book character:

> I think it's safe to say that up until the 1960s, the primary function of non-white peoples in comic books was to play stereotypical, formulaic roles. They usually fell into one of three categories:
>
> (1) The racial threat: They represented something alien and hostile to white, and thus civilized culture.
>
> Non-whites of this type were portrayed as menacing and frightening, a threat to the white race. This type was especially prevalent in jungle-adventure comics in the case of blacks and Western comics in the case of Native Americans.
>
> (2) The childlike dupe: This type was more benign than the racial threat caricature, but could still be dangerous, because they were so easily susceptible to manipulation by evil-doers or by enemy agents. Thus, the role of the white hero was to set them straight by exposing the false nature of their supposed leaders or "gods." This is more in line with the "White Man's Burden" theme running through popular culture. This type of story was especially prolific during World War II and the early years of the Cold War, as Africans found themselves duped by Nazi and Communist agents.
>
> I didn't find as many instances of Native Americans falling into this category, but I did come across some during World War II where Native Americans were duped by Japanese agents. I discuss a few of these examples in [*Comic Book Nation*].
>
> (3) The sidekick: This is a pretty familiar stereotype. Well-meaning, if still degrading, this type found non-white characters playing junior partners to dominant white heroes. Although I can't recall any specific examples of this where Native Americans are concerned, there were a number of characters modeled after the Lone Ranger's Tonto. At least these characters were portrayed positively as likeable and heroic, they were still never portrayed as more than mascots or subordinate partners.
>
> Sometimes superheroes took on a non-white sidekick as well, such as the Green Lantern and his Eskimo friend "Pieface" (late 1950s–early 1960s) [Wright interview].

The list of stereotypes goes even beyond Wright's list. Sadly, this trope of Native people carries over into modern times. Most of today's comic books repeat the sins of their literary ancestors, particularly in representing Indigenous people in only one or two generic fashions. While modern Native heroes may not have to share the spotlight with anyone, they still fall into a few specific stereotypes that serve only to generalize Indigenous people. While the majority of comic books offer this slanted view, happily not all comic books are guilty of stereotyping Native characters.

What are these stereotypes, disparagements, and misrepresentations? Specifically, how have people such as Columbus, Cooper, and authors of dime-store novels altered the way in which audiences perceive Indigenous people in popular media? How have Native American comic book characters progressed through the ages from generic enemy to impotent sidekick to central hero? What are some specific generalizations that are made about modern Indigenous heroes? Most importantly, why should we care about any of this stuff? What does the portrayal of Native Americans have to do with the average comic book reader? What do these negative portrayals say about the general public's attitude toward Indigenous people? Lastly, what does all this mean to those Native Americans who read comic books and, perhaps, find some intrinsic role models in these Indigenous characters?

As a member of this latter group, a Native American comic book reader who identified with the notion of mythic hero at an early age, specifically that of the Indigenous hero, I attempt to bridge the gap between the medium and the culture it portrays. Given this cultural affinity, I distinguish the real from the unreal — the falsely portrayed comic book Indian from the factual, modern Native American. Also from this vantage point, I am able to point out the place we Native people seek to attain in popular media: a position in which we tell our own stories, or in which we are at least illustrated in more humanistic terms and not just as caricatures of the past.

It is not my intent to investigate every comic book that even *mentions* the word Indian, as such an undertaking would itself constitute the never-ending story and would exhaust all my resources. Rather, my discussion covers those comics that serve as examples to the larger ideological representation. I discuss comics based on their popularity and on the effect that they may have on the plethora of *other* Indigenous comic book characters, and I focus directly on those titles and characters that provide insight into how we are represented in comic books.

In any medium, it becomes important that we as Indigenous people tell our own stories and offer our particular worldview. My discussion serves as just that: I relate to the reader what I see in comic books as a Native reader, and I offer insight into a Native worldview in this discussion of cultural misrepresentation in American comic books. It is my hope that this analysis serves not only that purpose but also offers a blueprint for future comic books to rid themselves of the shackles of misrepresentation. Until that time, when there are no more (not-so) "funny books" that misrepresent us, I suppose there will be just that many more comic books for me to read, evaluate, critique, and write about.

I am investigating not only comic books and Native American characters found within them, but also the understated meaning of the relationship of these two elements to each other. To understand their content, the collective meanings within a particular era they represent must be understood as well.

Many texts offer general information about comic books. In particular, these texts serve to describe the importance of the genre to understanding America as a whole. Thus, we must turn to a survey of the actual comic books themselves.

Besides obtaining information directly from the source (comics themselves), we can gain even more insight from interviews with the creators of these comic books. It is interesting to see not only what views the authors have about their character but also how much the characters change from inception to publication in order to meet commercial success.

This multitextural examination is not surprising to those studying Indigenous people in various forms of media. Stedman's *Shadows of the Indian* (which provides an excellent set of criteria to use when evaluating common stereotypes) extrapolates from many sources, including theatrical plays and romance novels to examine Native stereotypes. Similarly, Kilpatrick's *Celluloid Indians* finds source material in James Fenimore Cooper's work as well as Sherman Alexie's *Lone Ranger and Tonto Fistfight in Heaven*. Thus, when examining Indigenous representation in this medium, that is, in comic books, we must be flexible in our sources.

Most importantly, I am a member of the Caddo Nation, which allows me to provide a sense of how a Native American might view such portrayals. Yet it would be false to say that this research represents the viewpoint of *all* Native American people, as this is not the case. The following information and discussion encompasses the data gathered from published discourses, comic books and their creators, and my analysis (as an Indigenous reader) of the treatment of Native American characters in comic books. While I can attempt to give a serious and unbiased opinion from a Native American standpoint, in the end, the statements made are my take on the issue and mine alone. I do not speak for all Native people on this issue, nor would I want to do so.

CHAPTER ONE

The Mohican Syndrome and Super "Wannabes": Ain't Nothin' Like the Real Thing

*The deep, primitive woods of the New American — savage, brooding, home of strong passions and ruthless ambitions! ... but **Dan Brand and Tipi**, who had made the forest their friend, could make even the trees battle for justice....* —From the pages of *White Indian*

Inspiring Whites to Act Like Indians Since 1823: The Mohican Syndrome

Maurice Horn tells us that a "large segment of American literature has been devoted, sometimes obsessively, to the single themes of the frontier ... Fenimore Cooper's Leatherstocking saga" and was one of the "first to blaze a fertile trail" of this type in literature [173]. From 1823 to 1841, James Fenimore Cooper published a number of books collectively called the *Leatherstocking Tales*. In them, a Caucasian male named Natty Bumppo is the central character.

Raised by Mohican Natives, Bumppo later adopts the Native American way of life — choosing it above the aristocracy of white society. The theme of a non–Native completely transforming into an Indigenous person has become a literary standard for many stories since. As far as comics books are concerned, little has changed in literature since Cooper's time.

This *Mohican Syndrome*, in which a white man becomes Indian, manifests itself through non–Native participation in Indigenous ways of life. This formulaic participation allows the non–Native character to absorb all things seemingly positive about Native culture by some sort of osmotic metamorphosis. One only has to watch late night television and catch the film *A Man Called Horse* (Elliot Silverstein, 1970) to see a visual representation of this white-man-becoming-Indian-phenomenon in modern media.

Jacquelyn Kilpatrick expands on Cooper's influence:

Cooper's work wasn't the only one or even the first one to present a white male who managed to assimilate all the skills and other positive traits of a Native American, but his Mohicans story has been assigned reading for many generations now. It's been made into a film at least fourteen times, and it was a serial TV show, so it isn't surprising that it is also found in comic books. It's an important part of the American mythology because it is a statement that the Euro-American male is superior to the indigenous people and also unique from Europeans because he is of the land and of the people [Kilpatrick interview].

The Mohican Syndrome also serves as an introduction to a particular stereotype found in comic books. Many comic titles suffer from and are directly influenced by Cooper's ideals. Examples include *White Indian*, *Tomahawk*, and *Scalphunter*. In these books, the hero is a white male pretending to be Indian—an arrangement that seems to be very popular with audiences.

For instance, in *White Indian*, originally found in Frank Frazetta's *The Durango Kid*, which is set in Revolutionary War times, the main character, Dan Brand, becomes the White Indian who serves as a hero to frontier peoples.

As always (it seems), the white hero is provided with an ethnic helpmeet, in this case, it is his tiny Indigenous friend, Tipi, who, of course, represents a specific stereotype found in several comic books, namely, the notion of the Indian sidekick. While we will touch more on the notion of the Indian sidekick, let us for now investigate those comics that exploit this idea of the white Indian—the super "wannabe." With the Mohican Syndrome, a white man becomes Indian in every way that counts. In comic books, these individuals are not only transformed into the best representation of that Indigenous culture, but they also become heroes.

From *White Indian* in the 1940s and 1950s to more modern tales, such as *Scalphunter* and *Tomahawk*, these and others become mere pretenders of culture that outsiders view as exotic. In many cases, while no "super" powers inhabit these individuals, it is enough that they *act* like Native people. Pretending alone affords them the means of saving the day.

White Indian (Magazine Enterprises, *The Durango Kid*, October/November 1949)

> It is the white man I want! With him I will do battle. But if my red brothers stand in the way, then they too shall feel the might of my arm!—Dan Brand, *White Indian*

Danger! Spoiler alert: Do not let the name fool you. Dan Brand is not just a lightly tanned Native American, he is a white man. He is called *White Indian* because he has not only befriended many of the local tribesmen, he has also adopted their way of life. This series, illustrated by comic book legend Frank Franzetta, centers on a white man in colonial times who acts and dresses like an Indigenous person. Because of this charade, Dan battles and defeats any foe who happens to cross him, including real Native Americans. Once again, *White Indian* illustrates the Cooperesque idea of a non–Native becoming a better "Indian" than the real ones.

In one issue (*White Indian*, no. 12), Dan demonstrates his superiority over real Native Americans by outthinking them and outfighting them, and he effectively matches his skill in herbology with a holy man—all in the first few pages. Truly, the white

Indian is a much better Indian than the darker ones. Or so the comic would have us believe.

Later, in the same issue, Dan seemingly has no qualms about killing several (hundred?) of his "red brothers" by felling an entire forest of trees on the advancing attackers. Of course, the tension is heightened later when Dan, the "Mighty Forest Eagle," must rescue Tipi from a watery grave. Such action — whether it includes killing Natives or saving them from certain death — is nonstop in the Franzetta-illustrated pages.

However, what do we make of the cultural representation in *White Indian*? Does this book about a white hero who simply dresses in buckskins misrepresent Native American people and culture?

White Indian, despite the name, treats its Indigenous characters with a good amount of care and does not demean Natives with its vocabulary. Given the protagonist's choice to emulate this culture, Native people are not portrayed as alien beings nor are they described in such terms. As demonstrated above, Dan thinks of Indigenous people as his "red brothers [and sisters?]."

Despite the absence of the usual "ughs" and "-um" (as in "get-um up"), there is a distinct disparagement in the verbiage given to Native Americans in *White Indian*. Translation: the Indians do not talk like Tonto in this series; yet, as seen in countless Hollywood movies, Native characters' speech patterns in this comic seem overburdened with metaphors and similes. While this does indeed give them a sense of nobility (as opposed to savagery) and saves the Indigenous characters the indignity of sounding ignorant, still it amounts to one stereotype interchanged for another.

All Native people found within the *White Indian* comic books seem to belong to one large Plains-type tribe, based on their clothing. Despite the book's setting near the New England area and its timeframe during the late 1700s, the Indigenous characters all seem to live in tipis and wear buckskin. A more factual depiction of Native American life in this region and at this time would include images of thatched dwellings and quillwork adornments, but such is not the case in *White Indian*.

Occasional comedic interludes are centered more on Dan Brand's joviality and not on any characterization of Native Americans in the comic books, such as the stupid or drunken Indian. The Indigenous characters are always either very serious or very malevolent, but they are never the butt of some joke. While it is good that no jokes about Indians and the evils of "firewater" occur, this leaves out a vital element of Native life, namely, Indian humor. Again, we see one stereotype interchanged for another.

When dealing with any semi-historical comic, the question of whether Indigenous people appear to be extinct is a hard one. Surely, since this comic book takes place in Revolutionary War times (circa 1770s), the Native characters are "trapped" within its pages in a historical setting, but then so are all the other characters in the comic book. However, despite this fact, this comic supports the notion that Indigenous people exist only in the past.

The comic book seems to play Indigenous parts rather heavy-handedly. Yes, in many cases, Native characters are primitively savage, and/or naively led along the evil path, or they are supremely and sickeningly good. There seem to be too few shades of gray — or in this case, shades of red — to the Indigenous characters in *White Indian*.

Surprisingly, this comic book's tone toward Native American people is anything but patronizing. There is a palpable undertone of respect and seriousness in every Indigenous character. Much of this is also reflected in the artistry of Frank Franzetta and his visual portrayal of Indians. Never are the characters simply caricatures of themselves; rather, they have real and believable features.

In short, although some degree of humanity of Native characters shines through — in the serious tone and aesthetics of the comic book — not much else does. In essence, the Indigenous people within this series serve as scenery for the main (white) character. Despite Dan Brand's decision to become Indian, which could be argued as the ultimate homage, he makes little attempt to learn anything from the Natives. Of course, he has nothing to learn, for Dan is a better Indian than the Indians.

While this series has some shortcomings, it is surprisingly sensitive toward making Native American characters more human. Of course two major supporting factors to this are: (1) the Indigenous people are trapped in the past, and (2) the central character is white. Not bad, given the time period in which this series first made its debut (late 1940s–early 1950s).

CONCLUSION

Similar to the movie *Dances with Wolves* (1990), *White Indian* is a story about a white man with some Native Americans thrown into the background for flavor. Despite the savagely rugged artistry of Franzetta (love it) and the humanity of Tipi, this comic is difficult to bear. *White Indian* offers too little specific Native culture (which supplies the prowess and abilities Dan Brand is famous for) and instead celebrates the white protagonist's "greatness."

Straight Arrow (Magazine Enterprises, February–March 1950)

Strangely, while Straight Arrow appears to be yet another version of the white-man-pretending-to-be-Indian Mohican Syndrome, the exact inverse is true. Straight Arrow is actually a Native American who *pretends* to be white on occasion. In other words, while characters such as White Indian, Scalphunter, and Tomahawk have fabricated Indigenous secret identities, Straight Arrow has fabricated a white secret identity, namely, Steve Adams, a local rancher (French online "Straight Arrow: Nabisco's Comanche Warrior").

Similar to *The Lone Ranger*, *Straight Arrow* started out as a radio program (hosted by the Nabisco Company) before it was written for a comic book. While the radio program and its popularity deserves much discussion, the focus here will rest on the comic book representation of *Straight Arrow*.

Throughout the comic, there is no use of disparaging language toward Native American people. Indigenous people do not seem to be referred to as "red skins," "savages," or other, more derogatory terms. Perhaps this is due in part to Straight Arrow's own ethnicity or it may be just an oversight on the part of the other (white) characters.

It is fortunate that none of the Comanches featured in *Straight Arrow* speak as Tonto does, in broken English. Like Tonto, the Native characters do not use contractions. However, certain verbal pan–Indian stereotypes remain in the vocabulary. Such terms include, "squaws," "braves," and so forth. However, despite this generic use of pan–Indian terms, the Indigenous characters seem somewhat intelligent, at least when speaking.

The Native clothing found in *Straight Arrow* seems to border on stereotypical. Straight Arrow himself wears war paint, two "brave" feathers, and makes liberal use of fringe. Yet, the Comanche people are members of a Plains tribe: one among a large group of various tribal entities that follow similar ways of life and dress similarly. Thus, while there may not be any *specific* Comanche clothing, at least the "look" of the comic imparts a "flavor" of the tribes of the Great Plains.

There are few comic interludes to speak of in *Straight Arrow*. Similar to *White Indian*, this comic takes itself very seriously. Thus, there is no humor at the expense of making Native American people look stupid or less than human.

While these are good elements, it is sad that the Native People in *Straight Arrow* appear to be extinct. The characters seem trapped in the historical Old West. Nothing in the comic alludes to the survival of the Comanches into modern times.

Comics have a tendency to portray Native American characters as either noble or savage, with little room in between. Taking Straight Arrow as the ultimate noble Indian who always does the right and noble deed, other Comanche characters are portrayed as savages, ready to fight with little encouragement or reason. Never is a character portrayed as just a "regular" Native American who exhibits neither of these extreme characteristics.

Taking all of these elements together, while they are not overtly offensive, the overall tone of the comic book is somewhat patronizing. Indigenous characters seem semi-intelligent, yet there is still some generic language and clothing, and, with few exceptions, most Native characters are portrayed as either supremely good or supremely bad.

In this, while we can see that *Straight Arrow* celebrates a Native American central hero, and does so by reversing the Mohican syndrome, it does nothing to make Indigenous people more human. While Straight Arrow is Comanche by birth, the culture itself is not celebrated or explored with any depth. All one can tell from the limited cultural information inside the comic is that these are Plains-type Indians; the creators did chase a Plains people, the Comanche, for their subject, which may have been more by luck than by design. In short, while there are a few good points about *Straight Arrow*, overall it falls short in continuing to support a tired and limited view of Native American culture.

CONCLUSION

Straight Arrow seems to be on the right track in some ways: the central character is (supposedly) Comanche, but he only disguises himself as a white person. Still, there is very little exploration of specific Indigenous culture (do we know any more about Comanche people from reading this? No.) Given the blandness of this ready-made hero, it is little wonder that the series owes its origin to hocking crackers on a radio program.

Tomahawk (National Periodical Publications, September–October 1950)

The central character of *Tomahawk* is not an ethnic minority, and certainly not Indigenous, yet this particular comic book deserves mention for several reasons. First, the comic's title itself lends itself to mistaken identity. Anyone unsure of the Tomahawk character in history might mistake it for one with elements of historical Native American culture, based on its name alone. Second, this comic book illustrates the stereotype of the Mohican Syndrome in which a non–Native becomes the best Native there is. Lastly, while the central hero in *Tomahawk* is not Indigenous, many of the supporting players *are*, a fact that makes this a noteworthy comic. This discussion focuses on how Indigenous people are represented in comic books, not only on how the main characters are represented. In this comic book, the Natives are present but none serve as the main character or central hero.

Alvin Schwartz, a comic book writer who worked on *Tomahawk* in the early years, comments on his contribution to the series: "I would get handed an assignment, along with a few typical comics reflecting that assignment. 'Here — this is Tomahawk. We need a few new stories. Our regular writer is getting stale or died or doing something else, etc. Look them over and come up with a few ideas'" [Schwartz interview].

Despite this attitude and in spite of prevailing attitudes toward Indigenous people at that time, Schwartz wrote *Tomahawk* with some care. In one of his many online articles, Schwartz reveals his creative process on the series: "I know little about whom else may also have done *Tomahawk*, but I used this strip to introduce a new way of writing about Indians. Most of the time, pulp and comics writers (who were often the same people) made Indians talk like idiots."

Here, Schwartz refers to the Tonto-talk prevalent in comic books of the time. While replete with "ughs" and "make-ums," these comics did little but further the stereotype of "stupid Indian." Yet, Schwartz maintains that he took a different attitude. Speaking of the Tonto-talk, he states that there was no "effort at all to catch some of the idioms of the Indian languages and offer them to the reader. But I didn't like writing about Indians that way, and my editor, Jack Schiff, didn't like it either. But I also had a very special source of Indian lore."

Schwartz's source was his close friend, Herbert J. Spinden, who "knew most of the Indian languages" and "had acquired them because he'd been brought up by Indians." Schwartz explains: "There was still a frontier in the early [1880s] when [Spinden] was a lad, and in addition to what he told me about how Indians really sounded when they spoke to each other, so I could put them into my *Tomahawk* scripts."

What about the other early writers of *Tomahawk*? Were they also as enthusiastic to illustrate the way Indigenous people truly spoke to each other in their Native language? Schwartz states that he can speak only for himself in this matter: "I never met the other writers or artists. Just asked a few more questions about what the editor wanted — in this case, Jack Schiff — a good editor who shared with me a lot of what today would be called 'liberal ideas' [and he] was strongly anti-racist personally. (Others really didn't care.)"

While Schwartz seems to have had the good fortune to work for an editor who had "liberal ideas"—such as representing Indigenous people as human—not all were so lucky, or even cared to be. It seems that writers at this time had a mind of their own about such things, or at least Schwartz did. He says:

> I wrote my stories the way I thought I'd like to do dialogue for Indians instead of the pulp dialogue that inflicted the industry—and [I] got a lot of supporting information from my friend Spinden ... it was the kind of thing Schiff liked ... that's all there was to it. I was also writing a lot of other stuff at the time including the Superman and Batman dailies. End of story. Even if Spinden hadn't agreed with my approach, I probably would have written them that way anyway, but without the details he was able to enrich them with for me [Schwartz interview].

CONCLUSION

I think James Fenimore Cooper was part fortune-teller. He must have had some feverish apocalyptic dream in which he saw this very comic book, one in which a white frontiersman out "Indians" the Indians. *Tomahawk* offers very little substance for Native readers other than to serve as a representation of a tired theme that we must strive to overcome. In that, the series is very useful, save for Rachel Pollack's versions of the main character, which will be discussed later.

Scalphunter (DC, *Weird Western Tales* no. 39, March–April 1977)

PostCivil War America has been the setting for countless numbers of traditional western stories. This time period seems ripe for storytellers to tell many tales. In this comic, Brian Savage, also known as Scalphunter, roams America in search of himself. Along the way, he finds much adventure, and, of course racism as well.

In their *Scalphunter* series, DC touts him as "a man who lived in two worlds but was at home in neither." Created by Michael Fleisher and Dick Ayers, *Scalphunter* is set in the 1860s and centers on Brian Savage, a white man captured and raised by Kiowa people at a young age.

Thus raised, Savage obtains his Kiowa name: Ke-Woh-No-Tey, which (according to the comic book, at least) supposedly translates into "He Who Is Less Than Human." Of course, in reality, this phrase is simply gibberish, words that sound ever-so-slightly Kiowaesque. However, this fictitious element aside, the name he is given illustrates the idea of multiethnic complexity, despite Brian being white. The name and comic book reveal the belief that one cannot live in both cultures successfully.

While *Scalphunter* highlights the thematic quality of cultural misfit, the hero does not share in the physical heritage of the culture he seeks to be a part of; he is not biologically Indigenous. In other words, Scalphunter is about a white man who just happens to be raised by Kiowa people. This is the inverse situation of Johnny Wakely (*Red Wolf*), who was born Cheyenne and raised white (more on this character later).

At the outset, this idea seems to stand in direct contrast with the notion of the "white Indian." For example, in popular media, when a white person is transformed into a Native, he seems to be accepted by both Anglo and Native American worlds. The non–Indian can always become the "perfect Indian," and be accepted readily by both cultures as the real McCoy. On the other hand, the converse does not seem to hold true. If an individual is multiethnic or shares elements from two separate cultures closely, that individual is accepted by neither.

This theme pervades the entire book. Of course, that is putting it lightly. It is basically run into the ground, as it were. Almost every issue touches upon this subject of rejection by white society.

However, the comic book is not without other faults. Indeed, this comic book seems to contain many of the common stereotypes that mar other comic books that feature Indigenous characters. In this case, the central character is not truly Indigenous—he has merely adopted a Native American disguise. True, readers are led to believe that Brian Savage truly thinks of himself as Kiowa, yet Brian could regain his white status whenever he so chooses. Supporting evidence includes a major storyline in which Brian attempts to find surviving members of his Anglo family.

In *Weird Western Tales*, no. 51, readers are given more information about Brian's Anglo identity. "With both his White Father and his Indian brothers dead he needed an anchor for his drifting identity ... a white man in an Indian's clothing, he traced his sister's path from St. Louis to New Orleans, and finally to Atlanta ... through it all, he kept his sister's face before him." Eventually, Brian finds his sister but does not reveal his kinship to her. Unfortunately, the sister witnesses Scalphunter killing a man for her protection.

At the story's end, his sister inquires after Scalphunter's true identity. "The tall man looks into his sister's eyes, remembering the horror he saw there, during his struggle in the courthouse," then, while mounted on a rearing black horse, he shouts, "I am Ke-Woh-No-Tey! I am a Kiowa brave." Thus, despite having the freedom to choose which culture to call "home," Brian chooses the Indigenous culture as his own.

Although Scalphunter is biologically non–Native, it is important to include this comic book character in our examination for two major reasons. First, because the central charac-

"Animal Magnetism." Perhaps because of Brian Savage's (aka Scalphunter's) upbringing within a Native American community, he seems closer to the natural world — at least close enough to emulate the reflexes of a "human cat." *Weird Western Tales Starring ... Scalphunter*, "The Belle," vol. 9, no. 49, November 1978 (© DC Comics).

ter believes himself to be a member of the Kiowa people so fully that he adopts this identity completely. Therefore, Brian is not only Kiowa to himself, but he also makes sure that everyone else (all other characters in the comic book) believe it as well. Second, given the book's name and its Indigenous-looking cover and interior art, many readers might well assume that the main character really is Kiowa as well. While the notion of his adopted identity shall not be argued here, this last point can be put even more simply: *Scalphunter* should be examined for cultural misrepresentation because, at first glance, it quite honestly looks like a book about Indigenous people. With so much resemblance, the need to investigate its authenticity becomes apparent.

The title alone should allow readers to gauge just how stereotypic this comic might be. Why stop at the term *Scalphunter*? Why not just call the series *Wagon Burner*? Or, alternatively, *Red Devil*? Titles such as these would carry with them almost as many negative connotations as "Scalphunter" does. Almost.

Moving on from the disparaging title, the writing fares little better. Brian Savage, the Scalphunter, demonstrates almost every stereotype found in comic books. Although white by birth, Brian is painfully expressionless; keep in mind that many individuals associate stoicism as an Indigenous trait. In every panel, his face is devoid of any expression, except when he is enraged or prodded by others into battle. Then, of course, his face becomes a savage canvas of rage.

While there is no mention of what Brian's role might have been in the Kiowa society in which he was raised (did he receive training as a hunter, a storyteller, or maybe even village idiot?), he seems to be an excellent tracker. It seems that even though he is biologically white his cultural upbringing affords him an almost supernatural ability to survey and assess the world around him. In other words, since he has been raised as an Indian, Brian is able to track, hunt, and kill anything that crosses his path. In this respect, his senses function at levels that most normal human beings are unable to obtain. For example, while making his escape from a train wreck in issue no. 49, readers are informed that "Only a wild animal has the reflexes to *survive* a crash like this: only a *human cat* can move fast enough, sure enough ... only a man like *Scalphunter*..!" (emphasis from comic book)

There are only a few stereotypes that manage to escape Scalphunter's identity. Brian does not have an innate sense of spirituality, at least not like most shamans might. He cannot call upon his spirit-animal friends to come to his aid in times of need. He does not serve as comic relief to anyone within the series. In fact, there is little comedy in this book. Brian seems to be bereft of a sense of humor — something few real Kiowas would be without.

Culturally speaking, humor is a vital part of everyday life for Indigenous peoples. Deloria provides a detailed examination of Native humor: "It has always been a great disappointment to Indian people that the humorous side of Indian life has not been mentioned by professed experts ... the image of the granite-faced grunting redskin has been perpetuated by American mythology." Deloria continues: "Indian people are exactly opposite of the popular stereotype ... Indians have found a humorous side of near every problem and the experiences of life have generally been so well defined through jokes and stories that they have become a thing in themselves" [146–147].

What about the vocabulary — is it demeaning? The short answer is, most assuredly, yes! The long answer is that, throughout this series, the language used in reference to the main character, and therefore the culture he represents (in this case, Kiowa), is indeed demeaning. On page after page the reader can find someone calling the central character "savage" or worse. As stated above, even the comic's title is demeaning. It makes sense that much of the descriptive language used within would follow suit. Therefore, yes, the descriptive vocabulary is demeaning.

Of course, these slurs usually culminate in spurring Brian Savage into acts of vengeful retribution. In issue no. 47, Brian is called "Injun," "Redskin," and "stupid." "Suddenly, the joke isn't funny anymore ... suddenly, it's all deadly serious." Following this, several panels show Brain kicking butt. Yet, this "payback" does nothing to alter the sheer amount of negative labels that are applied within *Scalphunter*. True, the audience may well empathize with the central character and might feel some relief at witnessing justice for such slurs. However, there seems to be so much time invested in retribution that little time is given to celebrate what Brian feels to be his true culture, namely, Kiowa. In short, while much attention has been given to making sure that no one calls him any bad names (or else!), there is little space allotted for celebrating his adopted heritage.

These verbal attacks really have nothing to do with Brian Savage, the human being. The explicit language used is directed at the Indigenous culture Brian seems to represent (in this case, Kiowa people), but not at himself. For instance, if Brian were to change clothes and cut his hair, it can be surmised that he would never ever be called names like "savage" again. Yet, these slurs remain — directed at a particular group of people — with or without Brian Savage's participation within that culture.

Refreshingly, Brian Savage's vocabulary is not filled with guttural moans and "ughs" that we expect to find with Tontoesque language. Indeed, he seems to have a command of the English language equal to many other characters within the comic book. However, again, it is important to keep in mind that readers may well expect that Brian speaks English fluently, given that he is white by birth.

Sadly, the central character comes complete with stereotypical clothing: headband, fringe, moccasins, and one lone feather sticking up in back. There is nothing that would differentiate Scalphunter from any other generic Indian found within comic books. Nothing about his clothing or style identifies him as belonging to the Kiowa.

The comic book illustrates how much better Scalphunter is than everyone else because of his cultural upbringing. He is not stupid and he is not portrayed as such. While there may be some illustration of his naivety with respect to the technology of the late 1800s, nowhere within the series is he portrayed as just a dumb, drunken Indian.

In *Scalphunter*, there are several elements that point to the notion of Indigenous people as being extinct. First, the series takes place at a specific time in history, namely, the late 1860s. Unfortunately, just as many other media have done, this limited time period allows the audience to conceive of Indigenous people only as historical figures and not living, breathing, and viable members of society who survive into modern times.

Second, Scalphunter is the last of his kind. His adopted Kiowa parents were killed by white soldiers. In fact *Weird Western Tales*, no. 51, would have readers believe that there are no Kiowa people left at all. "Raised a Kiowa, he was cut loose from his Indian heritage when Union Soldiers massacred his tribe.... He believed himself totally alone in the world." Thus, this comic book would have us believe that Indigenous people, specifically the entire Kiowa tribe, have been wiped out.

Next, Scalphunter travels all over the United States, encountering many adventures along the way. However, despite this, there is little mention of other tribal groups within the comic book. Surely Scalphunter might feel just as comfortable in a similar tribal society. Yet, the readers never see Scalphunter with other Native Americans.

Finally, Scalphunter is really white. Thus, readers seldom see a true Indigenous person. Given this fact, there is little doubt that this series portrays Indigenous people as extinct.

Scalphunter is presented as both noble and savage. Brian always attempts to act based on a specific sense of right and wrong--he has a distinct morality. However, when he is mistreated or when others violate his personal moral code, Brian becomes a lethal animal of rage. Thus, both stereotypes (of the Indian as noble and the Indian as savage) are alive and well within the character of Scalphunter.

While the tone of the comic series may not be patronizing, its overt messages are ones of generalization; thus, the two cancel each other out. Within its pages, many assumptions are made about Kiowa people, using Scalphunter as an example. Thus, generalizations such as taking conquered enemies' scalps and superstitions about a photograph stealing one's soul (*Scalphunter*, no. 62) are commonplace in this production.

In *Scalphunter*, there is no specific notion of the humanity of Indians. It is true that Scalphunter is kept alive by his physical prowess, allotted to him by his cultural upbringing. However, it is his Indigenous side that allows him to be, dare we say, savage enough to allow his moral codes to overcome adversity. Being Indigenous, or, in Brian Savage's case, being brought up Indigenous, does not automatically make one a human. In *Scalphunter*, being Indigenous merely means that one is more dangerous than other human beings.

Therefore, *Scalphunter* seems to contain much cultural misrepresentation. Indeed, the problem is compounded by the fact that all this misrepresentation centers on an individual who is not truly Indigenous at all. Perhaps this lack of any authentic Indigenous identity is the core problem. Perhaps things might have been different if the character were truly multiethnic instead of just being dressed up to look that way. Since this is not the case, this comic must serve as an example of what *not* to do when creating comic books with Native Americans in them.

CONCLUSION

There is no way to put this delicately. *Scalphunter* is an abomination. The series does nothing to celebrate Native American (Kiowa, in this case) culture. Unlike other "wannabe" comics (in which the white central characters emulate Native culture), *Scalphunter* offers almost no actual Indigenous characters in which to compare or contrast Brian Savage's character. It is almost as if the series suggests that (1) not only are Indigenous people vestiges of history *only* in being an extinct species, but also (2) the only Indian left is a poor imitation of one indeed: Brian Savage all but single-handedly demonstrates many of the stereotypes we will explore in this book. For a Native reader, this series is both offensive and infuriating. Was that delicate enough?

Vertigo Visions: Tomahawk (No. 1, 1998, DC)

Years later, another (and very different) *Tomahawk* would be born in the pages of a comic book. This one comes from the Vertigo Vision group (part of DC comics) in a "one-shot" in 1998. This *Tomahawk* is a remake of the original title that started in 1950 [Overstreet 739]. In this story, the Creator Spirit of the Wampanoag people, Grandmother Wolf, chooses the main character, Thomas Hawke (or Toma-hawk as his Indigenous friends call him), as the champion of her people.

In essence, Thomas, much like the aforementioned Natty Bumppo, must shed himself of white "humanity" to become a Native American. He does this by first learning the Wampanoag language (under duress) and then later when he is forced to survive in the wilderness alone, with only the protection of Grandmother Wolf to care for him. Rachel Pollack, creator of the newer Tomahawk, takes a different stance on Thomas's transformation. "He does not 'go Native,' as the British used to say, but in fact finds his true faith" [Pollack interview].

His true faith seems to manifest itself only after he leaves "civilized" Boston life. "When I was writing it, I felt the story truly came together when I realized that Thomas was a Christian ... of course he is a Christian who accepts the divine powers outside the Church doctrines, because it is [the wolves] who brought him to himself." Given this evidence, while Thomas does not shed his white humanity to become Indigenous, he amalgamates the non–Judeo-Christian idea of the Indigenous Grandmother Wolf into an ethnocentric view. In other words, at no time does Thomas acknowledge the Wampanoag spirit's authority — the entity that enabled him in the first place. Rather, he credits all to his English God. Pollack states that, for her, "in some ways the key scene [of the comic book] ... was the moment that the wolves bring him everything to make the tomahawk, he does so, and thanks Christ for his deliverance."

All this seems fine at the outset, but there are many issues that misrepresent Indigenous people. As mentioned above, many non–Native individuals harbor the idea that anyone can become a Native American, *à la* Hollywood style. Comic books that uphold such notions do little to promote truthful and realistic representations of Indigenous people.

Is it too much to wonder if the Wampanoag spirit, Grandmother Wolf, might surely have wanted to pick someone more fitting to be her champion? Perhaps someone who had trusted in her and had been taught since conception her right and wrong ways? Perhaps some member of that particular tribal nation and not just some white guy named Tom? Maybe even someone who was Wampanoag? There is much food for thought here.

Kilpatrick comments on what, in this book, is identified as the Mohican Syndrome. In *Celluloid Indians: Native Americans and Film*, she discusses how Cooper's creation of the frontier-woodsman-raised-by-Native theme was used by Hollywood and how these non–Natives "were, in fact, generally better at being Indian than the Indians, just as Natty Bumppo always managed to be a better Indian than either Chingachgook or Uncas" [4]. Apparently, Thomas is one of these men who can become the better Indian.

Pollack clarifies that her intention was never to make Thomas the best Indian, only to illustrate Grandmother Wolf's keen insight into matters of the physical world. She states that "Grandmother Wolf does not choose him because he's superior but because she wants someone who can communicate in both worlds. She also wants a White person who can confront and overcome his terror of nature, not just of the Native people, and therefore act as a counter, at least somewhat, to the madness of the Europeans to destroy nature.... My idea was that Grandmother Wolf needed a White ally in the Revolutionary times."

Visually, the comic book *Tomahawk* is akin to many other comics in which a white man is "in cahoots" with Native Americans (or any other minority, for that matter). I refer to the fact that, visually, the non–Native is the prominent and central character with the Indians serving as background pieces. The story also uses the Indigenous people as background pieces to provide local color and ethnic authority with Thomas serving as the focal point of the story.

The thematic element is derived from the *Tomahawk* of earlier days as well. Yet, Pollack maintains that while the central character is indeed white, the Indigenous characters are integral to his character. Without the Indigenous presence, there would be no *Tomahawk*. Pollack concedes *Tomahawk*'s seemingly cultural one-sidedness, but she affirms it is her intent to make all characters, including the Indigenous ones, more human. "While I could not really portray their cultural view and life I tried to make them more central. At the same time, I would have to honestly say that the story still is about the White people, if at least more about their weaknesses and fears." Pollack states, "I hope to portray any character I create as a full person. And part of the Vertigo revisioning project is the chance to overthrow stereotypes."

Despite the creator's conscious efforts to make them seem more dynamic and truthful, the Native characters never seem as developed or as interesting as Thomas; of course, he is the main character of the series. From a thematic standpoint, this element is not surprising. Savage points out similar aspects found within western comics and especially in those comics with jungle themes, those in which the "lord of the jungle or 'jungle queen' tower over native Africans both physically and mentally" [76].

The vocabulary used to describe Native people in *Tomahawk* is at once both lightly disparaging and complimentary. Indigenous people are introduced to the reader as "savages." Yet, Pollack refutes this notion by stating, "It was meant to denote the bigotry

"Tomahawk Chops." In the Vertigo refresh of the character, Tomahawk projects his issues with his inner "savage" onto the native Wampanoag people. *Vertigo Visions — Tomahawk*, no. 1, July 1998 (© DC Comics).

of the people using it. One of the things I wanted to show in the story was how the White people looked down on, but also feared, the Native people, the same way they feared the wilderness, as powers that would expose their own 'savagery.'" To support this idea, the reader sees that as the central character, Thomas, learns more about the Wampanoag people and their way of life, negative terms are used less and less, which illustrates his acceptance of them as human beings instead of subhuman "savages."

The Indigenous people in this comic do not talk Tonto. The Wampanoag people speak eloquently enough when the words are translated for the reader. Pollack states that writing Indigenous characters that way "certainly was conscious. That foolish way Native people speak in movies and such can only have sense if they are talking a foreign language, English. Of course, when they speak to each other they will speak in their colloquial language, which we represent in translation as colloquial English." In a reversal of sorts, it is the Caucasian individual who begins to communicate in a Tontoesque manner, as he begins to learn the native tongue of the Wampanoag people. This element alone makes the book worthwhile reading for a Native reader.

As for clothing choices, the Indigenous people unfortunately do wear some feathers and fringe. However, they are not modeled after the Native American Plains tribes. The manner in which Wampanoag clothing is illustrated offers a refreshing alternative to the way in which popular culture usually stereotypically portrays Indigenous people and their historical clothing. Pollack comments regarding the Indigenous clothing choices: "I sent some images from my reading to the artist, not just of clothes, but of the tomahawk that of course was central to the story. At the same time, for purposes of the story we made them somewhat less Europeanized than the Wampanoag at the time of the Revolution. Later, I read that the Wampanoag were in fact farmers even before the first Europeans came."

Humor is sparsely found in this title and little of it has to do with the notion of "firewater" or Indigenous stupidity. Indeed, this comic book depicts the Wampanoag people and their guardian spirit, Grandmother Wolf, as a being of high intellect and resourcefulness. This element sheds a favorable light on the comic.

Unfortunately, while the above are positive elements of *Tomahawk*, the book also falls short in another area — one that is wholly unintentional on the writer's part. Given that the story is set in historical times — around the time of the Revolutionary War — the reader cannot help but view the Indigenous people as living solely in the past. While readers may also conceive of the non–Native main character as a being found only in the past, popular culture has long portrayed Indigenous people as a race of human beings that is entirely extinct. The historical imagery found in this comic book does nothing to lessen this flawed notion despite intention.

While there is some mention of Indigenous people as "savages," they are not portrayed as such and this negative nomenclature only serves to illustrate cultural ignorance of particular characters. Thankfully, this positive element of *Tomahawk* allows the reader to see the complexity of Native people. However, while this complexity is present, the Indigenous characters are, for the most part, little more than background pieces for the main Caucasian character. The overall tone is not patronizing and there is a general attitude of respect that the writer attempts to infuse into the story.

In all, *Tomahawk* portrays the Wampanoag as real human beings, which is tremendously important. However, in imitation of the original comic books series, the Indigenous characters mostly serve as thematic set pieces for the protagonist. Pollack expounds on this idea: "First of all, the basic idea [of the main character] comes from the older versions [of the comic book]. The funny thing is, when Vertigo started its idea of doing one shot revisions of old DC characters, and I tried to think who I might do, Tomahawk came immediately to mind." In the end, *Tomahawk* ends up painting a pretty, slightly misrepresented, picture of the historical Wampanoag people. Thus said, it does a much better job of representing Native American people than many, many other comics.

Thus, *Tomahawk* makes a serious attempt to portray Indigenous people accurately. While it falls short — though only slightly—in some ways, it succeeds in doing what many other titles do not do, namely, it allows the Native characters to seem real and human in many ways. Despite this, the comic book might benefit by making Indigenous characters more multidimensionally complex rather than having them serve solely as background pieces for Thomas.

CONCLUSION

Pollack has done a stupendous job revamping this character. She has attempted to create a balance between a hitherto ethnocentrically based character and the celebration of a specific Native American community. From the perspective of an Indigenous reader, such elements make the Tomahawk character not only bearable but enjoyable as well. While the fact remains that the central, and thereby entire story, revolves around a white protagonist, at least we now are given details about the Indigenous culture that empowers Tomahawk.

<hr/>

Chapter Two

Multiethnic Heroes: A Case of (Really!) Mistaken Identity

*I knew you when the world was young ... when forests stood where cities now grow. We are all of different tribes, yet we are all **The People**.*—Joshua Brand, aka Stalking Wolf

Within the context of the Mohican Syndrome, white heroes become the best Indians—even better than biological Indians. But what about those who are both white and Indigenous? Are there any comic books that address this issue of multiethnicity?

Here lies another common stereotype in comic books: the idea that a hero with ancestry from two cultures — usually Anglo and Native — will suffer for his or her mixed heritage. For such an individual, there is no ready acceptance in either culture, even with the blessing of a greater spirit or higher power.

Film, another popular American medium, has refused to even touch this issue of multiethnic children, which exemplifies, sadly, American attitudes toward multiethnicity. To ensure that characters in the stories remained culturally the same, with no mixing, unions were dispelled by killing the cultural "other" (usually the Indigenous woman). A prime illustration of this can be seen in the film, *Broken Arrow* [Delmar Daves, 1950], in which the main character marries an Indian maiden. The "bad" Indian later kills this young Indigenous woman the day after their wedding night — thus, ending any worries of mixed babies. Truly, Hollywood has offered no viable solution for the issue of being multiethnic.

Several comic book titles come to mind when examining this idea of multiethnic identity: *Red Wolf* from the 1970s and *Shaman's Tears* from the early 1990s. In each title, the idea of cultural mixing, and the subsequent friction this produces, is explored.

Red Wolf (Marvel Comics Group, May 1972)

In many comic books, when the hero is of both Anglo and Native American ancestry, the problem of "fitting in" becomes central to the story. Such is the case in Marvel's *Red Wolf*. The title character — an Army scout named Johnny Wakely — is a Cheyenne descendant of the Owayodata, a line of warriors whose job it is to protect the people of the Plains. While he is Cheyenne by birth and blood, he is raised by a white family.

In other words, he is biologically Indigenous, but he shares cultural ties with Anglo culture. This fact pervades the character's existence and makes Red Wolf a noteworthy character. While not genetically multiethnic, this character shares a strong cultural affinity with two distinct ethnicities: Cheyenne and white. In addition to being in an Anglo army, he is, as Horn puts it, "the last descendant for the Cheyenne's warriors" ["American West" 112].

Red Wolf is not able to easily fit into either the Native or the white world because of his mixed upbringing. This despite being hand-selected by a powerful Wolf Spirit — a selection process similar to Tomahawk's, but apparently less effective. In effect, the character lives as an outcast from both societies, as illustrated in Marvel's *Blaze of Glory,* no. 1 (1998). "*Red Wolf*— raised between the white man's world and red man's, trusted by neither, striving for a peace between the races that few seemed to want."

According to Wright, Red Wolf is "Marvel's first Native American superhero" [249] and warrants close attention. Horn states that "*Red Wolf* marked the first time that an American Indian had assumed the role [of mysterious avenger], and it certainly should be remembered at least for breaking ground in a new direction, even if it proved temporarily unsuccessful" ["American West" 113].

Perhaps Red Wolf's lack of success is due to the overall popularity of the comic itself. Many times, Native American comic book characters do not garner the same notoriety and acceptance that Anglo characters seem to enjoy. Jacquelyn Kilpatrick offers two possibilities for this: "I can think of two reasons for the lack of Native American superheroes. (1) The time freeze — how many comic books have 19th-century heroes? In the time period during which comics have been printed, Native Americans have been almost always seen as they were imagined to have been in the 1800s. (2) In the movies, Native American characters have almost always been sidekicks — Tonto, etc. A kid brought up watching westerns wouldn't expect to see a sidekick as a hero" [Kilpatrick interview].

Horn expounds on the idea of complexity: "The theme of the mysterious avenger is, of course, as old as comics themselves, but *Red Wolf* marked the first time that an American Indian had assumed the role, and it certainly should be remembered at least for breaking ground in a new direction, even, if it proved temporarily unsuccessful" ["American West" 13]. Horn continues this exploration of Red Wolf's complexity by tying the natural world to the cultural: "In *Red Wolf* especially the land was integrated into the main motivation of the hero. It was from the land and the generations of warriors who had personified it that the hero drew his strength and his justification, in the manner of a modern Anteus" [178].

When *Red Wolf* first appeared on the scene in the pages of Marvel's *The Avengers,* no. 80, in September 1970 [Overstreet 287], both whites and Native people, based on Horn's description, readily accepted the hero. "Wearing the wolf headdress, the *Owaya Ata' hae,* and armed only with his quarterstaff, Red Wolf fulfilled his mission to be brother to and protector of all men, be they red or white" ["American West" 113]. Yet, there is more to this character than just this romantic description coupled with a headdress and staff.

"Wolf Pack." Marvel's character Red Wolf (seen here with his companion, Lobo), is one of the comic book industry's milestones for Native American representation. *Marvel Spotlight on ... Red Wolf*, vol. 1, no. 1, 1971 (© 2008 Marvel Characters, Inc. Used with permission).

Indeed, as seen in his origin, found in Red Wolf, no. 1 (May 1972), he is a natural-born Cheyenne who was later raised by a white family. We have discussed the idea of multiethnic identity in comic book characters and its relevance to that person's cultural acceptance or lack of acceptance in some cases. Johnny Wakely, which is his English-given name, wants very much to fit in and find his proper place.

Within the story, difficulties with each culture present themselves to Johnny. At a young age, Johnny's Native family was killed in a brutal massacre by "pony soldiers." Johnny himself comes close to death at the hands of a genocidal sergeant bent on eradicating all Indians, including Johnny, because of his prejudiced notion of "nits make lice" [*Red Wolf*, no. 1]. Acting under orders, a sergeant offers the wounded boy to Mr. and Mrs. Wakely, who accept the young Native as their own son. Years later, after Johnny gains a degree of respect from his adopted Anglo parents, they are killed by a group of Indigenous renegades (possibly hired by white land speculators). At this point, Johnny gives up all hope of fitting into either culture. He feels that he belongs to neither his biological nor his adopted culture and he wonders where his true place lays.

Where does this need to align himself with Anglo culture come from? Johnny's adopted parents were good to him, but he never seemed comfortable with their racist views toward Indigenous people. Johnny's father tells him, "This land is rich, Johnny! The red men are savages and must be driven from it — that it can produce the food we need." In his mind, Johnny replies, "I do not agree with my white father — the Indian is not a savage! But I shall not argue with him!" Certainly, Red Wolf feels the need to somehow vindicate himself to his white parents, to make them understand (posthumously) that he and his people are not savages and do not have to act like savages.

This feeling most likely also stems from the attitudes toward Native people he witnesses at the fort. Upon arriving to take a job as a scout, Johnny is challenged to a fight, which he "throws" in an attempt to make friends. Johnny sees that losing the fight makes no difference: he not accepted into white culture. After being attacked by Cheyenne, a young woman becomes frightened at Johnny's Indigenous appearance, thinking that he is just another savage Indian.

He continually seeks acceptance into Anglo culture. After witnessing the evil shaman talking about attacking the fort, Red Wolf states: "Instead of glory — they'll find a trap waiting for them! I'll ride back to the fort and alert the pony soldiers! Colonel Sabre will know what to do! Thus shall I prove to all that I can walk the path of the *Ta' Kai Kih*— the white man!"

Perhaps it is because of all these reasons that Johnny seeks to find his way, and his balance, between cultures. When the power of Owayodata is revealed to him, indicating that he is a descendant of such a powerful entity, Johnny receives an epiphany. "I hear, Owayodata! I — obey! For you have shown the path which I must walk. Nether am I white man nor red. I am a man — a brother and protector to all peoples! This is my mission — this is my power!"

Another facet to the Red Wolf comic book is the social comment it makes on human nature. One may readily identify elements of evil or racism inherent in both cultures (white and Native) and thus feel that Johnny's multiethnicity serves to liberate him from such evils. Thus, in frustration, Johnny's reaction to becoming Red Wolf (protector of both Indigenous and white folk) serves to elevate him beyond such

"Best of Both Worlds." Red Wolf, a Native American (Cheyenne) raised by Anglos, strives to maintain harmony for both ethnic sides of the equation. *Marvel Spotlight on ... Red Wolf*, vol. 1, no. 1, 1971 (© 2008 Marvel Characters, Inc. Used with permission).

pettiness and to serve possibly as a demonstrated role model for future ethnic relations. Red Wolf as a semi-mystical Civil Rights leader? Anything's possible.

Horn describes the components that make R*ed Wolf* unique. "Only in *Red Wolf* was an intelligent attempt made at organically incorporating elements of the super-hero ethos into the Western mythos; because of its very sophisticated and intricate weaving of two distinct traditions, the experiment ultimately failed, and it is not likely to be tried again in the foreseeable future" ["American West" 205].

However, years later, Red Wolf was indeed tried again, but in a minor role. This time, there were specific cultural differences that disallowed Red Wolf from continuing his attempts to fit into white society. In this reincarnation — in Marvel's *Blaze of Glory*— Red Wolf does not wish to be culturally accepted as he once did. John Ostrander, creator of *Blaze of Glory*, uses this idea to his advantage.

Red Wolf's multicultural ties allow Ostrander to portray the character in a unique way. "This [multiethnic heritage], in my eyes, would create a conflicted character although, by the time of *Blaze*, his frustration at trying to reconcile the people who gave him birth with the people who raised him has gone past the boiling point. In *Blaze*, he has thrown off siding with the Anglo. After watching betrayal by betrayal of every treaty, how could he decide otherwise?" [Ostrander interview].

This idea of being pushed past the boiling point that occurs in the first issue of *Red Wolf*, as well as the notion that Ostrander presents, is certainly a realistic point of view and one that many Indigenous people can relate to in modern times. The notion rings sufficiently true that it could have come from an actual Indigenous person. However, Ostrander does not pretend to be Native, and he only comments on what he sees in life and in history in what he hopes is a realistic Native viewpoint. He relates the following: "I'm an Anglo. If I share an ethnicity with any of the tribal nations, I am not aware of it. I became interested in Native American myths and stories and this, in turn, led me deeper into Native American history and culture. I don't claim to be an expert by any means; I'm more of a storyteller who wants to get things right."

In many ways, Ostrander does get things right — at least from an Indigenous standpoint. For instance, in the opening of *Blaze of Glory*, no. 1, readers are given a glimpse into the Native American past that is somehow more than just a brief history lesson. Ostrander manages to provide facts of Native American cultural significance as well.

Take this excerpt from issue no. 1 describing the year 1877: "Hinmaton-Yalaktit of the Nez Perce — known to the whites as Chief Joseph — refuses to accept a treaty forced on them by the whites and successfully fought Federal soldiers as he and his tribe fled towards Canada." While readers may be familiar with the name of Chief Joseph, few may know his real name. By providing this information, Ostrander allows readers to share in a historical event with some added Indigenous cultural meaning.

Ostrander comments on his logic for this specific opening: "The theme of the story was the 'closing' of the West as it was traditionally known. I was setting the story in a very specific time and place and area. The flight/fight of the Nez Perce (which is an amazing story) came to symbolize one aspect of it, along with [Chief Joseph's] famous line, 'I will fight no more forever.' I wanted a context for that line and I felt it was important for the reader to have some sort of understanding of that event."

It is the context of *Red Wolf* that must be examined through a cultural lens. Here,

"Tough Love." In Marvel's remaking of the character Red Wolf in *Blaze of Glory*, he now has abandoned his quest for racial harmony in favor of western vigilantism. *Blaze of Glory*, vol. 1, no. 2, February 2000 (© 2008 Marvel Characters, Inc. Used with permission).

using Stedman's instrument, we shall examine the *Red Wolf* series for cultural misrepresentation. Both the old and the new series will be examined.

In *Blaze of Glory*, there is no language used that carries a negative stereotype. In most cases, when Indigenous people are discussed in the comic, their specific tribal affiliation is mentioned, such as the Nez Perce or Cheyenne. While mention is made of "red" people or folk, the tone used is one of respect and not disparagement. However, in the original *Red Wolf*, there is some sparse use of negative connotations, such as "savage." Overall, the language is respectful.

In addition to this descriptive language, we must also consider the language the Indigenous characters use themselves. In *Blaze*, no characters speak Pidgin English like Tonto. Only one Native character speaks with a slightly wooden tone, but perhaps this is because he is an old man. Red Wolf himself speaks in a slightly cryptic tone, but this may have more to do with the character's air of intrigue. Ostrander supports this idea: "He's also been sometimes described as the Native American avenger and I wanted to explore that. I wanted to make him mysterious; we don't know his thoughts although his words and actions tell us a lot about where he is [emotionally]." Similarly, the Indigenous people in the original series do not speak like idiots.

While the words provide accurate representation, the clothing leaves much to be desired in both the older and the newer stories. Of course, since Red Wolf is Cheyenne, his outfit is made complete with fringed buckskin. However, many of the Natives in *Blaze of Glory* appear to belong to the same tribe, if one uses clothing as the marker. While the story takes place in Montana, none of the Indigenous clothing stands out as anything different from the apparel worn by most Plains tribes. Writer Ostrander laments this oversight. "I do wish that the Native American female character in *Blaze* was drawn a little more authentically — the artist seems to have her wearing a miniskirt and a vest! Not something I had much control over. Also, her features are a little too Anglo for me."

Comic relief is sparse in this very serious comic book. Indeed, there are absolutely no comedic scenes built upon Indigenous stupidity. Native characters, including Red Wolf, seem very intelligent. For this reason, the series can be looked upon favorably by Indigenous readers.

Because the series is set in historical times, it is hard to say whether Indigenous people are portrayed as an extinct species or not. Certainly, *Red Wolf* places Native characters at a time in history and it does so with a modicum of accuracy. Despite this, Native readers must keep in mind that there are few stories with Indigenous central characters set outside of this time period. Therefore, while there are numerous positive elements, culturally speaking, there still exists a real need to portray Indigenous people in modern times and locations and it is for this reason that both *Red Wolf* and *Blaze of Glory* fall somewhat short of the mark.

On a positive note, the usual dichotomy of Native peoples as either noble or savage does not seem to occur here. Indigenous characters seem fully human — complete with complex emotions and intellect. As discussed above, Johnny himself serves as a case study in identity crises. This is a constructive step forward away from the stereotypes of both the altruistic Indian willing to sacrifice himself for the greater good and the villainous Native bent on destruction who never listens to reason.

There is no patronizing tone and verbal respect is paid to Indigenous people in the *Red Wolf* comics. Perhaps this respect is shown because the source of Red Wolf's power originates from an Indigenous source. Perhaps the reason stems from attempting to have an Indigenous character become the centralized hero. While this may not seem to be much of an accomplishment initially, popular media is filled with far too many cases of one-dimensional Indigenous characters, but relatively few examples that illustrate Native humanness exist.

Thus, based on Stedman's criteria, we see that *Red Wolf* is, for the most part, a positive portrayal of Indigenous people. While the issue of keeping Native people trapped in the past still exists, at least visually comic books such as *Blaze of Glory* do an excellent job of making Indigenous people very human and complex characters.

CONCLUSION

Red Wolf touches upon an important topic within Native American culture: the idea of negotiated status. Many Native people experience this difficulty even in modern times. Also, the series, in both its original form and in the several iterations (including *Blaze of Glory*) that have occurred since its introduction in the 1970s, offers much hope and inspiration for the viability of Native characters. However, the short lifespan of the original series dashes this hope somewhat. While still a good story and a good read, one gets tired of seeing a Native superhero in only an Old West setting.

Shaman's Tears (Image Comics/Creative Fire Studio, May 1993)

Shaman's Tears tells the story of Joshua Brand, a man of both Irish and Lakota descent. In this comic, the issue of mistrust based on mixed heritage associated with comic books is of central significance. Joshua is accepted wholly by neither race, simply because he is identified with physical qualities and features from the opposing ethnicity. While non–Natives shower him with derogatory slurs for his dark complexion, he is scorned by his Indigenous "blood-brother" for being an outsider.

Comic book readers (as well as many readers of American literature) have continued to be exposed to the notion of the Cooperesque white Indian: an outsider, usually a white male, who becomes the ultimate Native, capable of paternally protecting his red friends, whom for whatever reason he believes cannot protect themselves. Stedman states it best: "Traditionally the best Indian of all in a frontier tale is a white one" [205].

In all, these thematic elements culminate to form a view of Native American society as a sort of club or training program that non–Natives can join in a matter of months via wilderness survival courses. This is not (and never has been) the case. Indigenous cultures are learned over the course of an entire lifetime, not just by someone spending the weekend in the woods.

The fact that anyone would think otherwise is laughable at best. We owe this type of mentality to the ideas perpetuate in literature that stem from the Mohican Syndrome. Not much has changed in the world of literature concerning Native Americans since Cooper — but perhaps it is time it should.

Shaman's Tears and the Joshua Brand character will be discussed more in the section on Indigenous shamans. For now, the important thing to understand is that many

"Attack of the Totemic Power." Joshua Brand (aka Stalking Wolf) uses the power of the bear to say hello to his little friends. *Shaman's Tears*, vol. 1, no. 2, July 1993 (*Shaman's Tears* © Mike Grell).

times, characters with mixed heritage may automatically receive some negative attention. Given its prevalence in film and comics, this is not an uncommon element.

Conclusion

Without the benefit of insight offered by its creator, Mike Grell, which I will go into further below, *Shaman's Tears* appears to be just another example of the "Indian's Plight" as defined by Vine Deloria in his *Custer Died for Your Sins*. The central character, reluctant hero though he is, is mistreated on account of his mixed heritage. As we shall see later, with Grell's help, the character is more complex than at first he appears and much less so than Grell may have originally envisioned. Extra "cool points," though, for (finally) having an Indigenous comic book hero who lives in modern times.

CHAPTER THREE

The Indian as Sidekick: Falling Prey to More Villains' Traps by 10 A.M. Than Most People Do All Day

Find-um rock hunter's bark pup. Him real hungry, you betchum!—Little Beaver

For those familiar with Robinson Crusoe and his companion Friday on that fateful island, there should be little surprise that Tipi is Dan Brand's (aka the *White Indian*, Magazine Enterprises, July 1953) version of an Indigenous Friday. The white Indian received his own comic book title from the Magazine Enterprises group.

As is the case in many comics, Tipi's role plays out as a background piece to the central white character. Perhaps another of Tipi's functions as an actual "Indian" person in this comic is to lend Dan Brand some credibility as a white Indian. Whatever his role (comic relief, one supposes), Tipi's character is impotent at best. Tipi seems to show the white's superiority in becoming the "best Indian" [Steadman 43].

In one adventure (*White Indian*, no. 12), Dan and Tipi attempt to provide aid and supplies to the troops resting in Valley Forge. During this trek, they run into British spies. Thinking that Dan's "Indian training" has left his ability to use firearms weak at best, the British spies bully Tipi in an effort to goad Dan into a gunfight. The Indian-as-sidekick mentality lying just beneath the surface of the comic reveals itself here: the white man (Dan, in this instance) is seen as the protector of the helpless red man and must fight those who would do him harm. This type of paternalistic attitude is not surprising, given its pervasiveness historically throughout America's dealings with Indigenous peoples. Why would comic book characters be any different?

Horn gives us the following opinion about Indigenous comic book sidekicks: "The Indian sidekick was a staple of the medium: the Lone Ranger had Tonto, and Red Ryder Little Beaver, to cite the two most prominent cases; and while this is now seen as being patronizing it certainly was not perceived in that light by the artists." Horn goes on to explain: "Tonto displayed a bravery and heroism that most people themselves are incapable of, and Little Beaver showed more courage, initiative, acumen and resourcefulness than any of his white companions or schoolmates" ["Encyclopedia" 188].

While Horn may be right — that the artists themselves in no way meant to portray Indigenous people as less than human — a statement such as this demonstrates how
acceptable the notion of Indian sidekick was during the early days of comic books. Given
that these notions, which are now viewed as patronizing, were once commonplace,
according to Horn, it can be said that this mentality illustrates common attitudes of
the time. Surely many people living in southern states in the years before the Civil Rights
movement meant no disrespect by the term "Negro." However, the negative connota-
tion remains. The same can be said here. Indeed, artists may not mean to cast Indigenous people in a negative cultural light, but they may find themselves at the mercies
of prevailing social attitudes and industry norms, the views of publishers, and myriad
other pressures. To support this evidence, Alvin Schwartz — a comic book writer who
worked on *Tomahawk* in the early years — recollects about being a comic book writer
in the 1940s: "In the first place, I would get handed an assignment, along with a few
typical comics reflecting that assignment. 'Here — this is *Tomahawk*. We need a few new
stories. Our regular writer is getting stale or died or doing something else, etc. Look
them over and come up with a few ideas.' I never met the other writers or artists. Just
asked a few more questions about what the editor wanted" [Schwartz interview].

Schwartz seems to be one of those rare individuals who saw Indigenous people as
human beings and attempted to portray them as such. Despite this, he wrote for a comic
book that portrayed Indians as simple creatures of nature who served more as colorful
backdrop settings than as human beings. Yet we have discussed how Schwartz attempted
to portray Indigenous people as beings of logic. While *Tomahawk* may have had its
intentional shortcomings or no, the sidekick remains a popular, though troubling, character.

In his book, Savage attempts an answer to the question of Indigenous sidekicks
by illustrating why heroes with sidekicks, such as *Batman and Robin*, became so popular. "Arguably, they [Batman and Robin] owed much to the renditions of other media.
If, for example, radio's Lone Ranger and Tonto (no kid, granted, but clearly possessed
of limited talents and abilities and thus like a kid) had been demonstrating since 1933
that a hero and a half were better than one, Batman and Robin merely offered further
evidence" [7]. Savage alerts us to the fact that in some ways, Tonto was seen by his
readers not only as a child in many ways, but also that he was "half" a hero.

Yet, this half hero remains popular even in modern times. Indeed, one would be
hard-pressed to utter the phrase "The Lone Ranger" without automatically finishing,
"and Tonto." However, Horn points out that the "title 'Lone Ranger' was always something of a misnomer since the hero had in actuality at least two constant companions"
["American West" 37]. Tonto was only one of the Lone Ranger's companions — the
other was Silver, the Lone Ranger's horse. Indeed, popular belief is that Tonto was created only so that, for the radio listeners, the Lone Ranger would have someone to speak
to other than his horse.

Tonto even went on to have his own comic book in the series, similar to the success of Little Beaver. This spin-off, *The Lone Ranger's Companion Tonto*, lasted from
January 1951 until its demise in January 1959, with hand-painted cover art [Overstreet
548]. While it can be argued that both Tonto and Little Beaver were popular enough
to create an entire comic book series just about them, and therefore must have served

as prime examples of human heroism, we must examine the truth about such spin-offs. At the time, it was popular to have entire comic book series about a hero's horse — perhaps being a sidekick probably was not much of a step up from a horse, at least in the eyes of a publisher.

Little Beaver (Dell Publishing Co., No. 211, January 1949)

Originally, Little Beaver is found in the pages of *Red Ryder*. "The action of Red Ryder takes place in the 1890s after the last of the Indian wars.... Red Ryder owns a ranch ... oftentimes Red must come to the help of [his friend] old sheriff Newt; he then puts on his boots and his beat-up Stetson and with the aid of Little Beaver, the Navajo orphan he has adopted, he rides into the wilderness, ranging far and wide, from the northern Rockies to Old Mexico, in pursuit of some stagecoach robber or cattle rustlers" ["Encyclopedia" 578]. However, the sidekick soon scored his own comic book. Fred Harman created the characters during the 1930s. Horn illustrates the popularity of the Indigenous sidekick in comic books. The author states, "Even more popular was the *Little Beaver* feature which starred the little Navaho Indian involved in a variety of entertaining scrapes. So popular did he become that ... Little Beaver had his own comic book" ["American West" 72], which ran from 1949 to 1958 [Overstreet 544].

Little Beaver was the faithful sidekick to Red Ryder in a popular western series. Horn describes *Red Ryder* as the "first long-lasting Western success in the comic book field" ["American West" 67]. "Coasting on the popularity of the newspaper strip and later of the movies and radio program, the comic book enjoyed great success among the young readers" ["American West" 71]. One such Little Beaver catch phrase was "You betchum, Red Ryder!" Here, the sidekick is identified with his Tonto-speak. Why would a character with such verbal and perhaps mental limitations appeal to readers?

While the descriptive terms used to describe Native Americans in *Red Ryder* is not overtly offensive, Little Beaver's personal use of vocabulary is somewhat insulting. Certainly there *were* Indigenous people who had limited use of English (there still are some), but none use the generic "ughs" and "heap-big" type of terms, as Little Beaver does.

Additionally, Little Beaver's clothing does nothing to indicate his specific tribal representation. He looks like every other generic ever produced by Hollywood or the comic book industry: buckskin pants, moccasins, and a "brave's" feather. Similar to his demonstrated speech, his clothing is nothing but a cartoonish caricature that represents how non–Native people see Indigenous culture.

Little Beaver's main job is to provide comic relief for the heroic (white) protagonist, and he does his job very well, indeed. Yet much of the humor generates from Little Beaver's buffoonery. This portrayal of the "stupid Indian" does nothing to celebrate the culture, and it only demeans it.

As this comic book is a western, it shares the problem that all comic books in the genre do: the Native characters are portrayed as remnants of the historical past. While one may argue that the white character is also portrayed as a historical artifact in this genre, we must remember that the same predisposed attitude toward white people does not exist: no one who is able to look at the world around them thinks that white people only existed in the Old West. However, many do think this way about Indigenous people, especially in terms of Native culture.

Both the *Red Ryder* and *Little Beaver* comics seem rather ambiguous about their Native American characters, and perhaps this is fortunate. The Indigenous players do not seem fixed at either noble or savage polar extremes. Thus, while in many cases the Indian characters may not be overly well developed, at least they are not stereotypic "cookie-cutter" versions such as Hollywood uses to the nth degree.

Despite Little Beaver's many attempts to do good, fight evil, and right wrongs, the overall tone of both comic titles is condescending to Native people. Little Beaver is plucky and cute, but normally he cannot achieve success without the intervention of his Anglo protector (Red Ryder). What message can this give readers about Indigenous people? We *mean* well, but we are bumbling idiots? All Native Americans can be expected to utter such phrases as "You betchum"? This is not acceptable, despite Little Beaver's appeal.

In these comic books, there is nothing that speaks to the overall humanity of Native American people. Certainly, there is some appeal to readers; else, Little Beaver would have never warranted his own comic title. Yet, while the character may be entertaining to some degree, it does nothing to further celebrate Native culture or demonstrate Indian humanness.

While both comic books offer some entertainment value, neither offers proper treatment of Native American characters. While this treatment seems typical for the period (circa 1950s), the era in which these comics were created does not excuse the impropriety. These comics merely reinforce notions that were acceptable for general audiences back then. Perhaps treatment of the Lone Ranger's friend Tonto will fare better.

CONCLUSION

Little Beaver may be cute (to *somebody*), but his Indigenous "Stepin Fetchit" act is too hard to swallow at times. Certainly we might excuse the fact that he is a mere child; however, since his character never advances to become more fully developed — one with, perhaps, a better grasp of language skills — there really is no excuse for his stereotypic characteristics. What is troublesome is the popularity of this character to mainstream readers even with these deficits — almost as if mainstream audiences applauded this misrepresentation and defamation of a Native American character. Troublesome, yes, but not surprising.

The Lone Ranger's Companion Tonto (Dell Publishing Co., No. 312, January 1951)

Of all the comic book Indians, Tonto's character seems most easily recognizable. Much of this probably has to do with the longevity of the legend of the masked man and his Indigenous companion. Tonto's popularity is precisely what makes discussing this character a necessity.

Starting as a radio show in the 1930s, the *Lone Ranger* series gained enough popularity to merit a newspaper strip. Later, as a testament to the continuing attractiveness of the story, these strips were put together in the first comic book featuring the pair [Overstreet 548]. It is the later comic book about Tonto, whose full title is *The Lone Ranger's Faithful Indian Companion: Tonto,* which we investigate here.

Tonto's character embodies a plethora of idiosyncrasies that never fully illustrate the nature of the character. Tonto is both sides of the coin: he is a character who can be simultaneously respected and despised by Indigenous people. He is at once a shining example of cultural elements we take pride in as a people as well as the embodiment of some of the most foul stereotypes and distortions that can be placed on an Indigenous character.

Tonto is strong, athletic, compassionate, intuitive, an expert marksman and an excellent equestrian handler. He is also trustworthy: if Tonto says he is going to do something, he will do it, no matter what may befall him. Truly, Tonto possesses many characteristics that an Indigenous person — or anyone else, for that matter — would be proud to have.

However, Tonto is also portrayed in many ways that are less than flattering for Indigenous people. He is severely limited in his grasp of the English language. When he speaks, his intentions are barely translatable and one is reminded of the meaning of his name when translated into Spanish: dummy. While we will explore later how this limitation is limited to Tonto's English and not his actual mental faculties, for now it is important to understand that this limitation makes it easy to generalize that Tonto is just another stupid Indian.

Also, in the comic book, Tonto is always subjugated to the authority of the Lone Ranger. While the two men are supposed to be a team, the Lone Ranger ends up giving all the orders. There is no equality between the two men — there is only a member of a minority race doing the bidding for a member of a dominant culture.

To add visual insult to injury, we have no idea to what tribal affiliation Tonto belongs. Tonto's clothing style offers no evidence to help decipher his tribe of origin. In short, his buckskin jumpsuit and single feather are too generic to offer a positive role model for Indigenous people.

Tonto is indeed a mixed bag. Yet his character becomes even more complex upon closer inspection of the comic book. Take Tonto's problem with ESL (English as a Second Language). When he speaks, Tonto still uses the broken English we are accustomed to hearing from Indigenous people, complete with the "ums" and "ughs." However, when reading his thought-bubbles, there is a surprising change in the quality of language. In his thoughts, Tonto is very coherent and highly articulate — his thoughts stand very much in contrast to his verbal skills.

What could this mean? Well, for starters, comic book audiences have much more information about Tonto than anyone else. Only the comic book readers are allowed to read his inner thoughts, and they are the only ones to know that Tonto is not the simpleton he appears to be to others. In conversation with other Indigenous people, Tonto becomes quite eloquent.

Jacquelyn Kilpatrick comments on Tonto's verbal contrast: "It seems to indicate that he is intelligent and articulate in his own language but simply doesn't understand English all that well. That's a move in the right direction, but it probably doesn't have too large an effect. Too often, there is a prejudice in favor of American English to the denigration of all other languages. Americans have stereotypes attached to most non–English languages. Even the British have stereotypes attached because of their accent(s). That Tonto hasn't learned English well would still indicate a lower mentality to people who hold that stereotype in mind. The fact that the Lone Ranger seems to be profoundly monolingual doesn't seem to indicate anything except that he is a real American" [Kilpatrick interview].

Tim Truman, creator of Scout comics, offers this opinion about the Tonto series: "Some of the [1950s] Tonto comics were interesting. Alberto Giolitti actually seems to have done some research on the regalia of various Native groups. Also, in the Tonto comic — as opposed to the Lone Ranger comic — Tonto doesn't speak in 'pidgin English' when he speaks to other Indians. He speaks normally" [Truman interview].

Yet, Truman relates that much care had been given to illustrating the Native clothing properly. So much care in giving Tonto a fringed jumpsuit? While Tonto's garb remains unidentifiable to any specific tribe, much care is indeed given to the clothing of Indigenous people with whom he fraternizes. While most of their apparel still appears too much like that of the Plains tribes, there are certain intricacies that can be appreciated by Indigenous people.

Yes, there are several ethnically based slurs directed at Tonto within the comic book. Many times, Tonto is subjected to the slanderous terminology of those who would do him harm. However, these slights might have been offset had other individuals made comments that were not racially discriminating against Tonto. These offenses might have been offset in some small way had Tonto been granted the ability to take some "Native pride" in his particular tribal culture. Sadly, since Tonto's creators never deemed it necessary to allow him to belong to a specific tribal nation, the insults are not compensated for.

Tonto's verbal skills are atrocious. Yet, as we have seen, despite Tonto's inability to master English, he is no less intelligent for it. Indeed, while much of the outside world may think Tonto to be just another stupid Indian, he is intuitive and very brainy. Unfortunately, unless you are a person who speaks his native tongue (or just happen to be able to read his thoughts, as the audience is able), then you would never know this fact.

Sadly, Tonto and all subsequent Indigenous people seem to be part of some large generic Plains tribe. There is no mention of Tonto's specific tribe and he seems to be able to "talk Indian" with any Native person he comes across. This fact does nothing to convey a sense of the great diversity that exists in Indigenous cultures and therefore serves as a very negative stereotype.

With regard to humor, there is very little of this negative element within the Tonto comics. Most comic situations (if any) stem from the surprise of Anglo individuals at Tonto being a "good Indian" or besting them in some way.

Certainly, Tonto and others like him are trapped within the historical pages of the Old West. In this way, one might say that the Indigenous people are an extinct race, people who only existed when horses, and not automobiles, reigned supreme. Yet all characters, Indigenous or white, are trapped within the confines of the historical setting in which they are placed. Since the historical traditional view of Native Americans as living in days gone by has largely prevailed, there is a greater danger that the audience will think of them as a people only in the past tense. It is important to have stories with Indigenous people participating in modern events. No such happenings occur in Tonto comics.

To some degree, a patronizing tone is conveyed toward Indigenous people. Basically, the tone of the comics is one of subservience. Whether we speak of Tonto's slavery to the Lone Ranger or to the idea of western justice itself, it is pathetic to think that Tonto will never be allowed to have a normal life. He is bound to both the Lone Ranger and to the idea of frontier crime-fighting only because he is Indigenous. Because of this, he is imbued with special powers that no Anglo may possess: tracking, animal husbandry, getting hit on the head by whites, and so forth. Yes, the tone is patronizing indeed.

It can be argued that Tonto is more human than the Lone Ranger — he makes mistakes (good-natured ones) and faces the hardship of his racist surroundings. However, most comic book audiences are allowed to see Tonto only as subhuman because of his dismal English skills. Again, it is important to keep in mind the Spanish translation of Tonto: a dummy, foolish or fool. In the Lone Ranger's world — and it is indeed his world — Indigenous people are not human.

Dell Publications (and later Gold Key) produced many famous comics in its day, including *Tonto*, *Little Beaver*, and others. In *Comic Book Nation*, Wright maintains that "Dell's comic books remained steadfastly traditional in their cultural outlook" and were infused with "old-time moral and emotional values" by their creative teams [187]. Yet, surprisingly, comics such as *The Lone Ranger's Companion Tonto* offer a view of Native people as intelligent and compassionate humans.

Wright responds: "That's an interesting point. I think in the case of Dell, the 'traditional values' had more to do with a conservative editorial policy that didn't take a lot of chances and avoided anything too controversial, violent, or ugly in children's entertainment. And most of Dell's comic books were based on licensed characters, so they weren't going to deviate very much from what the characters were like on TV or in the movies" [Wright interview].

While he is a surprisingly complex character, Tonto leans toward being a negative stereotype. Sadly, this most recognized of Indigenous comic book heroes is one of the most detrimental to our culture. We must strive to create another character just as popular but one without the negative elements.

CONCLUSION

How can one not like Tonto? Ignoring Tonto's language deficiency for a moment, he is strong, efficient, and, well, "faithful" (as the title of his comic series suggests). In short, he gets the job done. Yet, it what he represents, rather than his actions, that constitutes an irritating thorn in the side of Native readers: Tonto represents the perpetual second-class citizen in a world dominated by whites.

Despite the laudable traits mentioned above, Tonto never rises above being someone's "companion." Just as Tonto never exists beyond "those thrilling days of yesteryear," he never advances as a human being beyond this subservient state. No matter how good, faithful, or reliable Tonto is, he will never be accepted as his own "man" or as a real human being. As Indigenous readers, the awareness of this fact sticks in our collective craw.

Yet, Tonto most likely represented an advancement in social equal rights during the comic book's initial run (1940s and 1950s), and he remains a popular character into modern times. While we can praise this advance for its innovations, Tonto remains a limited character, one who needs much improvement. We shall discuss later some revisionist comic books that embody many advances on the Tonto character.

Tipi (Magazine Enterprises, July 1953)

Tipi was a Native American youth who seemed to be ever at Dan Brand's (aka the White Indian) side. The two fought side-by-side against evil during colonial (pre–American Revolution) times. Interestingly, there are some very disturbing stereotypes as well as some groundbreaking innovations surrounding Tipi's character. Unfortunately, despite these brighter elements, Tipi was not able to warrant his own comic book title.

Normally, the terms describing Native Americans in the comic were tame, compared to other comics of the time. The occasional use of "redskin" or "savage" appears in the comic book pages. However, these terms were utilized to demonstrate a character's true despicable nature: those who used such terms were usually on the side of wrong. Despite these occasional occurrences, Indigenous people were presented generally in a respectful tone.

It is also a relief that Tipi did not speak in pidgin Tontoesque English. Tipi seemed very articulate and poignant at times. This alone is a pleasant surprise for a comic book Indian, considering the era and the general treatment of Indigenous characters by other comic books during this time.

While Tipi's speech marks an improvement, his clothing does not fare as well. Despite the comic's setting in the New England area, Tipi's clothing more closely resembles Plains Indian dress than what one might expect to find in this area. Still, there is something to be said for the fact that his apparel appears intricate and is illustrated with great care. Yet, based on his clothing alone, Tipi's tribal affiliation remains a mystery.

Unlike other sidekicks, Tipi is not a bumbling buffoon. While he finds himself in various predicaments and binds, it is not generally due to a lack of intellect. However, the downside to this is that this Indigenous character relies heavily upon the white protagonist for salvation and protection.

Similar to comic books set in the Old West era, this comic book traps all its characters within the constraints of the past. The presence of Indigenous people in today's society is a very important message to get across to audiences, and unfortunately *White Indian* does not convey such a message to its readership.

This comic title also tends to portray Native people in either noble or savage extremes. Many times, Dan Brand must battle Native Americans who seem rather bloodthirsty and do not think rationally. On the other hand, Dan often intermingles with docile tribesmen who seem ultimately "good" in nature. There are few cases in between these extremes to illustrate the complexity of what it means to be human.

Yet, the overall tone of the comic book is very respectful toward Native Americans. Indeed, Indian humanity and pro-Native civil rights prevail. The white Indian takes the stance that Indigenous people are not only important enough to emulate while fighting injustice in the new America, but they are also people who deserve to be treated fairly. For its time, this was a novel idea indeed and the comic's creators should be applauded for their efforts.

Conclusion

In many ways, Tipi is just a watered-down version of Tonto. While he may be the "good Indian," and he may even be a faithful companion, he does not exemplify those terrific traits Tonto had (namely, strength, cunning, and reliability). Tipi is completely dependant on Dan Brand for protection and guardianship. Sure, Tipi does not struggle with the same language barrier that Tonto had; yet, Tipi is a less redeemable character because he wholly supports a non–Native usurping and supplanting Indigenous culture in making it his own (translation: Tipi willingly aids and abets a super-wannabe). And I don't even want to begin discussing the homoerotic undertones conveyed in this series. Suffice it to say, while Tipi is a nice character, he is not one to elicit pride from Native readers.

CHAPTER FOUR

The Indian's Sidekick: Where's That New "Temp" We Hired?

Aw, %@$ **you**, ya cheap **spell jockey**! It'll take more kumiss than you'll ever **have** to put me on the **floor**.*—Weasel, Muktuk's spirit animal

With the advent of comic books such as *Turok: Son of Stone*, the Native American character finally gets a protégé to call his own. After years of fighting crime in the shadow of someone else, usually a white man, the Indigenous hero gets his own whipping boy. While this development is indeed a milestone, there are some inherent drawbacks.

In many cases, a Native American central protagonist does not warrant a human sidekick, but he must make do with a member of the animal kingdom. Thus, while white comic book heroes get an Indigenous helper, comic book Indians are only allowed an animal — and sometimes only the *spirit* of an animal — as assistants.

In many ways, having an Indigenous sidekick was very much like having an animal sidekick. Savage tells us that Tonto was only half a hero to the Lone Ranger's status of full hero [Savage 7]. Yet Horn perhaps best puts this notion of sidekicks in perspective. When describing Tonto's horse, Horn states that "Tonto also had a recognizable mount, the paint Scout, who was to Silver what he himself was to the Lone Ranger" [37]. One can surmise that Horn speaks of subservience here. It is not surprising that Horn discusses Tonto and horses in the same breath — both were looked on as helpmeets to the real hero. Still, having any sidekick at all (however marginal) is an improvement over being someone's sidekick.

Andar and Andy: Turok's Companions — in the Flesh!

Turok: Son of Stone was originally published by Gold Key comics and started in 1954, in *Four Color Comics* no. 596. This comic comprised an anthology comic series that highlighted other stories as well.

Of all the Indigenous comic book characters with a sidekick, perhaps the most important is Turok, for two main reasons.

First, Turok is allowed to have a real human being as his companion. Many others are allowed only a nonhuman totemic entity as their attendant. Turok, however, is afforded another Homo sapiens to keep him company. In the more modern version of Turok, Andar is replaced by his grandson, Andy. Thus, Turok gets a total of two sidekicks!

Second, the timeframe of *Turok* must be examined. The original *Turok*—in which first Andar appears—began in the 1950s. Thus, while other comics of the time had Indians as subordinates—*The Lone Ranger*, *White Indian*, and *Red Ryder*—in *Turok* an Indigenous hero was allowed to retain another human as his companion. Thus, because of the comic book's early appearance, the series must be noted for its innovation.

We shall discuss both the old and the new Turok comic book character in more depth later. Here, it is important to know that, while Turok's character may not have been a perfect one, the importance and innovative nature of the character cannot be denied. While it may seem logical that giving a Native American hero a real human sidekick so early in comic book history meant that the trend would continue, we shall see that, on the contrary, as time went on things did not improve for Indigenous protagonists—if anything, they got worse.

Conclusion

Andar may not be the perfect sidekick, but who is? Did Robin always do what Batman told him to do? No, of course not. Yet, just like the Caped Crusader, Turok was lucky enough to get a real, live human being as his sidekick rather than just an animal or totemic spirit. Frankly, the Native American hero should have been awarded a human sidekick long ago. While Andar, a young Native American, will do as a sidekick, real justice would be to have an inept white guy serve as a plucky assistant to a central Indigenous protagonist. Ah, well, maybe next time.

Lobo the Wolf: Red's Wolf's Four-Legged Buddy

Red Wolf's sidekick is Lobo, a grey wolf. There are far too many stories that rehash the idea of the great white hero and his faithful Indian companion. That Red Wolf is important enough to warrant his own sidekick is a mighty step forward indeed toward propagating a positive Indigenous representation in popular media.

Red Wolf has his own sidekick, which is a good thing. However, Red Wolf does not merit a *human* sidekick, only an animal. Sadly, this thematic element runs rampant in popular media. All too often, an Indigenous person is portrayed as someone close to nature—someone who can commune with the animals. Another common case is when a Native person has their own spirit animal or guide. Lobo seems to be a cross between both a character cliché of a being close to nature and a spirit guide for Red Wolf.

We must applaud *Red Wolf* for many reasons: The comic contains a character who is the first major Native superhero, one who is a complex character, more human than many other Indigenous characters, and one that even has his own sidekick. However, comic books such as this help to perpetuate the idea that Native people exist only in the past. Indigenous people are seen with their spirit animal too many times. While there is much to be celebrated in characters such as this, there is much to improve on as well.

"(Red) Man's Best Friend." Lobo, who is also a red wolf, resurrects himself to help the other Red Wolf defeat the bad guys. *Marvel Spotlight on ... Red Wolf*, vol. 1, no. 1, 1971 (© 2008 Marvel Characters, Inc. Used with permission).

Despite all of the comic's improvements, neither Red Wolf nor his lupine helper appealed to the general public. Perhaps readers were not ready for such a character. Regardless, the lack of popularity of *Red Wolf* may well indicate the dominant culture's preference for Indigenous characters who are misrepresented, such as Tonto and many others.

CONCLUSION

Lobo's presence seems fitting, given Red Wolf's canine affinity. However, having a wolf as a sidekick does not seem to command as much respect as having a human valet. Going back to the Batman example: would he have been as powerful a character if Robin had been replaced by a super–intelligent bat? It is hard to say for certain, but one would assume he would not be as popular had he been saddled with a bat for a sidekick. Perhaps this character limitation is one of many reasons for the cancellation of *Red Wolf*.

Gahn: Wise-Ass Chipmunk Guide to *Scout: War Shaman* (Eclipse Comics, March 1988)

Scout certainly got the short end of the sidekick stick. Not only did he receive a nonhuman assistant, not only was it only a spirit animal (and not substantially real), but it was one of the smallest members of the animal kingdom, the chipmunk.

While other Native American protagonists may boast of a mighty spirit animal on their side, such as Red Wolf's lupine friend Lobo, Scout merits one tiny chipmunk named Gahn. Yet Gahn's diminutive status actually manages to counteract a common stereotype.

As mentioned above, in many stories, across several genres, Native people receive large and powerful totemic spirit guides. In *Red Wolf* Lobo, for example, demonstrates the true inner and spiritual nature of the hero: powerful, in tune with nature, and potentially dangerous. By providing Scout with a chipmunk spirit guide, Tim Truman (creator) dispels such stereotypic notions about spirit guides. There is no need to have a large and powerful animal to guide him — Scout kicks butt even with a tiny chipmunk at his side.

Additionally, even though Gahn provides spiritual support to Scout, he serves up this support with a generous helping of sarcasm. The continual banter between Scout and Gahn provides a nice comic foil against Scout's efficient brutality (he is a *war* Shaman, after all).

In all, while no one really *wants* a rodent for a spirit guide, Gahn stands in sharp relief against generic Native totemic guides. The use of the chipmunk is subtle and ironic, both of which provide for an entertaining and thought-provoking use of a sidekick.

CONCLUSION

Granted, Native American protagonists are paired too many times with nonhuman characters. Yet, while Gahn is a totemic spirit, he certainly compensates for this fact with his pluckiness and humor. While this personification does not excuse this

"Every Chipmunk Shall Have His Day." Gahn, furry sidekick in *Scout: War Shaman*, puts in more than his two cents worth. *Scout*, no. 3, January 1986 (© Tim Truman).

choice, it certainly makes it easier to swallow. At the very least, the brevity and sarcasm displayed by the chipmunk turns the tables on the mystic Native shtick. Ask any chipmunk: sometimes, smallness really makes all the difference.

Weasel: Drunken Second Banana in *Muktuk Wolfsbreath: Hardboiled Shaman* (DC Comics/ Vertigo, August 1998)

So what is worse than having a tiny chipmunk as a sidekick? How about an alcoholic weasel with a smart mouth? This is exactly the character that Muktuk Wolfsbreath finds himself attached to, a companion who is simply dubbed "Weasel."

While Weasel may have a chemical dependency, it does not affect the quickness of his brain. Weasel is both quick-witted and quick to protect his friend Muktuk. Many times, the quick thinking and acting Weasel is the one that ends up saving Muktuk's proverbial bacon.

While these two make a good pair, the fact remains that the Muktuk character is not endowed with a human counterpart. Similar to Scout, Muktuk must battle for good with

"Meeting of the Minds." Weasel, an alcoholic spirit guide in *Muktuk Wolfsbreath: Hardboiled Shaman*, states the obvious while Muktuk narrates the story like a pulp fiction detective novel. *Muktuk Wolfsbreath: Hard-Boiled Shaman*, "Mommy's Girl," Vertigo, no. 1, August 1998 (© DC Comics).

only a totemic spirit animal by his side. While Muktuk is not exactly "Native" (see the "Instant Shaman" section for more details), he is close enough, thematically, to discuss here.

Weasel gives no end of grief to the protagonist. This is a far cry from earlier comic books, where the comic relief was supplied by the Indigenous person himself. Examples of the Indian sidekick can be seen in titles such as *Red Ryder* with his pal, Little Beaver, and (of course) the *Lone Ranger* with his Tonto. Horn describes Red Ryder as "the most popular of all western strips ... [which] was adapted into [a] comic book" ["American West" 578]. Therefore, having a sidekick that does not belittle our heritage is something new to a Native American reader of comic books. For this reason, *Muktuk* should be lauded.

Of course, given that Muktuk is a shaman and does much of his battling in the spiritual realm, it makes sense that his assistant would be a resident of that locale as well. But what about those Indigenous characters who do not fight in the spirit world? What sort of helpmeet is given the comic book Natives who fight in the "real" world against physical forces?

CONCLUSION

Similar to Gahn, Weasel wins a load of points with his humor. Certainly, it would be better to merit a human sidekick, but given Muktuk's vocation ("Hardboiled Shaman"), a member of the spirit world makes sense. In addition, the banter between the Muktuk and Weasel is written well enough to warrant an ongoing series. Now, if we could just get an Indigenous writer or artist on that comic book, it would be even better!

CHAPTER FIVE

Instant Shaman (Just Add Indian)

I am Coyote, the unique and invincible one! … I'm a god! A man! Coyote!!—
Sylvester "Sly" Santangelo, aka Coyote

The idea that all Indigenous people have some innate shamanistic/mystic ability is a stereotype found in comic books and other forms of popular media, such as film. Examples include elements such as animalistic (totemic) characteristics or just generic Indian "spirituality" (the latter is especially true when dealing with the idea of Indigenous person as shaman).

Why do writers depict Native Americans within the context of the spiritual realm? Certainly, there is some truth to this portrayal: there are indeed Native Americans that practice the shamanistic arts into modern times. Yet, why is there such fascination with the theme of Indigenous shaman?

For many, the idea of shaman may call up images of mystic chanting, animal sacrifice, and the occasional hallucinogen. In *Teachings from the American Earth: Indian Religion and Philosophy*, Robin and Tonia Ridington relate that "Shamanism is usually described as a magical flight into a supernatural realm" [192]. It is probably the irresistible combination of magic and the supernatural that attracts so many artists to create stories populated by shamans.

Yet a side effect comes with this trend: the assumption that within every Indigenous person there hides a potential shaman. Notably, the inverse is not true: within every Anglo, no one assumes that there is a latent priest/scientist/doctor ready to emerge without a moment's warning. No one truly expects everyone of Irish ancestry to somehow transform into a Celtic priest of old. People instinctively know that such vocations take years of training and practice. However, as an audience, we accept the subtle assertion that a Native person can become an instant shaman — despite the fact that fulfilling this role also requires a lifetime of knowledge, learning, and practice.

Comic books are no less guilty than other genres of using these generalizations. The literary vehicle of instant shaman or natural huntsman is not a surprising one, given a comic book's overall element of excitement and adventure. Really, what could be more exciting than suddenly finding out you are more than you were before or knowing that an evildoer can never escape justice from an Indigenous character because he can track

"A Comic Book Star Is Born." Coyote's origin utilizes Native American mythology to create a modern-day trickster figure. *Coyote*, vol. 1, no. 1, April 1983 (Copyright © 2007 Steve Englehart).

his prey wherever they may go? Comic books apply spontaneous transformation to seemingly normal Native American characters that morph into super shamans.

Of course, dealing with the shaman stereotype requires making use of typical shamanistic practices: sweat lodges, fasting, herbology, totemic practices, trance-induced song, and, yes, even the ingestion of naturally occurring hallucinogens (peyote in a few cases). Unfortunately, comic books usually offer a single crude amalgam of all these elements. Of these practices, comic book Indians seem to favor totemic application, namely, conversing with members of the animal kingdom and having a "spirit animal" sidekick.

Comic books in which this theme can be found include *Coyote, Alpha Flight, Shaman's Tears*, and *Muktuk Wolfsbreath: Hardboiled Shaman*. While not all these comics use the exact same shamanistic elements, the similarities are hard to ignore. And within this group there are some Native American characters who stand out as innovative and who attempt to throw off the shackles of misrepresentation; others, however, seem overburdened with these stereotypes.

Coyote (Marvel/Epic Comics, June 1983)

Coyote, from Epic Comics, revolves around a central character who is the embodiment of an age-old Coyote spirit. Because of this affiliation, the central character retains many of the characteristics normally associated with the Coyote found in Native American mythology. One such element is the ability to change into other physical forms, which is a primary component of the trickster figure, Coyote, in Native American mythos.

Just as in many other Indigenous cultures, Caddo (Hasinai) people have stories about the Coyote trickster. Our Coyote can also change forms. In one story, Coyote changes into a corn mill (the old mortar-and-pestle type) in order to get more food [Dorsey 108]. Similarly, the comic book Coyote can change physical forms. In *Coyote* no. 1, the reader is given a hint as to Coyote's origin. The comic book states that he can "shift his shape to resemble anyone he [chooses] or disappear altogether."

Throughout the first issue, there are flashes of stories about the Coyote spirit. These are done very well and appear to be represented in a way that conveys respect for Native culture. While the stories are set in prehistoric times, they do not convey the message that Indigenous people are found only in history. Indeed, the reader is led to believe that these origin stories occurred before humankind was ever around, when other entities ruled reality. In addition to these moments of insight to the Coyote spirit's past, the dialogue features a mixture of allegorical language and everyday slang. This alone breaks the mold of what one expects in literature in which Natives speak.

Coyote is highly articulate and does not speak in metaphors or in "Tonto-speak." When asked about his nonstereotypical character, creator Steve Englehart offers this reply:

> It's too bad that it seems like a great accomplishment, but I do know that all people have brains. (Again, early in my career, I wrote a French character who said things like "*Ah, mon ami, now we come to the maison, n'est-ce pas?*" and my agent at the time said flatly "Nobody talks like that." That really opened my eyes to the fact that

"How's Tricks." Coyote's trickster roots stem from a long line of Native American mythology. *Coyote*, vol. 1, no. 1, April 1983 (Copyright © 2007 Steve Englehart).

everybody talks perfectly coherently in their own head. Maybe Coyote's not thinking in English, but he's thinking articulately—and I'm writing *him*, not "look, kids, this is an Indian") [Englehart interview].

Again, this is quite a contrast to characters such as Shaman from *Alpha Flight*. All too often, Indigenous persons speak in metaphors or in broken pidgin English. In this respect, Coyote dispenses with tradition and negative stereotypes.

Englehart discusses the steps he took in creating a Native American character free of stereotypes. "I read half a dozen books and visited a few museums. In real life, that's way too much work for a simple comic, but not nearly enough to turn me into a [Native American], but I didn't want to make any obvious mistakes. I wanted the series to be as legitimate as I could make it." This effort to make Coyote legitimate was successful in many ways.

Yet why make such a character Indigenous in the first place? "I first conceived of Coyote—undoubtedly, I first learned of Coyote—while spending the month of June in Las Vegas, visiting a friend. We spent a lot of time out prowling the rocks and desert outside of Vegas—for which reason, I still think of Vegas as a place people live and work and visit the desert, rather than simply a glitzy Strip. So later, when I turned my idea into a comic, I made him a member of the people who lived around Vegas."

Coyote is a member of the Paiute people, usually located in that region. Coyote has a complex origin, but mostly he was a young Paiute boy who was raised by a magical couple. From this, he learned the trickster ways.

While this series is successful in avoiding many stereotypic pitfalls in which other comic books seem to fall, it is not free of blemishes. When Coyote is in his "true" form (and not assuming the form of a human, such as his alter ego, Sylvester Santangelo), he appears to be in traditional Native American clothing. Why not a cape? Alternatively, a mask? Similar to the protagonist in *Shaman's Tears* and Warpath from *X-Force*, why must this Native superhero be made to wear fringe?

Englehart supplies this answer:

> As a sort of "superhero," he needs a distinctive garb. Even though these were just "comic books," I, as a writer, try to do characters that are more complex than simple stereotypes—and as a thinking person, I try to be aware of the world around me. I [have written about] blacks, Asians, women, gays, and Native Americans over the years. I do not want to sound like I'm on a soap box or a pedestal; I just find stories more interesting if I have many different minds at work in them. So when I conceived of Coyote as a comic, I was fully aware that I should learn as much as possible about the [Native American] mind-sets, [and] I already knew that I wouldn't be going for broken English and eagle feathers. But having done so, I still needed a 'costume' for my hero, and since he was the incarnation of a primal [Native American] spirit, he gets to dress like traditional [Native Americans] (P.S. I know that [Native Americans] dressed differently in different parts of the country, and one area of ignorance on my part is whether a Paiute would dress like Coyote.) [Englehart interview].

Well argued. While Englehart has a valid point, it would be refreshing to see an Indigenous superhero without the buckskin. Warpath, one of Marvel's *New Mutants*, started out wearing a costume adorned with fringe and feather (for many years), but later, the character begin to dress more conventionally (in later issues of *X-Force*). While

"Steppin' Out in Style." Coyote's personal fashion choices take care not to fall into the same generic trap other comic books do, namely, fringe and bonnets. *Coyote*, vol. 1, no. 2, June 1983 (Copyright © 2007 Steve Englehart).

Coyote falls into this trap of fringed costume, it does not detract from the title's overall worth for Indigenous readers. Compared to many other comics, *Coyote* contains very few negative stereotypes, and Englehart should be congratulated.

For starters, the language used is anything but demeaning. Many of the stories are filled with a sense of respect for Native American mythos.

While many comic books do little to discourage stereotypic categorizations of Indigenous people, *Coyote* takes a slightly different approach. An approach, one hopes, in the right direction. Coyote is a carnal embodiment of the trickster figure seen in many Native cultures and folklore. As a trickster, Coyote is able to outwit and outmaneuver opponents. Thus, while maintaining a heroic style, and subsequently illustrating various aspects of Native American mythos, *Coyote* breaks some of the stereotypes that plague comic books. Yet, the comic is not without its faults.

Trickster tales abound throughout many of the Indigenous tribal communities in the Americas. While *Coyote* illustrates the cunning and mischievousness that a trickster embodies, the book fails to illustrate perhaps one of the most important elements about Coyote to Native Americans: his ability to instruct a culture as to the right way and wrong way of living. In Caddo culture, this instruction serves as the very core of the trickster himself; without such an ability to instruct people to follow the proper path in life, the Trickster fails to be part of the Native American ideology [Dorsey 89–90].

CONCLUSION

Coyote is a very interesting character: he is a product of modern times, he is not limited by any pan–Indian or Hollywood-type of clothing, and — much like the Native American trickster he is named after — Coyote offers a taste of the unexpected while still paying homage to traditional oral storytelling. Yet, it is unclear if Sylvester ("Sly") is really a member of an Indigenous tribal community (by birth) or if the Coyote spirit is simply reborn in him, with no regard to ethnicity or culture.

Based on conversations with Coyote's creator Englehart, Sly / Coyote is more than likely Native (as well as otherworldly from a different dimension perhaps). Add to this element the look, feel, and references to Native American mythos and the distinction becomes less important: certainly this comic books series directly *involves* Indigenous people, even readers are unsure of the central protagonist's tribal membership. *Coyote* is a worthwhile comic book to read, especially given its few stereotypes; however, the series could truly benefit from an Indigenous perspective on the creative team.

Alpha Flight's Shaman (Marvel, August 1983)

One shaman — whose superhero name also happens to *be* "Shaman" — is a team member of Marvel's *Alpha Flight*. Shaman, whose real name is Michael Twoyoungmen, is a member of the Sarcee tribe. Shaman received this heroic station via his special lineage, passed down from his grandfather. Within the pages of *Alpha Flight*, it appears that Shaman is more of a magician than a shaman.

In many cases Indigenous holy men, typically called shaman, perform holy feats only by establishing a direct relationship with the spiritual realm and, in many cases, they only do so to the benefit of their specific cultural kinfolk or community (Rasmussen

Opposite and top: "Coyote of Many Colors." Coyote offers a multi-tiered view of a Native American mythos while upgrading the story for modern times. *Coyote,* vol. 1, no. 4, January 1984 (Copyright © 2007 Steve Englehart).

Opposite and top: "Sometimes the Truth Hurts." Coyote sinks his teeth into his origins, which are not as simple as originally thought—and they bite back. *Coyote*, vol. 1, no. 4, January 1984 (Copyright © 2007 Steve Englehart).

13–19). Michael Twoyoungmen seems more the type to pull some magic out of his bag of tricks than to be burdened by a deep relationship with and concern for his people. Yes, *bag*.

Shaman receives much of his magical power from the medicine bag at his side. This bag is similar to the "light burden" that Turok (an Indigenous video game character) carries. Shaman also has many dealings with "gods," which seems to be the comic creators' interpretation of the Indigenous spiritual realm. There are very few tribal communities that come to mind who would refer to their respective spiritual denizens as "gods." This character too seems stereotypical in its affinity with the mystical power of magic.

For the most part, there is little demeaning terminology used in *Alpha Flight*. Of course, this may have something to do with Shaman's importance to the missions, as he the team's link to all things magical. Whatever the reason, Shaman is given a certain level of respect within the comic pages.

While heavy in his use of metaphors, Shaman does not speak in Tontoese. His character has command of the English language and demonstrates intelligence when he speaks. Perhaps this also references his education, as he is a trained medical doctor.

Shaman will probably never win any awards for "best dressed" with his headband and man-purse. Yet, his regular costume is relatively free of the standard pan–Indian headdress and fringed buckskin. Thus, while there are a few standard elements to his garb, readers are not presented with stereotypic clothing and accessories typically seen in many popular media.

Possibly because of his constant grief at being unable to use his magic to save his wife from death, Shaman is a very serious character and there are no comic interludes based on his character; especially none based on *firewater* or Indigenous stupidity. While the lack of these more disparaging elements are positives to his character, the complete lack of humor is still disturbing; there is no representation of the true Native American humor that so many Indigenous individuals possess. To present a more complete and accurate representation of Native American people, humor must not be neglected.

Shaman and the other members of *Alpha Flight* exist in the modern age. This illustrates cultural continuance, as Shaman is not shown in the light of the past only, which is typical of so many comics.

Michael Twoyoungmen (Shaman) is a complex character. While he does not demonstrate the Native humor element (discussed above), he is not portrayed as simply either noble or savage. His actions and choices are based on complex internal emotions and not just because he is the "good" Indian or the "bad" Indian, as is typically the case in popular media.

In all, while the Shaman character is rather stoic at times, there is some level of Indigenous humanity demonstrated. Certainly, his character (and his daughter) fall into the larger category of *instant shaman*, based on (Native) genetics alone; yet, from an Indigenous standpoint, the lack of stereotypes used to portray him and his presence in a modern-day setting make his character very human and acceptable.

CONCLUSION

In some ways, Shaman is a forgettable character, but that does not make him any less important from an Indigenous reader's viewpoint. His lack of "ughs" and feathers

"This Is My Bag, Baby." More than just a fashion accessory, Michael Twoyoungmen's mystic bag of tricks can surprise even him, at times. *Alpha Flight*, "Turn Again, Turn Again, Time in Thy Flight," vol. 1, no. 19, February 1985 (© 2008 Marvel Characters, Inc. Used with permission).

make him an important improvement in Native American comic book characters. Yet his primary function as a mystic supports the idea that Indigenous people are naturally children of the spiritual realm, based on genetics alone, which is troublesome, to say the least. Perhaps it is a good thing that Marvel has killed off this character (at the time of this writing); perhaps when they revive the Shaman (as almost *all* comic book characters get revived at some point), we can begin to see some positive changes and less stereotypes.

Shaman's Tears (Image Comics/Creative Fire Studio, May 1993)

Shaman's Tears is the story of Joshua Brand, a man with a multiethnic heritage who becomes "Wicasa Wakan" — the holy one. His heritage is both Lakota and white, but he does not feel comfortable in either world. A powerful earth spirit chooses him to fight for her and grants him special powers.

Many shamans or holy men are noted healers, and so apparently is Joshua Brand, protagonist of *Shaman's Tears*. His shamanistic power appears to take the form of self-regeneration: when wounded, he will appear whole again in mere seconds. Add to this skill, Joshua has great control over the environmental elements.

Joshua can control such elements as the wind, the sun, weather, and so forth. He retains special control and power over the totemic animal world (although his powers seem limited to those animals located in North America). From the birds in the air, allowing him to fly and see clearly, to the bear, which gives him strength, many of these border on the stereotypical Indian shamanistic powers found in many other comic books. Yet there are some differences.

Earth Spirit Woman chooses Joshua to be her champion as protector of the earth and its inhabitants. The "tears" of the shaman are the ones shed by Joshua (from one eye only) as the power from Earth Spirit Woman transforms him into Wicasa Wakan or "Stalking Wolf" (another name Earth Spirit Woman bestows upon him). This is certainly a redeeming quality of the comic as some Lakota holy men have been known to "cry" for their vision quests (Brown 20–21).

Shaman's Tears is an interesting comic to say the least. In short, this title seems to support a small number of negative stereotypes while attempting to transcend many others. The story, by Image Comic Groups, involves an attempt to imbue an Indigenous person with metahuman powers while allowing him to retain some sense of dignity. While the title has the feel of sincerity and deserves certain accolades, it is not without some flaws.

Shaman's Tears addresses the idea of negotiated identity and status by its main character, Joshua Brand, who is multiethnic. The first issue opens with a close-up of Joshua's face. Here, we see that he has Native features and coloring, but he has green eyes. Joshua is part Lakota, part Irish. This issue of ethnic identity is a difficult one at best for many individuals, including the fictitious main character.

Mike Grell — creator, writer, and illustrator for this series — explains this complex character and shares some personal history about how he came up with the idea.

> The choice was based on a number of things, including crass commercialism (we'll come back to this later) and what was the "hot" genre (superheroes) at the time. But mostly it was a case of what's near to my heart. I wanted to do a book that would

draw out the best in my abilities as a writer and an artist, something that couldn't be done by half measures.

Having grown up in northern Wisconsin, I've always loved animals and the outdoors. My grandfather lived among the Cheyenne for a number of years during the early 1900s and I've always had an interest in Indian cultures and traditions. So, when I first began the creative process on Shaman's Tears, I looked for a way to combine everything that I loved into a project that would force me to do my best work. Who and what Joshua Brand is was fairly easy. The superhero aspect was dictated by the simple fact that a company (Image) that was selling millions of superhero comics naturally wanted to continue that trend [Grell interview].

Yet, what of Joshua's multiethnic background? Why choose to create a character who is part white/part Native? Grell continues:

The multiethnic part was [also] easy — I'm Italian, English and Welsh, so for me [writing] from the viewpoint of a pureblooded Native American would be impossible. I do have many friends who are of Indian descent and I've been aware of a lot of the problems they face. I decided to focus on the shared aspects of human relationships that anyone can relate to: feelings of alienation; family problems; the quest for self-identity and an understanding of our place in the world. Brand is a man who ran away in search of himself, only to discover that he had run in a circle, back to his roots. By making him multiethnic it was easier to draw readers into the similarities in people while using the differences to create conflict and a more interesting story. Despite my own Welsh/Celtic heritage, I think the Native peoples have maintained a closer contact with the earth.

The idea of separation and isolation is a universal one, according to Grell. "From a purely dramatic standpoint, you need conflict for a good story and the differences that separate cultures have been a constant source of conflict since time began. I'm not claiming to have done a perfect job, but I tried to deal with real world problems facing real people by making those cultural and racial differences part of the story." Joshua feels that he does not belong to either specific cultural group. He makes the statement that his father was a "half breed" and that he himself is only an "Irish Indian." Joshua goes on to state that these ethnic identities have caused him much grief and he was "too much [Indian] for the white [people] ... [and] never enough for the Lakota" [*Shaman's Tears*, no. 1].

Joshua, being a product of a Lakota father and Irish mother, is raised on the Medicine Hat reservation. As a young adult he leaves the reservation for various reasons. Upon reentering the "rez," Joshua finds his mother in failing health. Her dying request is that Joshua should take his place in society by undertaking a vision quest. During his quest, which resembles the traditional Sun Dance, he discovers that he (like so many others) is chosen by a higher spiritual entity — Earth Spirit Woman — to be her earth champion.

This choice angers many younger "full bloods" of the reservation, protesting that Earth Spirit Woman's choice is an unjust one for two major reasons. Not only is Josh partially white but, more importantly, he made the decision earlier to abandon his people on the reservation. Conversely, non–Indians mistreat him because his physical appearance resembles Native culture. Thus, as Joshua becomes the "Warrior Healer: Wicasa Wakan," he is continually at odds with both cultures. Josh can find no culture that will fully accept him.

"Momma's Boy?" Joshua Brand (Stalking Wolf) is compelled to participate in a comic book version of the Lakota Sun Dance at the request of his dying mother. *Shaman's Tears*, "Warcry," vol. 1, no. 1, May 1993 (*Shaman's Tears* © Mike Grell).

Enduring hardships because of one's ethnic identity is an important thematic quality, yet it is not entirely a new idea. Marvel Comics' *Red Wolf* and DC's *Scalphunter* faced a similar fate. The main difference between these characters and Joshua is that they were simply *raised* by another culture (Red Wolf was Indigenous but raised by Anglos and Scalphunter was white yet reared by Kiowa people); Joshua, however, is the real McCoy in that he is *biologically* multiethnic. Obviously, belonging to more than one ethnic affinity has never been easy for anyone, even for comic book heroes. In this, *Shaman's Tears* makes an honest attempt to convey honest feelings that many multiethnic individuals experience.

The comic makes a good effort to illustrate the struggles one might endure during modern times because of mixed heritage. Many other comics only portray the struggles an individual might face in specific settings, such as the Old West in *Red Wolf*. *Shaman's Tears* is set in modern times.

Yet, the comic has some blemishes in other aspects of its representation of Native people. As Joshua returns to the reservation where he grew up, he runs into a childhood friend. Joshua and the friend turn out to be "blood brothers." This theatrical element too seems to be a favorite among story writers.

If we are to believe popular media, such as movies and comic books, it would seem that all young boys have an Indigenous blood brother at one time or another. In reality, many Indigenous cultures feel no need to shed blood to build social relationships. Many times Indigenous people are surrounded by individuals who are "cousins" in some way or another. In Native American culture, this has been referred to as a cousin "in the Indian way," illustrating no need of genetic or familial bonds.

However, creator Grell has a particularly different experience. When asked about any possible ethnic connection he might have with the main character, Grell states, "The only Indian blood I have in me was from becoming blood brothers (Cheyenne, Arapaho, Blackfoot, Pawnee, and Nez Perce). A Lakota pal once told me, 'you don't have to be Indian to have an Indian heart.'" Certainly, there are exceptions to any case and perhaps this idea of blood brothers was motivated by good intentions.

Despite these contrasting ideas of interpersonal/communal relationships, *Shaman's Tears* introduces several elements that are more widely accepted as true. Comments on how some of the Lakota sacred dances were once illegal and other hints to recent Native American history lend some legitimacy to the story. The comic book contains positive elements and, while the events are referred to in the generic sense, *Shaman's Tears* at least acknowledges the existence of religious diversity. There are many other titles that never touch on any of these concepts. Grell modestly addresses this positive addition by simply saying, "I have a rack of reference volumes."

There are some minor flaws in the way in which the book represents Lakota people. Joshua's mother makes a dying request of him that he undergo a "vision quest." Vision quests are typically done out of personal commitment, not at the behest of someone else. These quests are highly personal in nature. Thus, no one individual has the power to tell another that he or she should go on a vision quest. It must be a personal, voluntary choice.

While the quests are performed for personal reasons, many times the vision quest is a formal and spiritual request that the end product (the "vision," etc.) benefit the entire community of the vision seeker. In simple terms, one feels *intrinsically* compelled to go on a vision quest to gain some insight toward enriching the *community* [Brown 29]. Joshua is coerced into participating in a ritual that looks similar to a sun dance.

Joshua does not prepare himself with an open mind with the intention to seek the improvement of his community. He does it out of mistrust and negative feelings. Thus, *Shaman's Tears* offers a slightly skewed representation of a Lakota vision quest — at least according to Black Elk, a Lakota holy man who is quoted in the comic book.

As Joshua completes his vision quest, he is petitioned by Earth Spirit Woman to become her champion, her Wicasa Wakan or Stalking Wolf. During this time, the spirit imbues Joshua with many powers. Of course, it is no surprise that Joshua's powers are totemic in nature. He has the strength of the bear, the ferocity of the wolf, he can fly like the eagle, and so forth. These are the kinds of powers audiences of popular media have come to expect over the years. Much like the characters of Red Wolf, or Warpath, or even the television cartoon *BraveStarr*, Joshua is imbued with the power of the animals. Based on these components, it seems that Indigenous people are best suited to retain only powers that are totemic in origin.

Another peculiar aspect: when Joshua is chosen, he is instantly given new and colorful "hero" clothes. In addition to the colors, and perhaps because he is the chosen champion of Earth Spirit Woman, Joshua is outfitted in fringe and moccasins as well. While this is certainly an attempt to pay homage to his heritage, one certainly wonders: why not just give him a cape? Or a cool stealth suit? Why does it have to be fringe? (One could ask these very questions of Marvel's *Warpath* character as well.) Just because a superhero is Indigenous, must the costume reflect historical times?

Grell fields this question with a certain amount of candor. "In fact, the only reason he's in the costume you see is because of marketing research. The original sketch has fringe and a breechcloth, and was intended to be deerskin, but the publishers felt that bold colors and more 'superhero-type' costuming did better on the stands. I would have preferred to do it the other way, but you choose your fights and it's best to pick the ones you can win." Yet, this other choice of Grell's, too, seems to place Joshua's clothing within a historical setting, rather than a contemporary one.

This trend continues throughout the series. Later, Joshua is seen in his regular clothing, but he now wears a rather large eagle feather in his hair. While this feather illustrates Joshua's newfound respect for his people and heritage, it tends to strengthen a stereotype that many have about Indigenous people being stuck physically in the past. There is no real need for Joshua to start adorning his hair in such a fashion — it just serves to make him appear more "Indian."

Apart from the drastic wardrobe choices, once Joshua is chosen he begins talking in mystic phrases. He begins speaking to others about how the animals are his brethren. This is wonderful and it is indeed a part of several Native American worldviews. However, within the context of *Shaman's Tears*, and combined with the other elements mentioned, it comes off as being more stereotypic than anything else.

Grell shares his thoughts about Joshua's speech pattern:

> That's simple — he's speaking from the spirit. He's also speaking in the Lakota tongue, and I hate using the traditional comic book brackets or asterisked editorial notes like "translated from the original pig Latin.— ed." (As a kid, I could never figure out who

"ed" was — I thought he was the guy who did the translation.) If you want to see a great example of the use of language to establish characterization without resorting to subtitles, watch [the film] *Little Big Man* [Arthur Penn, 1970] and listen to Dustin Hoffman. When he's among the Indians he speaks perfect English (bear in mind that English is the language of the audience, not the character), but when he's among the whites he speaks as if he's an uneducated southerner [Grell interview].

While the comic book attempts to celebrate a new hero that is ethnically diverse, it does strengthen a few stereotypes about Native Americans. The diversity of the central character is a positive aspect, but it is closely followed by a few elements that can be easily misrepresented, such as the misuse of blood brothers and vision quests.

Also, after becoming metahuman, the central character devolves into a style of speaking and speech that derive from the world of the past. Overall, while this entails positive and sincere effort, it still lends itself to a few stereotypic treatments of the kind Indigenous people have endured for too long.

However, the above sentiments are not ones shared by the comic's creator. Grell feels that the central character is representative of a universal hero. "Let me say up front that I don't believe in super powers like Superman or Spider-Man have, but I do believe in spiritual and metaphysical powers, so for me *Shaman's Tears* is 'reality-based.' He draws his power from the same source that created us all, whatever you choose to call it. This factored into the decision to make him an agent for the U.S. Department of Fish and Wildlife, combining his connection with the earth and animal spirits to his law enforcement job (crime fighting being a prerequisite in superhero comics)."

Yes, there is some vocabulary demeaning to Indigenous people within this series. However, this language is used to illustrate villainy and wrongdoing. For the most part, *Shaman's Tears* respects Indigenous culture with its choice of words.

While no Native people in this comic *speak-um* like Tonto, the clichéd metaphors flow like water from a mountain stream. Surrounding the central character during his transformation are various quotes from famous Indigenous people. The protagonist himself also seems deeply rooted in the age-old tradition of Native people speaking in ornate metaphors.

Shaman's Tears also subscribes to another age-old tradition of popular media: its main character appears to be part of some pan–Indian tribe all of whose members wears buckskin and feathers. Understandably, the main character is (part) Lakota, which *is* a Plains tribe, and feathers may be in order. However, Joshua's outfit borrows little to nothing from Lakota culture or iconography. This clothing is generically Indigenous with no specificity, but with plenty of fringe. As stated above, this clothing choice is one made by the publisher (Image Comics) and not the creator.

Luckily, there seem to be very few jokes about Indian drunkenness or stupidity. While there are some derogatory insults to illustrate a character's flaws, there are no jokes made at the expense of Indigenous culture. There are a few visual allusions to Indigenous people partaking of alcohol, but they are not destroyed by it. Several issues of this comic illustrate Native people gathering at a bar or tavern, but drunken Indians are no where evident. This is a strong point of the comic book.

Another strength is the comic's portrayal of Indigenous culture as a viable and living entity. Simply put, the comic book shows that Indigenous culture exists into

"Badge? He don't need no stinking ... oh wait; he has one." Joshua Brand is not only a hero with special powers bestowed on him by a spiritual being, he is also a hero working for the U.S. government. *Shaman's Tears*, vol. 1, no. 4, December 1994 (*Shaman's Tears* © Mike Grell).

modern times. To support this idea, keep in mind that no illustrations of bows or arrows can be found in this series. Finally!

Unlike many comics of yesteryear, *Shaman's Tears* does not have the Indigenous character speaking in Tonto-like broken English. As explained above, the English is really a translation of the Lakota being spoken when Joshua transforms into Stalking Wolf. Still, while this is a personal choice of the comic's writer, it might be too subtle for many readers — readers who may see this as a cultural misrepresentation.

There is no patronizing tone in this comic book. Great care has been taken to present the Indigenous characters seriously, so while this comic has many misrepresentations, a tone that demeans Indigenous people is not among these flaws.

Shaman's Tears is complex to say the least. It features both major breakthroughs and some minor flaws for a comic book with a Native central character. Indigenous people are treated as both human beings and complex creatures within its pages. In fact, a special mention should be given here for Grell's development of supporting Indigenous characters, which are not only well-developed and well-rounded, but display an unusual amount of humanity compared to characters in other comic books. In short, the supporting Native characters exhibit a great deal of diversity, modernity, and (most important) humanity. These elements alone make Grell's work stand out among other comics.

Grell sums up his work on the series by relating his ideals in writing comic books.

> A writer's job is to tell a story. When I look at different cultures from a dramatic standpoint, I try to see more than just the sociological problems. It's the similarities that link us all, the shared human experience. But it is the differences that make it interesting. You have to be true to your source, sensitive to the nature of the people you're writing about, never condescending, but at some point you do have to take a stand and decide to face the issues head-on. That's why Shaman's Tears includes not only the positive elements of native culture and tradition, but the grim reality of the problems of alcoholism, teen pregnancy, family conflict, and crime [Grell interview].

CONCLUSION

Stalking Wolf is multiethnic (part white), he is the reluctant hero, he wields a myriad of powers (some of which border on stereotypic), and he sports some wild fringe in his costume. This character is by no means perfect — as mentioned, Stalking Wolf falls into the *instant shaman* category — yet, Grell's discussion offers some real insight into the creative aspects of comic book Natives.

Based on his comments, it seems that characters found in mainstream comics undergo many changes from the creators' original intentions. Yet, what we are left with here is a character who embodies much in the way of improvement in the representation of Indigenous characters (modern, centralized protagonists with powers based on traditional cultural elements that do not talk like Tonto), but who is still bogged down by a few cultural generalizations (he is an *instant shaman*, speaks in metaphors, is close to nature, and wears fringe *ad nauseum*). Grell has lofty goals and should be congratulated for his intentions (as well as his innovative supporting Native characters), but there is still room for improvement. Perhaps *Shaman's Tears* could be improved with Grell partnering with a Native American for future stories.

Muktuk Wolfsbreath: Hardboiled Shaman (DC Comics/Vertigo, August 1998)

This three-part miniseries from Vertigo is quite a well-written and well-illustrated treat. However, it is debatable whether this comic book should be discussed here. Despite a somewhat misleading title, *Muktuk* has little to do with Native Americans. But because of its very title, which alludes to those cultures that invoke shamans, such as some Native American and other Indigenous cultures, and because the characters' resemble early North Americans, a study of *Muktuk* seems fitting here. He and other Indigenous people in the story are handled in ways that break with many of the traditional ideas of how Indigenous people are usually portrayed in literature.

Muktuk is not a Native American — he is a member of one of the many Indigenous communities in the region of Siberia during pre–Columbian times. Yet this point does not detract from the comic's overall worth to a Native American reader. It is easy to identify Muktuk's similarities with other Indigenous peoples. Certainly, Muktuk is a shaman in a Siberian location a long time ago. His specific ethnic origin matters, of course, but his being associated (visually and textually) with other Indigenous cultures is just as important. While the bulk of this inquiry is about Native Americans in North America, the overall theme is about portrayal of all Indigenous people in comic books. Therefore, this comic book has much relevance here.

Muktuk's creator, Terry LaBan, says that he had no specific intent for making Muktuk Siberian rather than strictly Native American. He states that Muktuk is "not Native American but rather, Siberian. The two are related, at least if you believe the anthropologists, but obviously, not the same thing." LaBan continues, "I did use a certain amount of Native American — or really, Eskimo — mythology in writing the stories, though, and the character actually came to me after a visit to the Field Museum in Chicago, where I'd been really taken with the exhibit of Northwest Coast and Inuit artifacts, which included a lot of shamanic stuff. But the truth is, I only used the actual mythology as a jumping off point — most of what's in the stories is made up" [LeBan interview].

Muktuk does not speak in broken English and (unlike *Shaman's Tears*) he does not speak in metaphors about the Great Spirit. This alone makes him different from many other Indigenous characters in comic books. The setting occurs in prehistory and, while the clothing reflects this time period, characters speak in modern phrases and refer to current themes. Other Indigenous characters featured in this comic book are not included simply for comic relief or to serve as colorful backdrops for the main character, as they are in the reincarnation of *Tomahawk*.

Instead, comic relief is supplied by Muktuk's spirit animal, Weasel. Weasel has a drinking problem, but he appears to be a good companion to have on your side in a tight spot. This little fellow gives no end of flack to Muktuk. As with *Scout: War Shaman*'s chipmunk, Gahn, using a spirit as comic relief instead of an Indigenous person is somewhat of a novel idea. *Muktuk* provides a much-needed breath of fresh air for comic books featuring Indigenous people.

LaBan says this about the portrayal of Indigenous people in comic books: "I'm no expert ... [but] my impression generally is that when Native Americans are portrayed, at least in the last twenty years or so, they tend to be sentimentalized as some type of 'noble savage' or as bearers of wisdom that white people need to be receptive to." LaBan explains further about how the creation of *Muktuk* breaks with this sentimentality: "I'd read somewhere that shamans, Siberian ones, anyhow, weren't regarded as these wise, enlightened people within their actual societies. They were viewed as necessary, but people feared and distrusted them. I thought that was really interesting — they really were a lot like private detectives in a lot of ways. Then ... bingo!"

The amalgamation that resulted may have been somewhat serendipitous for LaBan, but it becomes vital for Indigenous people from a thematic standpoint. The mixing of detective genre with a distinctive cultural setting allows the main (Indigenous) character to become more solid in the reader's mind. Muktuk seems far more realistic and complex than say, Stalking Wolf (from *Shaman's Tears*), a character who seems ambiguous at times.

Muktuk constitutes a very positive example of how Indigenous people can be depicted with little use of stereotypes. Despite the fact the story is about a Siberian Shaman, there are many connections to Indigenous people in North America. These connections, coupled with the use of modern language and complex characters, make this comic book series a refreshing improvement on others. Comic book literature in general would benefit from the presence of more characters such as Muktuk.

While *Muktuk* is a good example of how Indigenous characters should be handled, Native people should also keep in mind the importance of communicating our own stories. Using *Muktuk* as a thematic launch pad, the next logical step would be to employ Indigenous authors to write comic books. Put simply, in addition to the appearance of good stories with few or no stereotypes, Indigenous people should consider authoring comic books. This topic will be discussed more later on.

CONCLUSION

Muktuk Wolfsbreath is a really great comic: Muktuk and Weasel offer a great demonstration of humor and the comic does a good job of amalgamating Indigenous oral tradition with noir-style detective stories. While the character Muktuk isn't technically Native American (he's more Siberian than anything), he's close enough from an Indigenous perspective. In addition, the iconographic style and thematic style suggest "Indigenous" to readers as much as anything.

Muktuk has too few blemishes (set in historical times and the presence of an instant shaman) to detract from its quality writing and effective story. Comic books would benefit greatly if Native characters were crafted as well as Muktuk (minus the few generalizations).

Manitou Raven (DC, *Justice League of America* No. 66, July 2002)

In the latest round of "Instant Shaman" characters, the DC universe has been graced with Manitou Raven, a North American Indigenous person from ancient pre–Columbian contact times. He wields magical powers on a universal level. It is rumored that he was inspired by Apache Chief from the "Super Friends" animated series. In this vein, he invokes the same magic word that Apache Chief used to grow tall: "Inukchuk!" (which seems to have no real meaning). This phrase would also allow Manitou Raven to use his powers.

The main points discussed in this section deal with comic books' use of the shamanistic stereotype when portraying Indigenous people. As illustrated in the cases above, the perpetuation of the "mystic Indian" is manifested in various ways. There are elements of the magical Indian (in some cases an "actual" shaman) in which the hero wields almost supernatural power, and there are also cases of Native Americans shown in close relationship to the natural world and, because of his or her Indian heritage, he or she is able to communicate with the members of the animal realm. This relationship may also help to explain the stereotypic view that many indigenous Americans are good trackers or have suped-up senses. The tendency to portray Natives as simpatico with nature and animals recalls the popular image of the Indian brave with his ear to the ground. Fortunately, there are some titles that attempt to go beyond such stereotypes — the *Coyote* series for one — but some limitations still prevent these comic books from going all the way in truly portraying Native Americans in a nonstereotypical light.

CONCLUSION

It isn't very surprising that DC killed off the Manitou Raven character, given the shift in focus to his wife, Dawn. From an Indigenous reader perspective this was a mercy killing. While Raven may not have been an *instant* shaman (there is little explanation of the origin of his powers), too many other stereotypical generalizations occur within the character to allow it to be enjoyable.

Native readers can be thankful that at least *one* stereotype was not used with Raven: he wasn't prone to "firewater" and he even went a step further (in his spiritual form, post-mortem) to encourage others (Major Disaster) to seek professional treatment for alcoholism. Despite this spark of humanity (in death), characters like Manitou Raven do nothing but add to the list of narrowly defined, one-dimensional Native characters that do little to uplift and celebrate the culture and only serve as "types" with little to no attention given to the character's development or to the meaningful illustration of Indigenous humanity.

CHAPTER SIX

Indigenous Trackers Union (ITU)

*It was **men** I hunted—evil men who rape the land, and **murder**, for profit!—*
Jason Strongbow, aka American Eagle

Another major stereotype in comic books is the portrayal of Indigenous people as skilled trackers with supernatural sensory perception. Expert trackers are usually seen in militaristic settings, and this idea has its roots in an era when the U.S. Army employed Indigenous scouts. Because these people had great familiarity with the territory involved, the idea grew that they were inherently excellent trackers.

While including every comic book Indian described as a "tracker" would exhaust the limits of this work, a few characters stand out in this category.

American Eagle (Marvel Comics, *Marvel Two-In-One*, October 1981)

A stereotype frequently found in literature is one that portrays Native Americans as imbued with enhanced sensory ability due to their "closeness" with nature. In a case comparable to this one, we can look at Marvel's character, American Eagle, aka Jason Strongbow.

The Official Handbook of the Marvel Universe (Marvel Comics, January 1983) tells us that American Eagle receives his special abilities from exposure to radiation while trapped in a cavern. While this exposure wondrously augments his strength, American Eagle is best known for his keen eyesight (like an eagle, one supposes) and other heightened senses. These senses serve him well as he tracks down his enemies during his first appearance in Marvel's *Two-In-One Annual* no. 6. He also sports a high-powered crossbow (of course) and adorns himself in a full-feathered headdress. "Jason emerged from the cavern with superhuman powers that he attributed more to the Great Spirit of his tribe that to the mutagenic effects of the radiation bombardment."

The *Two-In-One Annual* turns out to be a very interesting story about Native Americans. In addition to establishing the origin of American Eagle, the comic book deftly illustrates a real-life dichotomy, which many Native American people undergo.

Jason Strongbow (American Eagle) has a brother, and both men are charismatic leaders of their people. Jason believes his people would benefit from a more traditional way of life while his brother, Ward, leans toward a more progressive and therefore "white" way of life for his people.

The two brothers' differing points of view lead to some strong disagreements between not only them but also the people they lead. This division is one that many Indigenous people face throughout their lives: which is best — tradition or progression? Major divisions in Native life about this very issue cause some individuals to look down upon others who do not agree with their point of view on the subject. Unfortunately, the debate tends to force individuals into the narrow corners of becoming too "white" or being stuck in the past, depending on who is speaking.

One brother, Jason Strongbow (the traditionalist) in this comic book, while he does not feel that his more progressive brother has become too white, he does fear the corruption his brother may have learned from the whites. "I attempted to lead our tribe onto the path of nobility — but you, most of all, my brother, I had hoped to lead onto the path of greatness. Perhaps you learned **more** in the university than either of us at first understood — for you truly have learned from the whites ... but from the **wrong** whites!" [*Marvel Two-in-One* no. 6].

Despite this very philosophical discussion between the two brothers, the comic offers insight into Native American life, at least in a pan–Indian respect.

However, there are some less-than-stellar moments in the comic. Fantastic Four member, the Thing, reacts to his friend Wyatt Wingfoot (also a Native American and friend of the Fantastic Four) recounting a Native American legend in the following manner: "Awright, get on with it. What **did** happen ta remind the elders of that corny legend? No disrespect intended, y'understand."

While Wyatt took no disrespect, the overall tone is one that demonstrates impatience with another culture's spiritual aspect. Of course, one could effectively argue that the Thing's temperament was always somewhat abrasive, no matter the circumstance or even the use of the character as a simple plot device to move the story along. So, it can be conceded that the Thing's reaction to this legend was only natural to his character and did not reflect his opinion about Native Americans in general.

While this comic seems chock-full of Indians, none of them seem to suffer the sad fate of speaking like Tonto. In fact, we can go one step further and mention that few of the Native American characters speak in flowery metaphors either. Both of these elements are steps in the right direction for Native American comic book characters.

In a step backwards in the comic book evolutionary chart of Native American characters, American Eagle dresses in fringe and feathers. Given this generalizing stereotype (that all Indians must wear a feather headdress), the reader is given little way to identify his particular tribal affinity. Other than the comic book explanation that he is from "a neighboring tribe in the southwest" and Marvel Universe mentioning that his base of operations is "Navaho Reservation, Arizona," there is little that indicates his tribe. The feather headdress just confuses this issue more.

Yet, on the other side of this argument, Wyatt Wingfoot (friend of the Fantastic Four) wears everyday normal clothing. His character does not feel the need for fringe or buckskin. Moreover, what of the people in Jason Strongbow's tribe? They seem to dress normally. Sure, some of them wear headbands and have longer hair — but this sort of attire seems typical on a Navajo reservation in the early 1980s. Thus, the

AMERICAN EAGLE

Real Name: Jason Strongbow
Occupation: Tribal leader
Legal status: United States citizen
Identity: Secret
Place of birth: Kaibito, Arizona
Marital status: Single
Known relatives: Ward Strongbow, his brother, gained similar powers to Jason before being slain by a criminal's bullet.
Group affiliation: None
Base of operations: Navaho Reservation, Arizona
First appearance: MARVEL TWO-IN-ONE ANNUAL #6
Origin: Trapped in a cavern during an explosion of ore refining machinery, Jason Strongbow was simultaneously bombarded by radiation from an unknown isotope of uranium and the sonic vibrations of Klaw, the criminal master of sound, who happened to be present at the time. Jason emerged from the cavern with superhuman powers that he attributed more to the Great Spirit of his tribe that to the mutagenic effects of the radiation bombardment.

Height: 6'	**Weight:** 200 lbs
Eyes: Brown	**Hair:** Black

Powers: American Eagle possesses superhuman strength, derived from radioactivity that mutagenically fortified his body's cellular structure. At peak strength, he is able to lift 15 tons, sufficient power to uproot a tree.

The cellular fortification of his muscle tissue has also granted him superhuman levels of speed and endurance. He is able to run at a maximum of 65 miles per hour for approximately 5 hours before tiring to an appreciable degree. His body's endurance level is about 50 times that of an average human being.

The American Eagle's sensory organs have also been fortified by the radiation-induced mutation. Like his namesake, the Eagle has hyper-keen eyesight, able to see at 800 feet what the average human being sees at 20 feet. His senses of smell, taste and hearing are approximately three times that of an average human being.

Weapons: American Eagle carries a crossbow which fires specially designed bolts. He has a bolt to which a line of braided fiberglass is connected, enabling him to swing from overhead objects or to climb its length. He also has specially blunted bolts in order to stun an opponent at a distance.

"Definition of an Indigenous Hero." Marvel's Handbook offers little insight into American Eagle's heritage and worldview. *The Official Handbook of the Marvel Universe*, vol. 1, no. 1, January 1983 (© 2008 Marvel Characters, Inc. Used with permission).

"My Indigenous Sense is Tingling!" American Eagle is able to sense an oncoming attack just in time, due to his heightened Indigenous senses. *Marvel Two-In-One Annual! The Thing and Introducing American Eagle*, "An Eagle From America!" vol. 1, no. 6, 1981 (© 2008 Marvel Characters, Inc. Used with permission).

question of whether Native characters in this comic are dressed generically or stereo-typically is a hard one to answer. Certainly, it would have been better if American Eagle could have made his costume without the headdress (and possibly the moccasins), but overall the clothes found in the comic book are acceptable.

There are no scenes in which Native people are portrayed as stupid or drunk. In fact, there is little to be seen of Native humor in this comic book.

Indigenous characters are alive and well in modern times, according to this comic book, at least. While this may not seem like a large hurdle for Natives to have over-come, it is highly refreshing to see an Indigenous hero existing in modern times. Too many comic book Indians are marooned in times long past; happily, characters such as American Eagle and Wyatt Wingfoot demonstrate differently.

Native characters are not simply noble or savage in this story; instead, they seem rather complex when compared to many Indigenous characters produced in comic books. While there is the innate sense of good versus evil that the comic book story promotes, the Native antagonist is not some blood-thirsty fiend willing to fight any-one without a thought.

The overall tone of this story seems very respectful toward Native Americans. In fact, we can conceive of these Native characters as being very human — a quality not often found in comic books. Not bad for a "one shot" comic.

CONCLUSION

At first glance, with his headdress, fringe, and crossbow, American Eagle appears to be just another stereotypic character. However, his powers (supposedly) originate from radioactive material (though, there is a hint at the cultural legacy, too). I mean, what self-respecting character *wouldn't* want radioactive powers? If it's good enough for the likes of Hulk and Spidey, then it's good enough for a Native American charac-ter.

In short, while the character may have some inherent stereotypic issues, the fact that American Eagle's powers come from a non-ethnically based source (and not, say, the Great Spirit) marks a significant improvement for Indigenous characters.

Now if we could just have a Native character who had laser eye blasters as the source of their powers (instead of expert tracking abilities), all would be right in the (comic book) world.

Scout: War Shaman (Eclipse Comics, March 1988)

Scout by Timothy Truman is set in a not-too-distant post–Apocalyptic future. While, the Scout character could easily fit within the section on Instant Shaman, we discuss his character here based on his skill as a tracker of "monsters" (more on this later). He comes complete with a spirit animal, Gahn, who just happens to be a cute chipmunk.

Also, Scout uses peyote numerous times within the course of the comic book. This gives the impression to a non–Indian reader that all Native Americans take this med-icine. The real truth is that not all indigenous people ingest peyote. In fact, peyote is rarely used outside of two religious movements prevalent in the Native American com-munity: the Native American Church and the Peyote Way [Slotkin 96].

"The Education of the Thing." In a tender moment between the two, Wyatt Wingfoot asks the Thing to listen to a Native American story. *Marvel Two-In-One Annual! The Thing and Introducing American Eagle*, "An Eagle From America!" vol. 1, no. 6, 1981 (© 2008 Marvel Characters, Inc. Used with permission).

For those unfamiliar with the genre, Scout burst onto the comic book world in the mid 1980s with a violent and gritty realism. By the end of the decade, in 1988, the series transformed into *Scout: War Shaman* [Overstreet 659]. The comic book and its creator, Tim Truman, gained respect from Native American communities for the character's integrity.

"I've gotten tons of letters over the years from Native people — most of them Navajo, Hopi, and Apache — who have read Scout and they are always favorable. Some well-known Native creative people have also made it a point to get in touch with me over the years," says Truman. Along with Eric Schweig, a Native American actor from *Last of the Mohicans* (1993), Truman communicated with other Indigenous people in the film industry. "Sherman Alexi, the author, screen-writer and filmmaker is another guy who got in touch with me and we've had great correspondence over the years. Sherman had been turned on to my work by an Apache educator, Pauline Esquedero Shaeffer, who used the Scout comic in her classes at the University of Washington. Scout was the only book — comic or otherwise — in her curriculum that was written by a non–Native and which she thought was a positive portrayal of Native people in general or Apache people in particular."

Tribal Force creator Jon Proudstar supports the popularity of the Scout character among Native readers: "[In *Scout,*] Truman captured the spirit of what it is to be Native. I remember for a long time I thought that a Native had written the book. I liked Scout because for the first time it showed the complexity of walking two roads at once. That you could be American yet still, not. That spirituality was like breathing and our Gods exist like the air that we breathe" [Proudstar interview].

Simply put, this is a comic book about survival in a harsh, futuristic world. The main character, Scout, utilizes his wits as well as multiple firearms to aid in his battle against evil. Oh yeah, one more thing: Scout just happens to be Indigenous.

Set in a fictional post–Apocalyptic America where martial law rules, Scout is simply a man who must fight what he calls "monsters." Scout fights these monsters in various ways. Sometimes by hand and sometimes with a gun, and sometimes he fights them on a mental/spiritual plane. Truman relates the following: "In Scout's world, the disaster [nuclear holocaust] had already happened. America was practically destroyed — a wasteland, tapped out by corruption and greed, ozone layer gone, farmland gone, people reduced to virtual slavery. My hero had to be someone who could live in that world."

Generally speaking, the vocabulary used to describe Indigenous people in *Scout* cannot be termed demeaning. While there are occasional slurs toward Scout himself, the overall tone of the comic book is one of respect for Native American culture.

Scout is free from Tontoesque speech patterns. He is articulate and fully capable of expressing himself in English. This is a positive aspect of the comic book as too many Native characters are found babbling in incoherent monosyllabic sentences. Sadly, when this occurs, it makes the character seem unintelligent when compared to other characters given superior linguistic skills. Thankfully, Scout is free of such negative language stereotypes.

He is Native American but he wears neither feathers nor any stereotypic clothing. Truman comments on fringe and feathers: "I think that feathers and fringes add to stereotypes and contribute to the mistaken idea that Native Americans — no matter the

"Locked and Loaded." Tim Truman's Scout is ready for action and ready to face the dangers of an apocalyptic version of our not-to-distant future. *Scout*, no. 3, January 1986 (© Tim Truman).

tribal background — are a dead culture. Such portrayals also propagate a 'generic' view of Native people — that Native Americans were one big tribe that basically looked and acted the same way. They ignore the fact that each tribal group was very different form each other. Apaches were as different from Seneca as Chinese are from Russians. Cherokee are as different from Hopi as Spanish people are from Lithuanians." To punctuate this idea Truman states, "When I write about Natives, I came up with a rule of thumb: look at each group as a separate nation or country rather than as a tribal group."

Despite the lack of feathers, Scout has a single red line across his face. Could this be stereotypical "war paint" or a facial tattoo? Truman comments on the red line. "[Scout] did wear a stripe of 'war paint' across the bridge of his nose. It's based on the yellow stripes that Geronimo's group decorated themselves with. In Scout's case, the band is red. This is symbolic and, though unrevealed, is an important aspect of his characterization: red was the color of Crook's Scouts. They wore red headbands and, sometimes, war paint to mark themselves as U.S. Army scouts."

Scout seems free of comedy based on notions of the "stupid Indian" or "drunken Indian." There is a distinct lack of such scenes in which Native people are seen as drunkards or just plain stupid. Scout is a very serious character (a man at war with "monsters") and while there is a specific amount of natural comedy between him and his sidekick (more on the sidekick in a moment), none of this comedy occurs because of Scout's debauchery or lack of intellect.

Another positive note is evident in the setting. The character lives in modern (even futuristic) times. Too many times we find comic book characters trapped in the past. What is needed — and what *Scout* is able to do — is to allow a character to break forth from the past and live in modern times. We Indigenous people are not just historical pieces of notoriety; we are not just an interesting but extinct species. How refreshing that this character does not place us in a historical context. Scout's continuance even outlasts nuclear holocaust and goes a long way toward dispelling temporal misconceptions placed on Native Americans.

Scout also stands apart from other comic book Indians in that he cannot be squarely placed within the category of either "noble" or "savage." Scout is not some dignified Indigenous person who remains pure with child-like innocence. Neither is he a brute, unable to think rationally. Scout is simply a man with qualities good and not so good. He has no metahuman "super" powers; he has only keen physical ability. He is only a war shaman — one that prepares himself for both a physical and a spiritual war.

Given the complexity of this character, the overall tone of the comic book is never belittling but is instead respectful. Truman states: "I think ... most writers and artists — especially in the comic [book] community — rely on stereotypes and supposed archetypes when they create characters. They seem to use as their 'reference' and inspiration characters and portrayals of Native Americans in movies, books, and comics who preceded them rather than by getting deeply into actual historical and cultural backgrounds of various tribal groups."

Scout's character is human with flaws and strengths. He is not above reproach but neither is he unintelligent or completely incapable of logical cunning. He is not ripped from the fictional pages of history — he is a palpable individual placed in near-present times. Indeed, Scout is very human.

Scout is even accompanied by his own "hill spirit" named Gahn. This spirit is not what one would normally expect in a spirit animal. Most think of a great bear or screaming eagle of some sort when this term is mentioned. But Gahn is merely a tiny chipmunk who can be perceived only by Scout. Unlike other mystic spirits, Gahn chooses to speak in plain English and he can employ a sardonic tone with Scout. Scout is thus portrayed as not only a mystical Indian, but also one that must speak cryptically with his spirit animal.

While in certain respects Scout is portrayed as the Indigenous "victim" of society, he does not simply lament that fact and allow these obstacles to stop him from living his life. (The Native victim is not necessarily a literary stereotype found in comic books, but more of a generalization that has been made about Native Americans after the Red Power / AIM movement of the 1970s.) In one issue, Scout is asked about his past. In a single monologue, Scout tells of the wrongs committed against his parents by the government. Not only were his parents and his people bullied, but also his father was killed by government (B.I.A.) police. Because of his father's killing, Scout's mother turned to alcoholism and contracted a fatal case of sclerosis. Scout recounts how radiation poisoned and physically deformed many of his close family members (*Scout* no. 17). Yet Scout continues to fight on in spite of these adversities.

On his website, Truman states that "Scout [tells] the story of Emanuel Santana, an Apache warrior doing battle with crooked bureaucrats and mythological monsters in a post holocaust United States ... Scout proved to be popular and influential. Native American readers and educators have applauded the book for its respectful but non-patronizing portrayal of Southwestern Indian culture and beliefs." Perhaps this is true. One gets the sense that Scout's character was handled with care.

Truman addresses the idea of stereotypes in Scout when a reader complains that Scout's peyote consumption and communication with the Gahn (hill spirit) amount to just "a stereotype of American Indians." Truman states in reply: "The traditionally centered Apache seem to be on very intimate terms with their gods (as, in fact, are most religious people)—so intimate that the Apache refer not to their beliefs as 'religion,' but as 'Life Way.' To them all things contain Power and life-energy—particularly animals, but also inanimate objects and abstract natural phenomena. To get closer to these forces, some Native American groups—though not all—ingested ritual drugs. They felt themselves to be a part of the Earth, not Masters of it or a separate force in opposition to it" [Truman, *Scout*, no. 3]. It is clear that Truman has put much thought into his character.

Scout is not saddled with wearing fringe or turquoise apparel. He does not speak in broken Tonto English. He is the central character and is no one's sidekick. We can therefore surmise that Scout contains few negative stereotypes, despite the title's allusion to mysticism. This is a comic book that Native Americans can be proud to read because it dispels many misconceptions about us.

CONCLUSION

Scout is a really great comic book character from a really great source: Tim Truman. Truman puts a lot of research, care, and much of himself into his comic characters and Scout is no exception. Yes, some of Scout's methods (spiritualism, tracking, etc.) appear somewhat generalizing at first glance; yet, upon further scrutiny, Scout is presented in a respectful and genuine manner with tribally specific cultural ties. Scout is a title that, for its time, establishes many milestones for Native American comic book characters and one that Indigenous readers can read with enjoyment.

The Proudstar Brothers: Thunderbird and Warpath (Marvel)

The *X-Men* (Marvel Comics, September 1975) also spawned a Native American hero of their own. In clothing similar to American Eagle, Marvel also produced other Native superheroes with augmented strength and senses. This time the good people at Marvel decided to call their Indigenous champion Thunderbird, who is introduced to readers in *Giant-Sized X-Men* no. 1 tracking and catching a wild buffalo. His true identity is that of John Proudstar of the Camp Verde Apache reservation.

He and his younger brother, James Proudstar (aka Warpath), share basically the same powers: strength, speed, and elevated senses. Both brothers received their powers from their mother when she was exposed to radiation during government testing in the desert near their reservation (*X-Force* no. 1). James would later demonstrate his excellent tracking skills while hunting Charles Xavier and the other X-Men whom he blamed for his brother's death.

With his death, Thunderbird became a martyred hero as a member of the *X-Men*. Warpath became one of the original *New Mutants* (Marvel Comics, June 1984) and later in the pages of *X-Force* (Marvel Comics, August 1991). Never a well-defined character, conveying little insight into the Apache culture, James serves as a generic character at best. Thankfully, writers of *X-Force* later gradually did away with Warpath's stereotypical garb in giving him a more contemporary "street" style. Still, the imagery used to portray James Proudstar assumes that readers will accept a Native American figure who possesses augmented strength and sensory abilities. In other words, stereotypes such as the ones above prove to readers that Indians can run fast and see far.

James Proudstar, aka Warpath, has come a long way, from a fashion point of view. While he originally girded himself in fringe and feathers his look matured as the character himself progressed. Notice, however, that he still "sports" an eagle tattoo — albeit a very abstracted and "cool" version of one.

While we will go into more detail later on about these two Marvel characters, it is important to note here that these comic book Indians were portrayed as good hunters/trackers simply based on their biology. Similar to the notion of Instant Shaman, this stereotype relies on specific Indigenous ancestry. Despite the fact that there probably are many good "trackers" who also happen to be Native American, it is important that Indigenous people not be confined to generalizations based solely on their ethnicity. Tracking is a skill that, for the most part, is best learned and not one inherent to one's DNA.

CONCLUSION

Like many Indigenous comic readers, I have followed the Proudstar brothers for sometime with a sense of pride. Even with the elder brother's untimely demise (in *X-Men*, no. 95), the Proudstars remain major players in the Marvel universe. However,

"Where the Buffalo Roam." Despite the desert canyons' unfriendliness toward sustaining buffalo, John Proudstar (aka Thunderbird) plays a friendly game of tag in his homeland. *Essential X-Men*, 1996 (© 2008 Marvel Characters, Inc. Used with permission).

"Open Door Policy." James Proudstar (younger brother of the X-Men's Thunderbird) did not always adorn himself with feathers. Seen here in his first appearance in *The New Mutants*, his costume is very nondescript. *The New Mutants*, "Away Game," vol. 1, no. 16, June 1984 (© 2008 Marvel Characters, Inc. Used with permission).

"Comfortable in His Own Skin." Later in his heroic career, James Proudstar's costume changed and became less stereotypic (with fewer feathers); yet, taking pride in his heritage, there was always something to remind him of his cultural roots, as seen here with his abstract eagle tattoo on his back. *X-Force*, "Lower East Side Story," vol. 1, no. 65, April 1997 (© 2008 Marvel Characters, Inc. Used with permission).

as mentioned, their powers seem somewhat generalizing at times (especially the track-ing skills). Yet, if we keep in mind that these are simply mutants whose every *physical* aspect becomes superhuman, including hearing, sight, and olfactory senses, it becomes easier to understand the improved tracking skills.

This distinction should be clarified within the comic book pages and not in an outside source, such as this book. It is all-too-easy for readers to believe that the Proud-star brothers are good trackers just because they are Native American. Make this point clear and get rid of the fringe in their costumes — that's not too much to ask, is it?

CHAPTER SEVEN

Sepia-Toned Prison: Indigenous Characters as Historical Artifacts

Tonto only do what seem right! Now you take-um to sheriff!—Tonto, on morality

Mention the word "Indian," or even "Native American," and images of war paint, feather bonnets, buckskin, tipis, and horses come to most minds. Why? We are constantly influenced by mass media, such as cinema, radio, and yes, comic books, that strengthen this representation. Jon Proudstar, creator of the *Tribal Force* comic book, puts this in perspective:

> People and or companies tend to blanket Native characters into the best-known stereotypes from the Old West. It is from that period that they see us in our finest hour. Little do they realize that the Natives of that time were scared fathers and mothers defending their children and way of life from foreign invaders. Of course we were at our finest at that time. Much like the Americans during 9/11. That was a horrific event but it brought out the very best in all of us. Americans seem to forget that our 9/11 is when the boats hit our beaches.
>
> Comic books or media in general tend to mystify or romanticize the Native. They say we are a misunderstood race because we (in the beginning) were not cut out of the European mentality of divide and conquer. That we had a different set of values and religious beliefs [Proudstar interview].

The following comic book characters are trapped in a time warp. They are represented as historical figures only, with no hope of their continuing presence into modern times. While we have already discussed at length some titles in which Indigenous characters exist in historical times only, such as *Red Wolf, Scalphunter,* and *Tonto,* there are other titles that also propagate this stilted notion.

Turok, Son of Stone (Dell Publishing Co., December 1954)

While we previously discussed *Turok* for its innovation in having a Native American hero with a human sidekick, we must address the temporal issue that *Turok* raises as well. There are two incarnations of *Turok* that merit scrutiny: the first is *Turok: Son of Stone* from the 1950s and the second is a more modern version, *Turok: Dinosaur Hunter* (Valiant/Acclaim Comics, July 1993) and is Kiowa.

Comic book creator Tim Truman, who would write many issues of the modern-day incarnation, comments on the early *Turok* comic book. "I was a reader of the old *Turok* [comic]. I loved the art — Alberto Giolitti — an Italian artist was one of my biggest artistic influences. The stories were interesting, but really light fare. In hindsight, they're very interesting because the characters of Turok and Andar aren't 'noble savages.' There's no pseudo 'Indian religion' and they don't invoke any bogus 'great spirit.' They are hunters, but they rely on their brains more than their brawn. When they get into trouble, they use their wits or they run — just like real people. Very interesting."

Truman goes on to comment on the clothing depicted in those early comic books. "They look very generic, but the costuming is generally believable — no big headdresses and leather fringes, just simple attire. Then again, there is no specific tribal background named" in those early Turok comics.

Despite being transported to an alternate dimension — one with ravaging monsters and primitive humanoids — Turok and Andar remained (pre)historic characters, forever trapped within the pages of history and nonexistent in modern times. They seem permanently fixed in their timeframe with the illustration of this made complete by fringe and feathers.

Yet, Metcalf credits this notion with Paul S. Newman's skill as a writer. "The most extended example of this skill is seen in Newman's success at writing two stories for every issue of Turok comics for 27 years without ever letting Turok and Andar get out of the Lost Valley" [*Journal of Popular Culture* 152].

In this earlier comic book series, as well as many other characters with their own series, *Turok* conveys the idea that Native Americans exist only in historical times, not present in modern society. Not only is Turok not allowed to leave the Lost Land, no Indigenous comic book character is allowed to leave the confines of historical settings. Later, we will explore how Turok broke out of this temporal prison in the pages of the newer, more modern comic series.

CONCLUSION

Turok and Andar are relics of the past. Even when Turok is revived during modern times (in the Acclaim comic book), he remains an anachronistic relic. The new Turok creates some storyline and plot points and offers some brief views of modern Native Americans throughout the series, but Turok is still a character from the past.

His clothing reflects this, as he continues to wear his buckskin and feathers, no matter what time period he is thrust into. This makes reading *Turok* comics highly frustrating for an Indigenous audience. As seen in the later comic series, he can wield an automatic machine gun, but he can't change into some jeans and a jacket? We Native people exist today and need to be represented as such in comic books.

The Adventures of Browser and Sequoia (Saber Cat Comics, no. 1, March 1999)

It appears that this title was created with a younger audience in mind. Many of the illustrations, the scripting, and the physical humor of *Browser and Sequoia* appear handcrafted for a somewhat juvenile audience. Despite this, there are both positive and negative representational elements regarding Indigenous people within the comic book.

The storyline is set over 14,000 years ago in what appears to be North America. This is a double-edged sword for Indigenous representation. The comic makes efforts to offer a story of people who share a different worldview from others. For instance, in the introduction to the first issue, the reader is given a "Spirit Guide." This guide was once a human and now exists as part of the spiritual realm. This is a positive aspect of the comic and it helps to illustrate a worldview of spirituality that may be somewhat unfamiliar to non–Native readers. The idea of a human becoming part of the spiritual realm who provides guidance for everyday living is a notion that serves as a positive example of differing worldviews found in Indigenous cultures.

However, given that these are positive factors, the title's setting unfortunately contributes to the stereotypical notion that Indigenous people exist only in the past. It is important to remember that, as a people, Native Americans are still vitally alive and thriving today. They are not "stuck" in the past. While it is also important to understand the events of the historical past, especially when these events serve to educate the public about a specific people, the image of Native people living only in centuries long ago pervades most elements of the media. In other words, film, television, and print media all offer this idea of Indigenous people as existing only in historical times. The opposite is true: Indigenous people have survived to modern times and they are not just legendary people of days gone by.

That said, it is wonderful to have a somewhat accurate historical view of Native American events. During this time period, there were indeed animals such as "Super Bison" and "saber tooth" tigers. While setting a story about Indigenous people in a prehistoric setting limits them in many ways, it is good to see that care has been taken to ensure that elements within are somewhat accurate. The people of the time relied extensively on survival weapons such as the spear, and this reality is well represented within the comic book.

It is interesting to see comic book Native Americans without bows and arrows, which has become almost as much a representational standard as feathers. People of this time period would be more likely to have used the long spear to survive, and this comic does a good job of proving that not all Indigenous people must be pictured with a bow and arrow in their hands.

As for providing an image that the audience is used to seeing, these characters do adorn themselves in feathers. While it is true that Indigenous people did use feathers as signifying clothing, feathers serve as a visual reminder to non–Natives that Indigenous people dwelled only in the past. There is nothing particularly offensive about the use of feathers within *Browser and Sequoia*; however, just as is the case with the story's temporal location, these images come burdened with stereotypes that must be overcome.

"The Young and the Restless." John Proudstar, perhaps representing a growing concern over equality and cultural issues in the United States at the time (1970s), greets his first meeting with Professor Charles Xavier with a little open hostility. *Essential X-Men*, 1996 (© 2008 Marvel Characters, Inc. Used with permission).

On the whole, the characters of *Browser and Sequoia* demonstrate intelligence, humor, and compassion, and they display a wide array of human emotions. However, given that the characters do show a wide range of human emotion, their manner of speech is another matter entirely. The majority of the dialogue is peppered with cryptic statements that seem overly stereotypic. Phrases such as "run like the wind" and "the legend speaks true" give credence to the idea that Indigenous people speak only in semi-mystical metaphors. Unfortunately this amplifies the idea of the noble savage that Native people attempt to overcome.

Another aspect of the dialogue must be examined here. In the book, humans and animals are able to speak and understand one another. While this personification occurs in many types of stories, it is an important element within this text. Many traditional Native American stories contain this same element. Many times, animals are just players within the plot of traditional Indigenous stories. This same element shines through in *Browser and Sequoia*, where animals show as much intelligence and are able to articulate as well as their human counterparts. Much like traditional stories, the animal world plays an integral part in the life of the characters in *Browser and Sequoia*. For this, the comic book should be applauded.

Conclusion

Browser and Sequoia is a mixed bag at best. The intended audience appears to be young readers, generally speaking, based on the content. While there are some specific good points about the title — historical accuracy and introduction of diversified ideas of spirituality — the fact remains that the comic book is set in antiquity. This places Indigenous people well within the realm of history only, and the visual elements serve to exemplify the iconographic stereotypes that other media have used over the years, namely, coupling the image of Native Americans with feathers, which visually ties them to the past. While this makes a certain amount of sense, given that the story is set in prehistoric times, it is vital that we Indigenous are seen as people who continue to thrive in modern times, which is absent in the series.

Despite this, the comic does provide *some* accurate details about the past, including specific animal species, weapons used, and even popular theories as to origins across the Bering Strait. While the characters display some degree of depth, they still speak in a manner more suited to the noble savage. As we shall discuss later, there are perhaps better choices for young readers to gain an introduction to the Native American worldview.

CHAPTER EIGHT

Modern-Day Native Heroes: Now with 25 Percent Fewer Feathers!

We're two of a kind, she and I—mutants, the next step in evolution, born with extraordinary powers and abilities. Lucky us. I'm the maker. I build things—like this holographic display system.—Forge

There will probably always be some level of anachronistic representation of Indigenous people in some media somewhere, but there are also those few Indigenous comic book heroes who escape the trappings of historical setting.

This milestone is an important one for many obvious reasons: seeing Native Americans in modern settings allows the audience to view them as more than just pieces of history; placing Indigenous characters in more modern times forces creators to provide more modern clothing beyond the usual fringe and feathers; and putting these Indian characters into modern environments has the potential to get more Native people involved in the creation process. Writers and illustrators may have to rely on more than just history books to research their subject matter, and Native Americans themselves may even become comic book creators themselves as a result.

While the following characters certainly do not represent the entire population of Native American comic book heroes who are not trapped in the past, they do represent the cream of this tiny crop. Others not listed here, such as Talisman, Dani Moonstar, Dawnstar, and Echo, can be found in the section on Native American heroines. Later, we will discuss the important next step beyond simply putting an Indian in more modern times, namely, making an attempt to undo the stereotypes in a revisionist manner. For now, enjoy the following contemporary characters.

Thunderbird (*X-Men*, Marvel Comics, September 1975)

John Proudstar was recruited by Charles Xavier to join the X-Men and given the codename Thunderbird. Thunderbird came complete with a bad temper and a permanent chip on his shoulder. For this reason, perhaps it is better that his character was killed off so quickly in the Marvel universe. While this character is very important among Native American heroes, the short-lived Thunderbird is not without some specific stereotypes.

"Hell Hath No Anger." Thunderbird has a lot of unresolved anger, despite his fellow X-Men's attempts to help and understand him. Yet, this anger does not make him a "savage Indian" as seen in many media forms *Essential X-Men*, 1996 (© 2008 Marvel Characters, Inc. Used with permission).

"Living in the Moment." Scenes such as this one (which reveals John's discovery of his mutant powers), found in a special issue of *X-Force*, illustrate the Proudstar brothers' existence in modern times, instead of being portrayed within the confines of a historical (Old West) setting, as is the case all too many times in various media. *X-Force Flashback*, "The Brothers Proudstar," vol. 1, no. 1, July 1997 (© 2008 Marvel Characters, Inc. Used with permission).

Thunderbird is introduced to the world chasing a buffalo in Marvel's *Giant-Sized X-Men*, no. 1 (Summer 1975). While we pause for the allegorical element of this introductory image to settle in, we must first examine his location. Xavier finds Proudstar at his home on an Arizona reservation. Arizona? What about the buffalo he is chasing? Of course, many of us realize there are few buffalo (if any) to be found in Arizona. Yet, this element is added to perhaps give credence to Thunderbird's Indianness.

Unfortunately, what it does instead is to add to the already burgeoning amount of negative stereotypes out there. Obviously, Proudstar is chasing a buffalo because that is what Indigenous people do all day long, right? The major problem is that the imagery lends itself to the notion that all Native Americans, no matter their tribal affiliation, are intimately involved with buffalo. Of course, this is not so in the real world. In most cases, the Plains-type tribal cultures are the only ones that elevate the buffalo to a high place within their culture. This makes sense, given that bison are normally found on the Great Plains. Apache people found on reservations in Arizona are not (repeat: *not*) Plains-type Indians.

This initial observation being made, some negative stereotypes remain. Once Thunderbird becomes a member of the X-Men, his true temperament reveals itself. Thunderbird is a very angry man and this constant animosity eventually leads to his demise. Proudstar is angry for a number of reasons, but primarily, he is angry because of the treatment Native Americans have received in this country, especially given his status as a Vietnam veteran. "The white man needs *me*? That's *tough*! I owe him nothing but the *grief* he's given my people!" [*Giant X-Men*, no. 1].

Unfortunately, this attitude consolidates two general stereotypes: the angry Indian and the angry Indian Vietnam vet. While the latter might be better discussed by someone else, it is the former that must be addressed here. This idea of the angry Native is not a new one. However, the notion is not a surprising one, given the political environment at the time of its initial publication.

Wright supports this notion in *Comic Book Nation*: "A recurring theme found superheroes urging American Indians to abandon their traditional hostility towards the United States for the sake of the national war effort" [295].

Thunderbird, an angry young Native American male, surfaces at about the same time as the Red Power and AIM movements of the late 1970s. Many educated young Indigenous people became fed up with American policies at the time and they demonstrated in various ways, including grabbing the attention of the news media by unconventional means such as occupying an abandoned federal prison (Alcatraz) and forcibly taking over a federal building in Washington, D.C.

This rebellious spirit was also reflected in other popular media of the time. One need only mention the words "Billy Jack" (referring to the film of the same name) to a Native American and images of a kick-ass-Indian are instantly conveyed. The films centered on the Bill Jack character remain a big hit with Indigenous people and they remind viewers of the height of Red Power for Native Americans. Billy Jack, like Thunderbird, was an angry Indian newly returned from Vietnam.

Bradford W. Wright supports this by stating:

[Even] liberal, well-meaning comic book writers seemed to have trouble portraying Native Americans in a way that didn't conform to some stereotype. In the 1970s, that new stereotype became the "Angry Young Red Man."

Obviously inspired by revisionist Westerns like Little Big Man as well as AIM and the siege at Wounded Knee, this was the new image that sympathetic Anglos had of Native Americans. Thunderbird was the best example of that. Of all the new ethnic X-Men, he was the most stereotypical. Wolverine wasn't a Canadian stereotype (whatever that would be!). Nor was Nightcrawler a German stereotype. But Thunderbird was exactly what you would expect a Native American superhero to be in the 1970s.

How could they have broken from stereotypes? It would have required introducing characters who were Native American, but didn't rail about the "crimes of the White Man" every other panel. There was certainly a place for that kind of rage in any authentic Native American superhero, but it could easily become pretty one-dimensional. Comic books were rarely very subtle anyway, so any stereotype tended to get magnified [Wright interview].

This idea of the angry Indian has its drawbacks, such as losing identification from a more general (white) audience; yet, I can sympathize with, and on some level applaud, such demonstrative resentment. Much of America does not know or will not accept that Indigenous people have been and still are treated as second-class citizens and many times as invisible ones. While non–Native people should not be led to think that we are just angry hotheads waiting to retake Alcatraz at a moment's notice, this anger does serve to break some stereotypes of the stoic Indian and (hopefully) educate its audience simultaneously about culture inequality.

Does this anger border too closely on the notion of Indigenous person as "savage"? Certainly, there are elemental reminders of this savagery. Thunderbird's anger clouds his ability to reason and is the very cause of his death. However, he is not a morally corrupt individual because of this emotion. This contrasts with the idea of the bloodthirsty savage who is blind with rage and/or mind-numbing chemicals (usually alcohol, but occasionally the "savage" is improperly portrayed as a peyote user).

As many readers may already know, the *X-Men* series was never about disparaging or bad-mouthing specific cultures. It is evident within the comic pages, that the X-Men served as a metaphor for those ethnic and minority groups that were underprivileged, misunderstood, and discriminated against.

When dealing with Native American characters, this standard holds true. Thunderbird is not called a "redskin" by his teammates, nor do his enemies refer to him as a "red nigger." However, it must be noted that since this character existed for such a short amount of time, we can only guess that, at some point in the future, he may have been verbally insulted, if only to provide a little drama for the story.

While few invective references are used in the descriptive vocabulary, John Proudstar's own command of the English language must be discussed here. First, and most importantly, Thunderbird does *not* talk like Tonto. This is a milestone that must be celebrated. While the character still uses phrases such as "horned-one," when speaking to a nearby buffalo and "white-eye" (*Giant X-Men*, no. 1) when first addressing an Anglo, Charles Xavier, his overall use of language contains mostly contemporary and slang elements of modern times.

"Even the Mighty Fall." Thunderbird's pride and honor may have led to his fiery death, as depicted here. The real reason for his death comes from Marvel's decision to kill off his character, perhaps based on his overall lack of popularity. *Essential X-Men*, 1996 (© 2008 Marvel Characters, Inc. Used with permission).

"Fringe Makes the Man." While he later assumed a less stereotypic style, through most of his heroic career Warpath is adorned in this particular costume, complete with fringe and feathers. *The New Warriors*, "Ruins," vol. 1, no. 31, January 1993 (© 2008 Marvel Characters, Inc. Used with permission).

Thunderbird has the misfortune to wear two small feathers sticking out from the top of his headband. While there are some tribes that use feather adornments in this way, this choice aligns the character with an iconic stereotype of all Indians dressing similarly. Besides, Apache people do not wear feathers in this manner.

There are no comedic elements about this character. None. Thunderbird takes everything seriously; as mentioned, he has a proverbial chip on his shoulder. Thus, there are no notions of the stupid or drunk Indian. However, there are no scenes that show Native humor either.

Given Thunderbird's presence in modern times, along with his teammates, the character illustrates that Native Americans exist and did not all die out in the 1800s. This is a very essential element that should exist in more comic books, movies, books, and *any* stories with Indigenous people. The message should *always* be: "we are still here and we will remain."

Thunderbird does not align exclusively with either the idea of the noble Indian or that of the savage Indian. True, while his anger does end up killing him off in the end, his character is complex, compassionate, and conversely, logical, at times.

As mentioned, the overall tone of *X-Men* is one of deep respect for all humanity, whatever the ethnic, cultural, or political origins of the characters. Never does this tone lend itself to discrimination against Native Americans.

Respect for Indigenous humanity is the message conveyed found throughout *X-Men* and the character of Thunderbird. The character is important not only because the character is found in a highly successful comic book series, but also because the character is portrayed as representative of the political and cultural climate of the time. It is no wonder that characters such as Thunderbird inspired Native readers, such as *Tribal Force* creator Jon Proudstar (who took the Indigenous X-Man's name to heart) to become better people and heroes in their own way.

CONCLUSION

The Thunderbird character combines an interesting mix of nostalgia, martyrdom, and a dash of exploitation (for flavor!). There are many things to like about his character: he was a super-strong warrior and filled with Native pride. The nostalgia stems from Thunderbird's association with some of the most popular X-Men of all time (Cyclops, Wolverine, Storm, etc.). It is also easy to martyr a character whose storyline has long been terminated (except in some alternate Marvel universes). Like rapper Tupac Shakur, Thunderbird becomes even more popular, posthumously, than he ever was while living.

Yet, looking back on Thunderbird's short career, depicted as the "angry Indian," we cannot help but see some parallels with the American Indian Movement in the mid 1970s. Similar to characters in *Blaxploitation* films, the Thunderbird character may have spoken to a particular ethnically based demographic at the time. Whatever the case, his depiction seems somewhat skewed by this exploitation, in hindsight at least.

We can only hope that, had Thunderbird lived, he would have gotten rid of the fringed jumpsuit at some point. Maybe that's why he was so angry all the time; he couldn't get a good tailor at the X-Mansion!

Warpath (*The New Mutants*, Marvel Comics, June 1984)

Warpath has many positive and negative elements, at least from a cultural point of view, and it is difficult to say which outweighs the other. In the early years, when Warpath was first introduced in *The New Mutants*, no. 16 during the mid 1980s, the character was one-dimensional and full of stereotypes [Overstreet 599]. As the years advanced, so did Warpath's character. Yet, despite this growth, James Proudstar seems limited as an Indigenous hero.

James Proudstar is the younger brother of John (*X-Men*'s Thunderbird). Warpath was originally called Thunderbird II (he later changed it) and his costume was almost exactly like that of his older brother's for many years. The costume itself is unfortunate.

Like many of his heroic predecessors, during his early career Warpath was decked out in fringe and feathers. Not that there is anything wrong with fringe and feathers. Again, however, it is important that Indigenous people be portrayed as living entities and not relics from the past. While it is extremely important to maintain one's personal cultural identity, there is a need for Indigenous people to be viewed as members of a vital and modern society and not only as reminders of the past.

Over the course of its run, *X-Force* (Marvel Comics, August 1991) began to portray James Proudstar in a more contemporary light. By issue no. 65, Proudstar's image had finally become something other than stereotypic. Gracing the cover of this issue, Warpath looks like any other modern hero.

Of course, having a Native American as the main hero is quite an accomplishment in itself. Actually, having an Indigenous person as a central character of any kind — hero or villain — is quite a change from the earlier days of comics. One recurring theme found in a multitude of earlier comic books is the mass, almost faceless, identity of Indigenous people. Horn provides the following insight on Native characters *en masse*. "While there has been an occasional Indian villain in comic strips, these were not singled out as such. The Indian menace was always portrayed as collective" ["American West" 210]. The same holds true for Indian heroes: there have been very few that stand apart from the faceless mass.

Warpath is a mutant. Like many others in comic book land, his powers come from radiation. These powers include enhanced strength and senses. Warpath can see extremely well (even in the dark) and he has very acute hearing. Instead of these senses being celebrated, perhaps as, in DC, Superman's senses might be celebrated, these senses remind readers only of Warpath's excellent tracking abilities. In other words, even though Warpath is a metahuman with superpowers, the powers only serve to highlight abilities stereotypically associated with a Native American.

In many ways, this character is just a rehash of the American Eagle character from Marvel. Both characters are adorned in feathers and fringe. Both have tremendous strength. Both have improved sensory perception, including keen eyesight. Even the origin of their powers is the same: mutagenic effects of radiation. Oh yeah, and both are Native American. Hmm.

The fact that Marvel has maintained a character such as James Proudstar over the years is quite a statement indeed. While this is worthy of accolades, the character is far from flawless from an Indigenous cultural standpoint.

However, while Warpath may have had some character flaws from a cultural standpoint, he was still a character whom many Indigenous people admired. He was big, strong, and highly dependable in any given situation. Certainly, as a younger reader, I looked forward to each new issue that *might* contain Warpath. Indeed, one supposes the same can be said of the comic book Indian Tonto [Dell Publishing Co., no. 312, January 1951].

During its hey-day, the Tonto character may have been the best representation of Indigenous people popular media had to offer, given the strong, dependable characteristics of the character (similar to Warpath's characteristics). On a positive note, James Proudstar does not speak in Tonto-talk or in flowery metaphors. That alone speaks volumes to the worth of his character, as many Indigenous central characters speak in one or the other. As an Indigenous reader who is aware of all the flaws, nevertheless it would be interesting to see this character in his own titled comic book series. One can hope.

Apparently, there has been enough interest in this character to warrant a special *Flashback* edition of *X-Force* (labeled as issue "Minus 1"). This issue gives some background to the special ties that the Proudstar brother's had with each other. In addition, this issue provides some historical information that sets the stage for a specific subplot of the *X-Force* series.

As for demeaning vocabulary, there are still some remnants of racial slurs found even in later issues of *X-Force*. In issue no. 65, Risque — another Indigenous character — calls him "Geronimo" simply because he mentions that he is Apache. In the same issue, the Blob calls James, "Injun."

While this word alone may not be overly harmful, the connotations that it carries are detrimental. Of course, Native Americans were called Indians in times past, but almost every person with any degree of education knows that we are not from India. The word "Injun" is slang for the word "Indian." "Injun" is just shorthand for another word that is entirely incorrect. The context in which the character uses this word is, of course, belittling and demeaning.

As for James Proudstar's speech, he is thankfully free of Tontoesque utterances. Warpath has always spoken in an articulate manner. These two elements alone convey his intelligence. Unfortunately, Warpath belonged to the "Feather-Bonnet" tribe for a number of years. By this, I refer to his ubiquitous use of fringe and feathers. Verbally, James always takes pride in being Apache. However, there seems to be no trace of any traditional Apache garments to his superhero outfit. The fringe/feather combination illustrates a pan–Indian look that does not place him within any particular tribal affinity.

As far as comic interludes, there seem to be few that deal with "firewater" or Indigenous stupidity. James has never had much of a chemical dependency problem. In fact, he has helped a fellow teammate in overcoming her alcohol dependency. In issue no. 72 of *X-Force*, there is an Indigenous person who is drunk. However, there is no mention of "drunk Indian" or any other slur and there is nothing humorous or funny about this scene. It is not meant to be funny. This character was simply depressed and scared, and therefore he turned to alcohol out of desperation.

Much of the humor surrounding Warpath comes from his own good-natured joking. After Risque, a character with whom James becomes intimately involved, comments that his wardrobe is too "cowboy," James teases her about her choice of

"Return of the Mack." With the introduction of Forge in *X-Men*, readers are finally given a Native character with very few noticeable stereotypes. *The Uncanny X-Men*, "Lifedeath: A Love Story," vol. 1, no. 186, October 1984 (© 2008 Marvel Characters, Inc. Used with permission).

"Naked Truth." Forge reveals himself, and his origin, to Storm in his hi-tech penthouse. *The Uncanny X-Men*, "Lifedeath: A Love Story," vol. 1, no. 186, October 1984 (© 2008 Marvel Characters, Inc. Used with permission).

words. "Watch who you're calling cowboy. I'm a full-blooded Apache" [*X-Force*, no. 65].

While Warpath certainly seems to be alive and well in modern times, his costuming indicates otherwise. Because of his pan–Indian choice of feather/fringe, Warpath places himself in a historical context. Typical of so much depiction in popular culture, it is hard to think of an Indian without also thinking of feathers. Costuming such as his (at least, the costume he wears for the majority of his time on the comic book page) does not help in combating these preconceived notions.

Despite this, Warpath appears as neither noble nor savage. While he may be ferocious in battle, it is not because he a primitive in any way. Also, he does not speak in metaphors and thus, he does not share in this concept of Indigenous nobility. He is simply a man who happens to be both a hero and Apache. Thankfully, Warpath is not stereotyped in this way and it adds to the believability of his character.

Finally, *X-Force* has little to offer in the way of patronizing tone. While there are some themes that deal specifically with Indigenous culture, the overall tone is one of respect. This is an important quality as most times popular media tends to belittle Indigenous culture.

Thus, given the criteria discussed earlier, Warpath has surprisingly few stereotypes. While he could still stand to lose the feathers (and *has*, in recent times), he is a character that warrants much respect in that he is portrayed with very few cultural misconceptions. Hooray!

CONCLUSION

Warpath has been a staple character within the Marvel universe for quite some time. While he has not garnered (at this writing) his own series, he has been an important player for the *New Mutant* and *X-Force* titles. In his introduction, Warpath (then known as Thunderbird [II]) is depicted with few stereotypic generalizations: even his costume is "normal" (as all members of the Hellions — a group he was initial a member of — wore the same uniform). Later, he would adorn himself with feathers and fringe.

However, Warpath has matured over the years and he now demonstrates cultural specificity without crossing the line into Hollywood-type generalizations (for the most part). The creators of the character are to be commended for this as well as for endowing the character with features that demonstrate Indigenous humanity; however, as noted, this Native character is only one supporting character among many in a comic series. Yes, the character strikes the needed representation balance; yet, a step further in the right direction would be to give Warpath his own comic book series with him as the central protagonist. Perhaps if his popularity increases among readers, Marvel will allow that to happen.

Forge (*Uncanny X-Men*, no. 184, Marvel Comics, August 1984)

Forge is a mutant with a special ability to create any device his mind can imagine. While not a member of the core X-Men team, he has always been an integral part of their ongoing saga and has played a part in major events within Marvel storylines.

"A Real Class Act." Forge demonstrates some of his finer qualities and good taste to his fellow mutant, Storm. Noticeably, Forge does not speak in broken English and seems quite eloquent at all times. *The Uncanny X-Men*, "Lifedeath: A Love Story," vol. 1, no. 186, October 1984 (© 2008 Marvel Characters, Inc. Used with permission).

Yet there is more to him: Forge is also Cheyenne and he has a specific destiny associated with this cultural group — more on this later.

Given his unique power for creating machines, Forge's main employer is the U.S. government, which pays him to create machines that only he can dream up. While these machines are not always used for strictly humanitarian causes, he creates them nonetheless. Forge is no stranger to the U.S. government as he spent much of his life as a soldier, during which time he lost his right hand and his right leg.

"I got too close to a bomb" [*The Uncanny X-Men*, no. 186], he declares to Storm, another mutant. To compensate, Forge created a prosthetic hand and leg for himself, using his mutant talents.

"If not for my own ... knack at inventing, I'd be hobbling about on a steel pin and wearing a hook where my right hand used to be. I didn't believe it at the time ... but, I'm a lot luckier than most. Too many buddies came back unable to walk at all — some even to move — or they came home in boxes."

Despite Forge's ability to overcome physical challenges and despite his ability to create the impossible, there is another side to him. As mentioned, he is Cheyenne by birth. Within this tribal identity, Forge is also imbued with magic and mystical powers. While this particular power may seem to fall in line with the idea of the "mystic Indian," there is more to Forge than first meets the eye.

Forge's mystical force does not come from the usual herbal or totemic sources. Similar to Marvel's *Dr. Strange,* Forge's powers have sometimes overlapped with otherworldly and alternative dimensional entities that also tap into this power. This is a distinct change from the idea of an Indian mystic who uses elements of the natural world to commune with the spirit realm, which is the usual representation [*The Uncanny X-Men*, no. 224].

Despite a seemingly alien connection (at times), Forge has this power because of his Native American heritage. This lends itself to the idea of "instant shaman," in which a Native person is more likely to become a holy person based upon their cultural biology than based upon a lifetime of learning the holy ways. Yet, Forge's involvement in the supernatural realm is less stereotypic than many existing portrayals in comic books, such as *Alpha Force*'s Shaman.

None of the *X-men* comic books that Forge appears in use language that belittles Native Americans in any way. While Forge may have left much of his cultural heritage behind him, Native American culture receives respect. Instead of traditional Native mysticism, Forge chooses science as his totem.

Neither Forge nor his friend, Naze (a Cheyenne holy man), speak in pidgin English. Forge is highly educated and epicurean in his tastes. Unlike other comic book Indians, Forge can speak using contractions ("isn't," "don't," etc.).

Forge dresses in modern clothing and, for the most part, does not have an identifiable "costume." This comes as a relief and stands in contrast to most Indigenous comic heroes, who are adorned in fringe or feathers at all times.

There are very few comic interludes. The tone of the comic book (*Uncanny X-Men*) and Forge himself are both very serious. Indeed, Forge is introduced within a highly dramatic storyline ("Lifedeath").

Laudably, Forge and other Indigenous people are shown in modern times. They are not trapped in the pages of history. To go a step further, Forge is a master of technology, the very tool of modern times. Both elements combine to make the character a highly important one among Native American characters.

Neither of the stereotypes (noble or savage) apply to Forge. He is simply a human being (well, a mutant) with all the emotional complexities that come with being so.

There is nothing about the *X-Men* series that pokes fun at being Native. The series was in fact created with ethnic diversity in mind. Forge's ethnicity benefits rather than hinders his level of involvement with the X-Men.

Forge's character may be the most "human" of all Indigenous comic book characters. He has made big mistakes and has complex emotions that do not fit into any neat category. As mentioned, he does not fall into stereotypic traps that other Native characters fall into: he is "modern," he chooses technology advancement over generic mysticism, and he does not need to dress in fringe.

In more recent times, Forge has appeared in console video game titles, such as *X-Men: Legends* (Activision Inc., 2004). While the ramifications of this will be discussed a little later, it is important to know that Forge's character is so integral to the X-Men's comic book world that he is included in an electronic celebration (the video game) of the characters.

CONCLUSION

Forge is a favorite because his character is steeped in modern technology (his mutant power gives him the ability to create and utilize technology in any way he sees fit). Because Native American characters are often seen as either dim-witted (as simple children of nature) or as belonging to history *only*, this use of hi-tech firmly grounds Forge's character in ultramodern times.

Of course, one cannot overlook his inherent mysticism, based solely on his Indigenous heritage. However, add to the mix his lack of fringe and feathers and the fact that he is part bionic (he has a cybernetic hand and leg, both of which he created) and Forge stands out among Native American comic book characters.

Street Wolf (Blackthorne, 1986)

Street Wolf is the story of one man's fight against a city filled with crime. The man, Nathan Blackhorse, is Native American (possibly Navajo). With the help of a friend, Martin "Toots" Sweet, Nathan has trained his body and mind to be the ultimate fighting machine. He is a *wolf* among the city's scavengers; Nathan is the *Street Wolf* due to his predator-like skills in the urban setting.

He has no super powers and he is not metahuman. He is just a normal man who has extensively trained his body and mind in the martial arts. In this particular instance, he is a man with Indigenous ethnicity.

In the series introduction (issue no. 1), editor Mark Wayne Harris explains the inception and development of the character and his traits.

From Harris's description, it seems the choice to make an Indigenous hero was not a conscious one. "When I conceived *Street Wolf,* I couldn't decide what nationality to make him; or rather, what race to make him — black or white. I was really

getting upset, but Darrell [Goza] calmly shrugged his shoulders and said, quite mat-
ter-of-factly, without hesitation, and with annoying simplicity: 'So? Why Don't you
make him an Indian?'" Harris goes on to say that this is the "single greatest contribution" and "the perfect answer" for the development of *Street Wolf.* However, Harris fails
to mention why this choice was a good one and why it is the perfect answer.

Despite this omission, there are some positive elements about *Street Wolf.* While
Nathan is indeed Native American, there is little that is stereotypic about him. He does
not wear feathers. He is not a great "tracker." He does not have special totemic powers — meaning, he does not have the speed of the jackrabbit or the strength of the don-
key, which is a common stereotype in media. He is not a natural healer or shaman. He
is simply a man trained in martial arts who seems to have a tender heart.

This alone makes this comic book stand apart from the others. While Nathan is
Indigenous, his cultural heritage has little to do with being a superhero. His identity
is that of protector first and Native later. Like many others, Nathan must deal with
probing questions about his ethnicity. Therefore, this comic illustrates ideas of negotiated identity that many individuals struggle with.

Our Native American ethnicity is not the entire sum of our parts; it is only one
sliver of the entirety. The same holds true in *Street Wolf:* he is not just a Native American, he is a hero who happens to be Native American.

While this is a positive element in *Street Wolf,* there are also some negative aspects
to the character. After an African American female reporter asks him what kind of
Indian he is, Nathan reminds her that it is also important to just be American. He goes
on to emphasize this by asking her, "Do you know just what kind of African you are?"
While the message is still present — that an Indigenous person can be more than just
his or her ethnic identity — there are still some inherent problems with this exchange.

While there may be some specific tribal similarities between Native American peoples and those of African descent, the two worlds are vastly different. The collective
experiences of these people are different, for the most part, even in modern times.
Therefore, having a Native American ask an African American what kind of African
they are makes little sense. Yet, this exchange may spur others to rethink the nature of
the question entirely, so it is not without merit.

However, one gets the feeling that this type of exchange is included to illustrate
the lack of stereotypic behavior. In fact, the African American woman appears to have
learned this lesson, perhaps as the reader is supposed to. After being rebuked by Nathan,
the woman says that she was wrong to think that "all Indians are bitter and [are] on a
heritage kick." Perhaps it is the intent of the author(s) to destroy such a negative Indigenous stereotype by presenting it this way. However, it seems to actually reinforce the
idea that most Native Americans have a chip on their shoulder, and it therefore casts
them in a negative light. Still, despite this, the episode merits discussion of the kind
above, and maybe that is at least a starting point to begin creating open minds in a
comic book audience.

An important element in *Street Wolf* is that Nathan is very verbally articulate. He
is able to form complete sentences and complex phrases. While it may seem unusual
to bring this item up, it is important when comparing *Street Wolf* to other comic books.
Nathan does not speak in broken English or in cryptic mystical allegories. He speaks

"The Butcher Block." Despite the addition of a few feathers to his outfit, John Butcher is an interesting representation of an Indigenous character in modern times. *Butcher*, vol. 1, no. 1, May 1990 (© DC Comics).

American English in the same way as does everyone else in the comic book. This is a refreshing break from the verbal skills of other characters, such as *White Indian*'s Tipi, who speaks in Tonto-talk.

Street Wolf also contains fewer other stereotypes than do many comic titles. While the main character is Indigenous, he does not dress or act in a certain manner because of this ethnic affiliation. He illustrates intelligence in his ability to converse in everyday American English, an ability many other Native American comic book characters lack. He is simply a hero who has a specific ethnicity. In this, we are given a character who is treated fairly, intelligently, and with dignity.

First, the vocabulary used in *Street Wolf* is anything but demeaning. In fact, there is hardly any mention of the character's ethnicity. In issue no. 1, there is only a single mention of *Street Wolf*'s being Native American — an exposition that lasts for one individual panel. He is asked what kind of "Indian" he is, to which he replies that he is "Navajo." That's it.

As for use of speech, Nathan is highly articulate. He is a city dweller and has a college education. In fact, Nathan went to an Ivy League school, Princeton. There is no Tonto-speak here. Also, Nathan does not speak in flowery metaphors. He seems very aware of stereotypes and comments on this verbally. Recalling his memories of his mother, he adds, "and, no. She didn't make rugs and paint pottery for a living." Nathan makes a specific attempt to diffuse certain stereotypes by speaking skillfully about them, *sans* "ughs."

This language illustrates that Nathan is neither noble nor savage. Again, while he is educated, he does not speak in haughty language. Plus, while he is a trained expert in combat, he is not a savage who acts without thinking. He is simply a man.

As for clothing, Nathan is one of the few Indigenous comic book characters not introduced to the reader in either feathers or fringe. He does not belong to "Feather-Bonnet Tribe" [Stedman 243]. Thankfully, this omission allows the reader to view this character as one who lives in modern times instead of one who is a member of an "extinct species."

In no way is the tone of this comic book patronizing toward Indigenous people. It takes great pains not to be — so much, in fact, that his ethnicity is minimized to the point that it is hardly mentioned at all. While this does wonders at combating negative stereotypes, it leaves hardly any room to celebrate Nathan's ethnic identity. That's ok, though.

Finally, Nathan is only one man. Given this, he is also very human. His ethnic origin in no way takes away from this fact. Indeed, it adds to his human complexity and makes him an enduring, original, and accurately represented character. *Street Wolf* has very few misrepresentations.

CONCLUSION

The Street Wolf character is typical of the *indie* comic book explosion during the 1970s and 1980s when publishers placed an emphasis more on personal artistic choices than on marketable demographics. In this sense, the comic is able to explore and express notions of cultural identity without attempts at commercial visibility. Case in point: Nathan does not wear a costume and is not therefore visually marked by the typical buckskin or feathers (which is a good thing).

Although certain elements of the Street Wolf character seem stilted and one-dimensional, the title does a good job of avoiding major misrepresentations while still maintaining an Indigenous protagonist. For this alone, the comic is worthy reading.

The Butcher (DC, May 1990)

John Butcher is a Lakota man from South Dakota with a personal vendetta to avenge the brutal slaying of his parents. In an effort to muscle them off of their land, and the precious natural resources it contained, Butcher's parents were killed in a massive explosion. After serving his time in U.S. Army Intelligence, Butcher returns from martial arts training in Okinawa to learn of this horrible tragedy and he begins his quest, vowing to find and vanquish his parents' murderer.

As is the case with many other comics featuring an Indigenous person and the central protagonist, *The Butcher* contains very few racial slurs against Native people. Sure, similar to Jon Proudstar's *Tribal Force* comic, there are the normal rednecks-in-a-bar spouting off with phrases like "bunch of redskins," "stay out of a *white* man's bar," and "We can't have no goddamn redskin using the head ["restroom"]" [*The Butcher*, no. 3], but for the most part, all vocabulary used in referring to Indigenous people is fit enough for polite conversation.

Also an important point: John Butcher not only can *speak* eloquently, but he even has a very dry sense of humor, which allows for a blend of his cultural heritage with modern witticism. When asked if his statement that a "wife who bakes is like money in the bank" is an "ancient [Lakota] Sioux proverb," Butcher smiles and replies that this expression comes from a more familiar source; namely, "Betty Crocker" [*The Butcher*, no. 3].

In contrast to this progressive element, the Butcher chooses to adorn his costume with several feathers, a choker necklace, and a new-wave-style breechcloth and breastplate combo. While it might be supposed that Butcher has a ninjaesque spy jumpsuit underneath these emblems, the point remains: why not just give the character a superhero outfit?

Why the feathers? Certainly these elements are indicative of his particular tribal community (Lakota), yet aren't there enough Native comic book characters out there with feathers? Why add to this already-played-out depiction? Yes, some readers may *want* to see some visible semblance of his heritage, but there should be other ways to display this than through the character's costume.

Moving away from this onto a more positive note, there are no references to the stereotype of either the "drunken Indian" or of the "stupid Injun." As mentioned, there are brief comic interludes, mostly due to Butcher's humor, but nothing that demeans Indigenous people in these ways.

As an added bonus, since John Butcher is a product of modern times (with worldly training in Army intelligence and martial combat) and also exists in the present era, the stereotype of Native Americans as an extent species is notably absent. Thus, this character fits well into our theme of modernity, as do the others listed here.

Yet there are stereotypic elements that follow even this most modern of Indigenous comic book characters. While not giving too much away about the story's narrative, there are remnants of the "noble Indian" versus the "savage Indian" dichotomy, with (you guessed it) Butcher being the noble one. Still, despite this setback, the story is quite enjoyable (to find out more, please read the comic).

To round out this discussion, there are some important elements of *The Butcher* that should be celebrated. The overall tone of the series is not patronizing to Indigenous people. In fact, the tone is both respectful and empowering as Butcher draws from his unique cultural perspective to save the proverbial day.

Arguably, the most important element in any comic book featuring Indigenous character is that they are treated in a way in which their humanity is recognized. While John Butcher may have a few cultural setbacks, the comic book series demonstrates both Native Americans' presence in modern times and their complexity as a central character, both of which go a long way toward combating Indigenous stereotypes in popular media.

CONCLUSION

Butcher is like the sliver of pickled ginger that comes with sushi: it is really meant to cleanse the pallet, but truly becomes just another part of the overall package. The comic means well and does indeed turn some stereotypes on their head; but, in the end, *Butcher* is just another story that uses elements of Native American mythos to support its plot.

Don't get me wrong: John Butcher is an enjoyable character and the series is fun to read. However, the inclusion of various (seemingly random) Native-themed spiritual visions seems a bit heavy-handed to me. Still, John is a complete well-written, character who is thoroughly steeped in modernity (thus, establishing cultural continuance). Thus, *Butcher* is a *cut* above many others.

Turok: Dinosaur Hunter (Valiant/Acclaim Comics, July 1993)

In the early 1990s, Acclaim comics revived a popular character from yesteryear. *Turok: Son of Stone* was reborn into *Turok: Dinosaur Hunter*. In this incarnation, Turok was identified as a member of the Kiowa Nation. Kiowas are known for many things — warrior societies, cradle boards, and so forth — but not for their dinosaur hunting abilities. This fact, however, did not stop Acclaim from cashing in on an old favorite. This time, the character would not be permanently trapped in historical (or even prehistoric) times.

On the official Turok website, readers are given more information about this Indigenous comic book character. The website indicates that the Turok character was revived by "Valiant Comics, which had begun publishing in 1989 by signing a licensing agreement with Western Publishing (the original publishers of Gold Key comics)" [Official Turok website].

Thus, Turok began his rebirth into modern comic book readership. By 1993, Valiant Comics had started publishing the *Turok: Dinosaur Hunter* series. Of course, there were a few changes and updates to this character since his premiere in the 1950s. The dinosaurs were upgraded to "Bionosaurs, mechanically enhanced dinosaurs" and the Lost Land became another dimension that had somehow propelled Turok into modern times. "The Son of Stone found himself a man displaced in time, but now able to use modern weaponry to continue his fight against the Bionosaur threat which had expanded beyond the Lost Land and onto Earth itself!"

Turok: Dinosaur Hunter lasted for 47 issues, until 1996 [Overstreet 748]. This comic book helped set the stage for the Turok video game, which will be discussed in further detail later.

There is a certain amount of demeaning vocabulary used throughout the series, including the generalization of calling the main character "the Indian" and other usual slurs. However, readers can see that this is mainly the term other characters (wrongly) employ in describing Turok.

At no time is Turok's speech pattern remotely close to Tonto-talk. While Turok may not prefer to use contractions most of the time, he wields the English language with a considerable amount of aplomb. With this linguistic ability, the character is portrayed as an individual of intelligence. "In the Lost Land your grandfather and I watched the animals fight ... to learn what their weaknesses were! When the three-horned beasts fought ones like this ... they would always strike at the belly!" [*Turok: Dinosaur Hunter*, no. 9].

Turok does not wear a war bonnet (thank heaven!). However, he does wear a breastplate and fringed buckskin breeches, in addition to his occasional use of moccasins. However, it must be said that Turok is a member of the Kiowa tribe (at least in the later *Dinosaur Hunter* series from Acclaim). The Kiowa are a Plains tribe who wear traditional clothing, similar to what Turok is wearing, at various ceremonial times.

Does Truman feel that Turok's clothing accurately represents the Kiowa culture? Truman says, "No, but it was as close as I could find. I looked at both Turok and Andar and tried to find things about their 'look' that suggested a particular culture to me. I was adamant about giving them a particular cultural background — not just make them 'Indians' from some fictional 'ungaboonga' tribe or whatever. If I had a cultural background for them, I knew it would help keep me away from making them too generic. It seems that 90 percent of the world thinks that all Indians come from one big tribe of some kind. You and I know that different Native American cultures and groups are as different from each other as Italians are from Chinese people" [Truman interview].

Another dilemma concerning Turok's apparel is that it seems stuck in the past. Yes, admittedly, Turok is a man from the past; however, he readily uses new technological advances in weaponry (automatic rifles, grenade launchers, etc.), so why does he not attempt to utilize technologically advanced clothing?

Truman answers the question of why Turok still wears fringe.

"Because of something called a trademark. The character has to look a certain way so that licensors can make him look consistent over a broad range of products — an ugly fact [of the comic book industry]. If I'd have been the writer to kick the character off, things would have been different, I guarantee you. My [other] characters always change clothes! But I was assigned the job after the series started, and had to work with what they'd established."

Greg Metcalf quotes Paul S. Newman, one of the main writers of the early *Turok* comic book, about his reaction both to the new Turok title and to the comic book industry ("post–Stan Lee") in general:

The book looks so gorgeous and then I looked inside and they've turned him into an AK-47-toting killer. Where I had written about an intelligent inventive optimistic Indian lost in a prehistoric world of dinosaurs and primitive people, the new publisher has turned Turok into a killer. Where the art of Alberto Giolitti had shown a face of wisdom, experience, and understanding, the new artist's ink lines had slashed out a face of anger and angst; while the original Turok looked humanly strong, the new Turok came from the superhero school of steroid art, muscles bulging like braided intestines, and his skin looking flayed [Journal of Popular Culture 157].

Truman clarifies his position: "One thing to understand: Turok is iconic in many ways. When I wrote the story, the theme that I most often worked with was that Turok was a man out of place in the setting he'd been thrust into. He wanted (!) to remain true to his old ways, dress and traditions. One of the things that first occurred to me was the fact that, if he was hunting dinosaurs [in modern times], the first thing he'd have gotten rid of was that damn bow! He'd be packing real heat — an HK, an elephant gun, a grenade launcher, whatever! Yet, the bow had become part of his 'look' and trademark. So I had to come up with back-story for that."

Truman further asserts that at least one Indigenous character in the series is not trapped in the past. In issue no. 4, Turok is reunited with his old companion, Andar. Upon his death, old Andar makes Turok promise to become a teacher to his grandson, young Andar, or Andy. Andy is brash, radical, and bull-headed.

Truman says "Turok and Andar relationship is based on a literal 'traditional' Native person teaching a younger 'modern' Native person his traditions and values. I had fun with Andar, because he is so modern in every way. He dresses modern, thinks modern, and the closest he's gotten to anything resembling tradition is the fact that he's hung out with a few A.I.M. guys around the rez. He's a horrible hunter. (I had Turok say that the 'old' Andar, Andar's grandfather, was a horrible hunter, too. Doing this, I took a stab at dispelling the myth that all 'Indians' have this mystical, natural instinct for hunting and survival.)"

While the central character infiltrates a few different bars throughout the course of the series, he has never gotten drunk. Thus, humor derived from the idea of the drunken or stupid Indian does not hold here. When he (Turok) consumes alcohol on these occasions, there is nothing comic or funny about doing so. In fact, the true comedic value of this comic book can be found in the subtle Native humor that Turok possesses and, not in illustrations of the stereotype of the drunk/stupid Native.

In issue no. 4, Turok teases Dr. Reagan, a supporting female character, about how his people (Kiowas) eat dogs in harsh times. Later, in issue no. 6, Turok comments on Dr. Reagan's "nice butt," there is a specific sense of what might be labeled Native humor (which can be described as self-deprecating and somewhat subtle, but is best described by people like Deloria in *Custer Died for Your Sins*).

Truman wrote twenty-nine issues of the *Turok* series for Valiant. When asked about his ability to successfully infuse the comic books and, subsequently, the Turok character with an inherent form of seemingly Native-style humor, Truman replied: "I tried for that.... It's something that I'd noticed about native people I'd met. Also, I'm sure that my studies came into play here. I was reading a lot of books by Native writers at the time — stuff by [James] Welch, my friend Sherman Alexi, Tony Hillerman (not a Native, but he does a great job getting into Southwestern Native culture, I think) stuff like that. Those guys get into a lot of subtleties like that."

Turok is definitely portrayed as a cultural anachronism. In fact, he is sometimes paired against an enemy who resembles a primitive cave man (*Turok: Dinosaur Hunter*, no. 9). However, in other cases, Turok is by no means the last Indian in the world. Turok is introduced to a group of Tanoan-speaking Indigenous people in the Southwest (*Turok: Dinosaur Hunter*, no. 4). This is done, so the reader is told, so that Turok might become acquainted with modern people who share some of his cultural identity (there is some allusion to the connection between Kiowa language and the Tanoan linguistic stock of some Pueblo tribe). Therefore, Turok is by no means the last Native in the world. What led Truman to choose this particular group of people for Turok to connect with?

"Andar's clothing was really the key here. The old Turok looks like a generic 'Plains' type, but Andar has more of a Southwestern feel to him. Plus, 'Lost Land' of the old Gold Key Comics has a southwestern look to it. Branches of the Kiowas had a lot of contact and roots with the Southwest. So it seemed to be a good compromise."

Turok does not fall into the categories of either noble or savage. Turok uses logic and wits to survive untold dangers. Failing that, he also relies on physical prowess. There is nothing in Turok's manner that suggests nobility — save for the fact that he has a strong sense of moral conviction. Yet, in no way is he simply a savage, even when he is the most aggressive. During these times, he is still able to apply logic and reason, which many portrayals of savages do not do.

There is no demeaning tone present in the Turok series. Of course, there is the occasional drunken redneck who mouths something similar to "chief" or "Injun." These utterances only serve to indicate cultural ignorance and intolerance, both of which Turok remedies with a show of physical force.

Turok is indeed endowed with human traits by his creators. His internal emotions and feelings are explored in depth. This element alone makes the series stand out among others. Readers are privy to Turok's inner thoughts by way of first-person narration (Turok's standpoint). This stands in direct contrast to titles like *Scalphunter*, where the narration is third person and little attention is paid to the central Indigenous character's intrinsic values and feelings.

So is *Turok* a comic filled with cultural misrepresentations or not? For the most part, no. Turok makes valiant (pun intended) attempts to dispel many stereotypes about Native Americans. Readers are allowed to view the Turok character in many different lights: a person with intelligence, reliability, a sense of humor, and most of all, humanity.

Care has been taken to insure that tribal specificity (Kiowa) is given to the character. Yet, the series is not without its idiosyncrasies. Turok's clothing is stuck somewhere in history — a pan–Indian generic history at that. Truman sums up the character best by explaining why he agreed to write for the series.

> I didn't want to do the series when it was first offered to me! I thought they were going to go for too stereotypical of an approach. Also, I didn't want to become stereotyped myself—"Tim Truman, the Indian guy." At that time, any time a company wanted to do a Native character, I got a phone call. Most of the time the projects

were so steeped in Hollywood style pseudo "Indian b.s." that I turned them away. For some reason, I finally warmed up to doing Turok. I told them I'd do it as long as we could make him look a little less "Hollywood," and I think we did that. The Turok that I worked on looks much different than the Turok that appeared in issue no. 1.

CONCLUSION

Both the fact that the original Turok series lasted for so many years *and* the fact that Acclaim decided to revive the title should tell you something about the character's popularity. Despite this popularity, and despite major revisions from sources such as Truman, the Turok character is unable to shake off some of the clinging stereotypes.

Even this new character, who is well endowed with logical thought and Indigenous humor, and who is able to use AK-47s with aplomb, is still limited in being depicted wearing only traditional, historical clothing (much to Truman's chagrin, I might add). To boot, the *Turok* video game, inspired by the comic, includes none of the more positive elements noted above. The video game character is merely a heavy-weapon-toting character with braids.

To come so close to the mark, to have a Native character such as Turok evolve into a modern, well-rounded, and well-written protagonist only to be fettered by vestiges of old misrepresentations is somewhat disappointing. As Native comic readers, we can only hope that the continuing popularity of characters such as Turok will open the door for creation of Indigenous characters who are completely free of misrepresentation.

CHAPTER NINE

Indigenous Revision

Now and then, Kemosabe, why don't you just shoot someone in the head?—
Tonto to the Lone Ranger, on becoming more efficient

Alongside more modern heroes — Thunderbird, Warpath, Street Hawk, and Forge — there are a few comic books that feature characters who present a more modern and more revisionist image of Native Americans.

Why use the term "revisionist?" Because the wheel has to be reinvented as comic book creators continue to make attempts at disarming generic stereotypes. To break the bonds of past misrepresentation, Native American comic book characters must be presented in a way very much unlike any past Indigenous characters. To combat this negativity, writers, artists, and comic creators must revise past versions of what is "Indian" in comic books. Thus, these elements — ones that embody significant change — seem to exist best in a revisionist environment.

The following are just a few examples of comic books that do an excellent job of reinventing the Native American comic book character.

Tonto *redux* (*The Lone Ranger and Tonto*, Topps Comics, August 1994)

Another revisionist comic is Topps's *The Lone Ranger and Tonto* with art by Tim Truman. While this is yet another retelling of the radio-born classic, the comic is unique in that we see Tonto in more specifically human terms. The best illustration of its thematic purpose can be seen in the very first splash-page, where Tonto can be seen punching the Lone Ranger's lights out.

Predictably, there are several descriptions in this comic book series that demean Native Americans. However, these elements are used to illustrate ignorance or intolerance. When Tonto offers a smart-aleck remark, the ostentatious governor of Texas replies: "You ignorant **savage!** You're **never** to speak that way to me! In fact, don't speak to me at **all!**" (issue no. 2) Clearly, this character is portrayed in such a reprehensible manner (killing for sport, barking orders, and using his clout for personal vendettas) that the audience is easily able to see that calling an Indigenous person "savage" is not a choice a good person would make. Luckily, both Tonto and the Lone Ranger are able to even the score for this major slight.

In this comic book, Tonto talks *nothing* like Tonto; at least not like the Tonto many of us have known over the years in radio, comics, television, and film. Translation: this Tonto does not speak in the broken pidgin English that many of us have come to expect with this series, based on previous standard usage. "Of course, Kemosabe. Maybe when we talked I should use that 'me Tonto' stuff, way they write about me in the dime novels. You'd like that, wouldn't you?" (issue no. 1) Clearly, this is a comic book created with the intention to take previous notions and expectations of what a comic book Indian should be and completely rewrite them.

In this revisionist version of the famous pair, Tonto is dressed in ways both similar to and dissimilar from the reader's expectation. He wears the ever-familiar (at least, familiar to anyone who has ever seen the serials or read the comic books) buckskin jumpsuit with fringe accents. Yet, there is a uniqueness to his ensemble that has never before been seen. There are now several additions to this familiar costume: red bandana, scalp lock, and earrings. These elements alone impart a new message to the audience because they are starkly different from the character's normal depiction.

While the Tonto character itself may be far from perfect, this newer version, at least, gives some diversity to the all-too familiar character. The use of these items of apparel allows readers the chance to view Tonto in a more personal and specific light, rather than the generic cookie-cutter Indian image we have been given for so many decades.

Also in this series, comedic interludes lean toward demonstrating Tonto's sarcastic wit and acidic tongue. This is quite a change from expectations stemming from the Lone Ranger and Tonto characters in comic books of the 1950s (and all other media he is depicted in), where Tonto plays the faithful, but sadly uneducated Indian companion. The stark contrast results in the following: the old Tonto was very brave but he demonstrated little humor (if any); the new Tonto is full of vim and vinegar and has a very dry, sardonic sense of humor.

Despite the revisionist theme, this comic book is still set in the "Old West," that is, sometime between 1860 and 1900. Thus, all characters, both Native and non–Native, are portrayed as antiquities of a bygone era. While there may still be some individuals who call themselves "cowboys" in modern times, this title represents more a lifestyle choice (most times) than a demarcation of cultural mores.

Yet, the same does not hold true for Native Americans for whom Indigenous is not just a lifestyle choice (despite the lessons given in Mohican Syndrome stories, which attempt to convey the notion that *anyone* can become a better Indian than the real Indians). Unlike, some *urban* cowboys, being Native is not just a choice of which spurs go with what bolo tie. Rather, it is an ethnic, political, spiritual, and cultural affinity that cannot be emulated by simply dressing up on a Saturday night. Put another way: Indigenous people having been stereotypically portrayed in the past so many times, readers usually compartmentalize Native Americans into a dinosaur category (for example, see characters such as Turok). However, surely some readers are able to logically accept that there are Native American people living and breathing in today's world.

Thus, while the Anglo characters (and more specifically, the Lone Ranger) are shown as living in the past, audiences understand that there are "cowboys" (by choice) in modern times. Yet, understanding that the same is true for Native characters becomes a bit more of a challenge, especially for readers who have a limited scope on who Indigenous people truly are.

As Tonto is the main Native character in this series, he must be a litmus paper of sorts for how Indigenous characters are treated. Tonto is human and is depicted as neither noble nor savage — just human, with all the faults associated with this state of being. Tonto illustrates that he is not above petty bickering. He says: "Yes. I was looking for a conceited jackass in a stupid mask" (issue no. 4).

Going further, there is no belittling tone toward Native Americans in this comic. The revision takes great pains to portray Indigenous people in a way that allows them to come across to the reader as being more multidimensional. In short, the title offers much in the way of character development by both dispelling negative stereotypes from the old series (via comic book and television) and replacing them with a more believable character, who possesses human traits that include flaws.

CONCLUSION

Tonto *cold-cocking* Kemosabe in the jaw? Like the Toyota commercials of yesteryear, "Who could ask for anything more?" This revisionist comic series is worthwhile for this imagery alone.

Yet, there is more to this comic than just this simple gratification. Here Tonto has been transformed into a character we Indigenous readers know he could and should have become long ere now: more rounded and more humorous, still just as brave and athletic, but *way* more human, all way around.

We could use more revisionist comic books like Topps's *The Lone Ranger and Tonto*, where Native American humanity is well on display in its characters. In fact, if you took the Old West theme out of this comic — thus, demonstrating the cultural continuance of Indigenous people into modern times — this series would be just about perfect. Until we get something like that, I am content in hoping for more comics such as this one that revise readers' existing notions of Native characters.

Doot and Cusick the Tuscarosa (*Timespirits*, no. 1, November 1984, Epic Comics)

Timespirits is a rather pleasant surprise, especially when one has low expectations beforehand. This statement is actually no slight against the comic itself; it is easy to expect certain stereotypes based upon cover illustrations alone, which initially appear to support the notion of *Instant Shaman*. In the *Timespirits* case, where many of the covers feature a young Native American male in buckskin and feathers alongside a wizened shaman-like elder, it is easy to make certain generalizations about what one might expect within its pages.

As mentioned, I am pleasantly surprised at this title's treatment of Native American characters. There is no vocabulary demeaning to Native Americans found in its pages. Great care is taken to treat the Indigenous characters with humanity and to convey their complex nature. One humorously interesting note: Doot, the young Native protagonist, is mistakenly referred to by another minor character in the second issue as a *Piccan* (not to be confused with *pecan*, although being confused with that would be interesting, too), a people noted for their short stature and dark skin.

Despite the fact that Doot is an Indigenous person living around the sixteenth century, he is not portrayed as having a limited vocabulary. Cusick, another Native who serves as his mentor and traveling companion and who seems to be centuries older than Doot, also speaks with clarity and ease.

What about the clothing? It is tough to say whether the Native people in this series are given stereotypic clothing, as the two characters are usually dressed quite differently. While the older and more wizened Cusick dresses in field boots, a fedora, and eyeglasses, Doot clings to the buckskin and feather accoutrements of his particular timeline.

Additionally, it is hard to say whether the Indigenous characters are portrayed as members of an extinct species for this same reason. Certainly they easily adapt to new stimuli in each different time stream, but are there any Native people in the future times they visit? Since many of their adventures occur in mystical, magical, and semi-historic settings, it is difficult to say for certain.

As a positive element, there are no comedic scenes depicting the drunken or stupid Indian. While refreshing, this is not surprising, given that the two central characters are Indigenous: the reader can more easily identify with main characters that are not treated as stupid or easily plied with liquor.

Another positive ingredient in the mix: the Indigenous characters are neither noble nor savage. As mentioned, they are treated with much complexity. Thus, their actions are not driven solely by high-standing morals in being good nor by a savage, bloodthirsty will in being bad. This adds to the overall reverent thematic tone of the series.

To sum up, as mentioned, the humanity of the characters shines through in *Timespirits*. Doot and Cusick are treated with respect and possess few of the major stereotypes and misrepresentations typically found in comic books with Native characters.

Initially, readers may think that this comic is another example of the "Instant Shaman" stereotype, in which an Indigenous person becomes a magical being, simply based on their heritage, but this is not the case. Certainly, some high level of mystic power resides internally in Doot, but this is not based on biology. The other mages Doot meets along the way are not beings whose various powers are based on their Native ancestry; rather, they simply *are* powerful for one reason or another, despite their ethnicity. Thus, Doot has magical power beyond compare — he just happens to also be Native while possessing these — and that is the best kind of comic book shaman.

CONCLUSION

Timespirits is highly entertaining. Is it perfect in its representation of Indigenous characters? Of course not. At a minimum, this is still a story about two Native Americans who have shamanistic spiritual powers, which lends itself to the notion of "Instant Shaman." However, it does do a fair job at depicting their humanity, rather than caricaturing it. Plus, the storyline is fairly well laid out, which makes reading it a bit easier.

As mentioned, judging this book by its cover really does it no justice. Thankfully, *Timespirits* offers more complexity than its cover art suggests. For example, an element that offers a unique perspective is the actual treatment of Indigenous culture found within the comic. Even though the main characters (Doot and Cusick) are Native American, they do not act, nor are they treated, in a particular way to suggest this. They are just *people*, and that in itself is a rare commodity in the treatment of Native characters in comic books.

Tribal Force (Mystic Comics, August 1996)

Jon Proudstar, creator and writer of *Tribal Force*, has a very interesting history.

> I am Yaqui, Mayan, Jewish, and Mexican. I am a high school dropout. I did not get my G.E.D. until I was 26. My background is mostly working with high risk youth. I started at the age of 12. I formed Arizona's first peer mentoring group, which I called "The X-men" after the comic book of the same name. Basically what we did was take the structure of a street gang and implement it toward the positive. After a few years the reputation of the X-Men grew and I was invited to help set up Peer Mentoring programs across Tucson. Years later I would work for Our Town Family Center, Charlie Family Car, La Paloma Family Services, and Sonora Behavioral Health. I later went to work for the Sunnyside School District as a Native American adviser for seven of their schools. I would eventually work with the Tohono Odham and Pasqua Yaqui tribes as a school counselor. From there I worked with gang intervention and prevention with both tribes [Proudstar interview].

Proudstar shares his inspiration for the series. "As we know Thunder Bird had a very short lived life in the Marvel Universe. When they killed him off it was like they killed off any chance I had of ever having my own Super Man.... But then one day it hit me, like a bolt of lightning from Grandfather. Would Crazy Horse or Zapata stand by and do nothing? No. So with renewed fervor I began to develop the concept of *Tribal Force*" [*Tribal Force* interior note].

Proudstar maintains that, from a very early age, he saw the need for more Indigenous comic book characters written from a reader's standpoint. "I think it hit me at a very early age. I often wondered why we weren't represented. That's when the daydreaming began. I started to imagine what it would be like if some of the major heroes were people of color. Not fake color either. I'm talking ghetto folk that I was raised with" [Proudstar interview].

In *Tribal Force*, there is only one demeaning reference made toward Native Americans made during a brief encounter with a white man: "I don't owe you red skins squat. Now ya got a problem with that?" *Tribal Force* is unique in that it is a medium created by a Native American (Proudstar); therefore, all viewpoints (in this case descriptive vocabulary) illustrate best a nativecentric view. Thus, there are no negative terminologies used, only those that uplift the culture paired with the occasional demonstration of bigotry toward that culture.

To further illustrate this concept of an Indigenously centered view, notice that no Native people speak in Tontoese. All characters have complete mastery over the English language. Take the words of Adee, a living totem-like thunderbird as an illustration. As he reveals himself to a young Native female, he thinks, "This isn't going like I planned it. She's gonna freak."

"Force to Be Reckoned With." *Tribal Force* is one of the first comics containing Native American characters created by Native writers and artists. *Tribal Force*, "Special Edition," no. 1, August 1996 (© War Drum Studios).

The costuming of the superheroes in *Tribal Force* is not simply generic feather and fringe. The comic stands out as the main hero, Thunder Eagle, sports a costume fashioned after Ghost Dance shirts. The comic book creators give a detailed definition of both the Ghost Dance itself and the shirt worn during these dances.

While it is true that a particular scene in *Tribal Force* takes place during a bar fight, the Native Americans involved are neither drunk nor ignorant.

Since the comic book is set in the very near future, Native Americans are viewed as members of a culture that has survived beyond historical times. This is a step forward even above those characters who exist only in the present time, as it shows a living presence even into the future and beyond.

The Indigenous characters in *Tribal Force* are complex individuals and they cannot be simply placed into the category of either savage or noble. The majority of Native American characters introduced to the reader are the heroes of the tale. Even so, these characters seem imperfect and are not simply the noble do-gooders one might expect.

The contents of *Tribal Force* speak volumes about the amount of love and care poured into its Indigenous characters. Native American characters are endowed with superhuman powers and efforts are made to educate readers about Indigenous culture. At the back of the book, one can learn about the origins of the Ghost Dance and its importance to Native American tribes.

Indian humanity is not only recognized in this comic book, it is also saluted and extolled, leaving readers wanting more.

Conclusion

Tribal Force rocks hard, even if it *is* only a one-shot comic. Despite the limited run and other minor setbacks, we need more comics created and controlled by Native people. While there are a few others that do this (to be discussed in a later section), there still are too few comics created by Indigenous writers.

The comic books referenced here all demonstrate different ways to rethink the idea of Native American comic book character. Topps's *Lone Ranger* revisits the modern American mythos and adds some much-needed equality to the Indigenous character, Tonto. *Timespirits* avoids many stereotypes common to Indigenous characters. *Tribal Force* takes both of these elements and creates an entire world in which Indigenous characters are (super) empowered to take matters and their destinies into their own hands — an element not usually seen in comics. Thus, revisionist comics are important because they provide an alternative view of Native characters by offering some character balance, empowering them, and stripping away tired old stereotypes, all of which should occur in mainstream comics anyway but usually does not.

CHAPTER TEN

Independent Voices: Native American Comic Books from Smaller Publishers

*Every time I went back, even when the tribe was forced to move, or their land
was taken away, everyone was still a Chickasaw. And they were proud of it.—*
Johnny, from *Chickasaw Adventures*

Many of the comics discussed thus far are produced by the "big players," DC and
Marvel. But what about the smaller presses? Certainly there are some notable works
out there that do not originate from large publishing conglomerates. Also, smaller
presses may have more artistic control over their material than artists at the larger houses
(too many cooks can spoil the comic broth, it seems).

Smaller titles may not accurately represent the reading tastes of the masses; however, it is this narrowing of interest that makes them a fascinating read — a thematic
foil of sorts. While these independent comics may have more freedom, they can fall
victim to many of the same tired stereotypes that are found elsewhere. Refreshingly,
though, some small comics make good progress against these misrepresentations, especially in those places where Indigenous people are included in the creative process and,
at some, are even at the helm.

Educational Comic Book Series (the Mille Lacs Band of Ojibwe, 1996)

Similar to *Chickasaw Adventures*, the Mille Lacs Band of Ojibwe produces its own
comic books that attempt to highlight and celebrate culturally specific values. The two
titles, *A Hero's Voice* and *Dreams of Looking Up*, are geared toward a younger audience
in having central characters that are young children.

Filled with traditional Ojibwe language, stories, and images, the books visually
present the tradition of oral storytelling. It is perhaps for these reasons that books such
as *Chickasaw Adventures*, *A Hero's Voice*, and *Dreams of Looking Up* end up as products
of independent publishing groups and not large comic publishers such as DC or

Marvel. It is unfortunate that books rich in cultural perspectives might not be commercially successful.

Noticeably, the Mille Lacs books contain few, if any, stereotypes. Nowhere in either book is there any mention of terms such as "savage," "redskin," or even a disparaging version of generically calling a character "chief." This is not surprising, as these books are meant to celebrate Ojibwe culture, not offend it.

Similarly, no Indigenous characters babble in Tonto-talk. For the most part (with the exception of the very young ones in the books), the characters speak clearly and use contractions (something that Tonto always struggled with in the comics). A specific bilingual sense exists, as all the main characters speak both English and Ojibwe.

The Ojibwe's material culture is also well represented. Both titles show Ojibwe characters in traditional clothing distinctive to their people and not like the generic Hollywood fringe-and-feather Indian.

The inclusion of characters in historical garb does not mean that these books depict Native people as surviving only in the past. Rather, the central message of the comic books seems to be continuing relevance and that young (Ojibwe) people should do their part to continue the traditional ideals. Grampa, a character in *A Hero's Voice*, explains this best: "It's hard work to keep these stories alive. But it's worth it because it keeps our culture alive."

Are the Indians either noble or savage? While celebrating the culture, does the presentation of positive role models lend itself to the idea of "noble" Indians? Meaning, since many of the stories told in the books are about Ojibwe people standing up for their culture, does this support the stereotype that all Native people are inherently "good" or noble?

While one would think that this would be the case, *Dreams of Looking Up* demonstrates otherwise: no one is perfect, even if they *are* Ojibwe. When his younger sister tries to tell Junior about how important the old stories are, he cuts her off, with unintentional sarcasm. "Wow, Mary. That's such a nice little story." Later, Junior explains his seeming indifference: "How am I supposed to feel when I come back here and Mary thinks I'm the enemy because I don't think the same way about sovereignty that Gramma did?"

Is Indian humanness recognized? This is a subtle point, as Junior later tries to make amends for his oversight, but the stereotype of the angelic Indigenous person who never makes mistakes is not present in the Ojibwe books. Both books go a long way toward demonstrating some basic humanity in their characters. The characters may not have superpowers and the target readership may be narrowed a bit in favor of younger Mille Lacs, but the more universal messages of continuing existence and Native humanity make these books worthwhile.

CONCLUSION

Basically, the name says it all. The Mille Lacs comics are a specific product targeted to young readers to educate them on the importance of their culture. This fact itself should be celebrated.

While the books may share the same commercial success as those comics published by heavy-hitters (Marvel, DC, etc.), they *do* score a cultural coup by offering detailed information specifically about the Mille Lacs. Comics, like any other medium, have the ability to teach, educate, inform, and entertain. In this instance, entertainment takes a backseat to the first three elements.

Yet, entertainment is not completely absent from the Mille Lacs comics. This series seems well thought out and professionally written, illustrated, and colored. Every tribal nation should produce similar comic books to celebrate our culture and educate readers on its importance.

Peace Party (Blue Corn Comics, 1999)

Peace Party creator Rob Schmidt sums up his personal project: a "multicultural comic book featuring Native Americans" [*Peace Party* "Author's forum"]. For the most part, *Peace Party* lives up to this intention.

While Schmidt is non–Native, he maintains his suitability to create a comic with Indigenous people based on his "many years working and living in Indian country [where] he has developed a knowledge and sensitivity to the issues and the cultures" [*Indian Country Today* online]. Schmidt adds to this authority by including several Indigenous people on *Peace Party*'s Board of Advisors.

The central characters are also Native — Hopi, to be specific. Billy Honanie and Drew Quyatt are "[two] young heroes [who] fight everything from prejudice and pollution to super-villains and the supernatural" [*Peace Party* "Author's Forum"]. The two received their powers from a supernatural being in the first issue.

Is the vocabulary demeaning? While Schmidt mentions prejudice above, there is very little language demeaning to Indigenous people.

Neither Billy nor Drew speak in broken English like Tonto. Both not only speak well, they are also able to employ puns and subtle humor, in other words, they are able to play with the English language. Speaking to a somewhat dim-witted gangster about to pummel them, Drew pleads, "Right! We only *thought* we saw you about to shoot this poor, helpless man" [issue, no. 1].

While they are in their nonpowered human form, the central characters dress in everyday modern clothing: basically shirts and jeans. However, when the two heroes' transform into their metahuman alter egos, their clothing also transforms. The costumes more closely resemble traditional Hopi and Pueblo culture than they do the typical Plains Indian version of buckskin and headdresses.

One character, Rain Falling Down, looks very similar to a stylized Hopi Kachina while the other hero, Snake Standing Up, has face paint and clothing similar to what one might expect traditional Hopi dancers would wear. Suffice it to say, this clothing is not the stereotypical sort normally found in comic books featuring Native Americans.

There are no comic interludes built upon "firewater," though there is mention of the "drunk Indian" stereotype in the comic itself (issue no. 1). After a car wreck in the middle of the night, the main characters, Billy and Drew, comment on how easily this stereotype can occur. Billy asks, "Take a look at us. What will a passing motorist say if he sees one of us in our bloody clothes, with our complexions, walking along a road at dawn?" They both answer, "Drunk Indian."

"Cultural Competency." *Peace Party* contains culturally accurate depictions of traditional Hopi style. *Peace Party*, vol. 1, no. 1, 1999 (© Blue Corn Comics).

"Grand Opening." The main characters, Billy and Drew, receive their powers from an ancient source in the opening pages of *Peace Party*. *Peace Party*, vol. 1, no. 1, 1999 (© Blue Corn Comics).

The entire series is set in a modern timeframe. Both central characters are dressed in common, contemporary clothing. Their tribal nation (Hopi) is also featured, thus demonstrating that Indigenous people are not extinct and did not die with the passing of the Old West.

Another positive aspect of this series is the treatment of Indigenous characters in a complex manner. The main characters, whether in their regular human form or in their super-powered alter egos, are simply confused young men trying to help their people and do the "right" things. They do not fall into either the noble or the savage category.

Schmidt's work is respectful of the Indigenous people represented in the series. Nowhere in its pages is there a patronizing tone. The comic book series also promises to give back to the Native community by pledging that "10% of *Peace Party*'s profits" will go to select non-profit organizations including, the "American Indian college Fund, the First Nations Development Institute, and the Hopi Foundation" [issue no. 1, back cover].

Is Indian humanness recognized? One of the most important aspects of this comic book is its attention to creating and representing complex Indigenous characters with a spark of humanity, not just a stymied one-dimensional caricature. Billy and Drew are realistic people and have various nuances (Billy is a tribal lawyer, Drew is a contemporary artist, etc.) that make them interesting and *believable* characters.

In short, while this series certainly achieves a significant degree of success in avoiding many of the major stereotypes, it has not reached the commercial success enjoyed by larger publishers, such as Marvel or DC. This is unfortunate, because more comics like *Peace Party*— ones that avoid negative stereotypes of Native Americans — are needed in the industry. Despite the fact that Schmidt is not Indigenous himself, he not only intimately identifies with the issues and needs of various cultures, but also he has made serious attempts to involve various Indigenous people on the comic book's Board of Advisors.

Conclusion

Schmidt has put some very hard work into this title. As mentioned, while he is non–Native, he does do his homework and he includes Native Americans in the creative process as well. The books are entertaining, well written, and well illustrated.

Schmidt has receive a large amount of feedback, both about the comic books and about the nature of Indigenous misrepresentation in media, much of which can be found on his website.

Now if we could just get *Peace Party* in color! However, this may be taken care of in Schmidt's upcoming graphic novel. It will be interesting to see what is in store in future for this franchise, especially with the potential for interaction from Indigenous creative forces.

Chasm, Guardian of Grand Canyon/EcoSqaud (Canyon Comics)

Indigenous comic book characters turn up in the most surprising places. On a recent trip to the Grand Canyon National Park, my wife and I and another couple

"A Taste of What's to Come." Billy and Drew begin learning to control their powers in *Peace Party*. *Peace Party*, vol. 1, no. 1, 1999 (© Blue Corn Comics).

"Coming of Age." At the close of issue no. 2, Billy and Drew begin to gain full control over their powers. *Peace Party*, vol. 1, no. 2, 1999 (© Blue Corn Comics).

stumbled across the *Chasm* comic books. I picked up these comics, which appeared to be a cross-hybrid of promotional advertisement and educational tools, with little expectation. While the story and art did little to move me, one character stood out among the others.

One of the heroes, or "Guardians" of the Grand Canyon, is a female Indigenous character named Soothsayer. While there are some generic stereotypes associated with this character — we shall explore the Soothsayer character more in the section on Indigenous women — this publication is notable as it comes from a smaller press.

CONCLUSION

Unlike many other people, my mother *never* said to me, "if you can't say anything nice, don't say anything at all." However, as this seems like a good rule of thumb, I will refrain from disparaging the *Eco Squad* comic here in print.

Suffice it to say that we can applaud the fact that these comics intend to celebrate and educate readers about the Grand Canyon and its various elements. This is a positive thing.

Yet, in a comic book that educates readers, this series seems to totally miss the mark on representation of Native people. Small press or not: *Eco Squad* could (and should) do a much better job at Native representation.

Chickasaw Adventures (Lane Morgan Media, 2003)

The *Chickasaw Adventures* is quite a different creature. The series is one of the most original, authentic, and refreshing "Indian" comic books available. Most notably, the series is produced in part by the Chickasaw Nation.

In this series, the central figure — Johnny, a young Chickasaw adolescent with little knowledge or respect for traditional Chickasaw ways — is mystically swept away and encounters various "adventures" through time, taken from Chickasaw lore, legend, and factual history. While the comic is not perfect, its positive elements outshine any minor stereotypes.

Writer Jen Murvin Edwards explains the comic's origin: "The idea of creating a comic series for the Chickasaw Nation was originated by Marty Brickey, owner of Layne Morgan Media, Inc., after a conversation with Governor Bill Anoatubby of the Chickasaw Nation" [Edwards interview].

None of the comic's descriptive language demeans Native people in any way. Given that the central theme resonates with Chickasaw culture, the vocabulary celebrates rather than ridicules Indigenous people.

Even when Johnny is transported back to the past, none of the Indian characters use the Tonto version of English. In each of the adventures, Chickasaw people are portrayed as intelligent people, able to effectively communicate ideas to one another without the usual "ughs" or "you betchums" readers usually encounter in historical Indigenous settings.

Edwards agrees with this finding:

> The Native Americans in this series speak like anyone else. Johnny, our main Native American character, speaks like your average kid. Back in time, the Native American characters speak normally; some of them use certain Chickasaw language, such as

"The Adventures Begin." *Chickasaw Adventures* is an excellent example of a Native American tribal entity creating comics that celebrate their specific culture. *Chickasaw Adventures*, no. 1, 2004 (© Layne Morgan Media).

"Feather of a Different Color." Because of the Chickasaw Nation's involvement in the creative process, scenes such as this one more accurately depict tribal-specific clothing and traditions (notice the authentic headwear, which is not just another "war bonnet"). *Chickasaw Adventures*, no. 1, 2004 (© Layne Morgan Media).

Chukma, for "Hello." Tonto-ish speaking has *no place* in our series, whatsoever. All the characters are well spoken and articulate [Edwards interview].

In each of Johnny's journeys into Chickasaw history, the Native people he encounters maintain a look and a style of clothing that is characteristic to Chickasaw culture. When Natives are seen, they do not resemble every other comic book Indian. The style of clothing may contain feathers or fringe here and there, but the overall clothing style is distinctive and not pan–Indian (Plains) style.

Edwards supports this idea by explaining how the Chickasaw Nation became involved in the creation process.

In this first book, we fixed mostly art issues: due to the extreme lack of resources about the Chickasaw Nation, the Nation had to communicate to us important cultural elements known only to them. For example, we changed all hairstyles of the book from Mohawk-style to roaches. We also changed the Minko's, or Chief's, headdress from eagle feathers to turkey feathers, as in the Chickasaw Nation turkey feathers were the highest reflection of status. We also removed a panel where Johnny, who has now taken over the identity of a young Chickasaw in the past, hugs his Uncle; in the Chickasaw culture of those times, men did not show affection [Edwards interview].

Overall, while the adventures take place in historical times, the Indigenous characters are necessarily depicted as an extinct species. How is this? Indigenous continuance is demonstrated at the beginning and end of each adventure: Johnny is a contemporary Chickasaw youth who travels back in time to participate in a particularly important moment in history — yet, he always comes back to the present (modern times) armed with important knowledge of how Chickasaw people have been able to survive despite harrowing adversity.

Edwards explains: "This is what I love about our comics: in *Chickasaw Adventures*, we get the best of both worlds. Our series tells the story of Chickasaws in *both* present and historic settings. We completely break this stereotype because our main character is a *real* and *modern Chickasaw kid*— we see him in school, at home, with his Grandfather and mother, with his friends. Nevertheless, we also see Johnny go back in time, where we get to experience all the benefits of a historic setting: experiencing historical events first-hand, hearing historical characters speak for themselves. It is essential to see those historical events, but it is also essential to see how Johnny uses those lessons now, in the present — Johnny is a real, modern kid who takes his historical experiences and applies them to his life as a twenty-first-century Native American."

This series portrays all the Indigenous characters in realistic terms. There are no bloodthirsty savages or supremely noble do-gooders. The Native Americans are realistically rendered as ordinary people who possess the normal ranges of emotions and mores. Edwards elaborates: "One stereotype we wanted to avoid in our series is depicting Native Americans as solely warriors, fighters, or killers. We wanted to show the multifaceted nature of the Chickasaws as not *only* warriors, but healers, mothers, fathers, brothers, and proponents of culture."

There is nothing patronizing in the tone of this comic: given the amount of interaction Chickasaw people had in the creation of this project, the tone is very respectful and adds a sense of pride in what it means to be Chickasaw.

"Great and Mighty Warriors." Introducing some self-deprecating humor (also known as "Indian Humor") not only adds dimensionality to the Indigenous characters, but it also breaks some stereotypes by demonstrating that not all Native people are great warriors or trackers. *Chickasaw Adventures*, no. 1, 2004 (© Layne Morgan Media).

"Mix and Match." Images such as these depict Chickasaw people in part traditional / part European clothing, which would be common at that time in their history. Accuracy like this comes from the interaction with the Chickasaw Nation. *Chickasaw Adventures*, no. 2, 2004 (© Layne Morgan Media).

This message — what is means to be Chickasaw — is one of the most important elements of the *Chickasaw Adventures* series. As the stories and depictions instill pride in Chickasaw culture, the Native American comic book characters, generally speaking, are treated as real humans — more so than in many other comic books. It is this care and concern to infuse a sense of Chickasaw pride that makes this series a model to which comic book creators should look when creating Native American characters.

The comic book series has gained a certain degree of acceptance and popularity. Edwards explains, "The series was originally four books, but after the first book was presented to the Chickasaw Nation, they were so enthusiastic about the series that they extended it to a total of twelve books."

CONCLUSION

This is truly something to get excited about: a tribal nation producing their own comic book? Stupendous. What's that you say? They hired someone else to create the book for them? Well, what is wrong with that?

As mentioned, the Chickasaw Nation provided not only the initial project vision but also the cultural oversight to this series. Using ("contracting out to") a professional creative team only serves to support the importance of this project (not to mention, it adds to the overall *professional* quality of the books themselves).

Also, if the series is tribal-specific, it adds to the importance of Native people telling our own stories. *Chickasaw Adventures* is entertaining and it provides readers with ample insight to the culture itself. Not many books are able to do this. More tribal nations should take on similar projects and produce their own comic books.

The Raven (October 2004, Darkwing Productions)

The Raven is another comic book from a smaller press featuring a Native protagonist. Reminiscent of *Tribal Force*, this comic book series has an Indigenous person at the helm. Jay Odjick, a member of the Algonquin tribe (in Canada) created, wrote, and illustrated *The Raven*.

Odjick explains:

> As kids, my brothers and I read a lot of comics.... One of the things that always seemed kind of strange to me, was seeing native characters represented in comics; they tended to come across as somewhat caricatureish, and stereotypical. So, an effort to flip that preconception on its head played a factor, I wanted to create a Native character infused with supernatural elements who would be, in essence, "the good guy." [Also,] I tried to create a story that people of many walks of life, or racial backgrounds could identify with, but with a special hope that Native youth could recognize something in these series that doesn't get put across in mainstream comics or films: That we are all trying to figure out in our own way, exactly what it means to be a modern day Native person.... Ultimately I wanted to create a series and character that were as cool as any other. Lofty goals! (Laughs) [Odjick interview].

While the series does not have the big budget *polished* feel of work from Marvel or DC, it does do a good job of staying away from general stereotypes. The central character, Matthew Carver, is an Indigenous male with a mysterious and lethal power

Opposite and top: "History Lesson." Throughout the series, the *Chickasaw Adventures* continually infuses Chickasaw-specific elements, such as the White Dog and the Kohta Falaya, within its pages. *Chickasaw Adventures*, no. 3, 2004 (© Layne Morgan Media.)

inside of him (the Raven) that demands to be unleashed. While there are hints that the metahuman power may have manifested in another Native person years ago, there is no mention as to whether the power is directly linked with Indigenous heredity.

There are very few instances of derogatory or inflammatory language toward Native people used in this series. While there are several brief uses of the term "chief" from a thug, there are only a few references to specific ethnicity (i.e., "reservation" and "Running Bear" [a last name]) of any sort in the series. While this may be a plot device to create suspense or mystery, the lack of specific tribal affiliation has both pros and cons.

One pro is that Matthew is just a guy with metahuman powers who happens to be Native; he lives in New York and tries to have a normal life (at first). The focus is less on the ethnicity of this person than it is on his power. All too often, comic books seem to illustrate the idea that Native characters always knows every single thing about their heritage and cultural history, which is not always an accurate depiction (i.e., sometimes an Indigenous person has only a limited knowledge of his or her cultural history).

Odjick shares his aim for doing this:

> I wanted to do a story where the main character was Native, but *that* wasn't the main thing about him. In other words, a story that any reader could pick up and go, "Oh, this guy is Native," but doesn't come packaged with the preconceptions and stereotypes present in most mainstream comics representations of Native peoples ... it's edgy, it's cool, it's modern, and the main character just happens to be a Native character, without too much emphasis being placed on that in terms of dialogue and story. Do we know where Bruce Wayne's ancestors are from? Peter Parker's? No, and I wanted to something where people could read a story about a Native character but not need to know too much about Native myths, legends, and lore coming into the books, but have these elements introduced through the telling of the story in a way that was organic and entertaining.

However, this also demonstrates a con: without some explanation of the character's cultural connection, there is little to celebrate about his people. While this element does not always have to be present in an Indigenous comic, it certainly is an important consideration and may add to the overall humanity of the central character.

Odjick responds to this criticism: "At the onset or launch of the original mini series, I decided to keep that aspect of the character intentionally vague, in hopes of appealing to more Native readers. In a way, I wanted to create a character aimed at them, and was worried that by actually coming out and revealing what band or tribe the character Matthew Carver belonged to, I could alienate those youth. We are doing a new comic through Arcana Studio ... in the new series ... we talk more about the character's tribal affinity, in part because this book will deal more with Native folklore and myth than the previous series did, and I wanted to incorporate more Algonquin, or more specifically, legends and stories from my own community, Kitigan Zibi."

Matthew's humanity is demonstrated in other, nonstereotypic ways. He does not speak like Tonto in broken English. As mentioned above, Matthew lives in a highly dense urban area and speaks fluent English like everyone else in the book.

Also, given his locale (present-day New York), the central character does not adorn himself in fringe and feathers, even when he changes into the Raven. Raven's costume

"Creative Native." *Kagagi: The Raven*, by Jay Odjick, is another example of comics with Indigenous people at the helm. *Raven*, no. 1, 2007 (© Jay Odjick).

reflects fewer stereotypes than those found in many other Native American comics. Sleek body armor and lethal claws are the basic elements of the Raven's gear with no need to throw a feather in his hair (*à la* early Warpath costume). Odjick elaborates on this choice: "I think to create a modern day Native superhero, the character's costume has to be indicative of not only the modern superhero style attire, but the sensitivities of modern Native people as well. The short answer, also, is that ravens are black, so his costume is black! (Laughs)."

Another positive: there are no comic interludes of the Indigenous character drunk on "firewater" or demonstrations of the "stupid Indian" character. Matthew/Raven is a sober and intelligent person whose character does not succumb to this stereotype.

Matthew's modern urban location also speaks to another element that breaks common stereotypes. Because he exists in the present day, the central character is not a product of history nor does he descend from an extinct species. His existence demonstrates continuance of Native people into modern times. Why make this choice? Odjick states, "because the story dictated it. It's a story about a modern-day Native person, and I couldn't have told that story if it had been a period piece. As well, I wanted to present a Native character in a light that mainstream readers weren't accustomed to, which included having him live in a modern city and time. Some people would argue that really is not all that novel a concept, but ... as a first Nations person myself I have rarely seen this done in mainstream entertainment."

Yet, the concept of the Indigenous character being either noble or savage is somewhat unclear, given the limited number of issues (at the time of this writing) in the series. Matthew is certainly a good and moral person; he jumps headfirst into a dangerous situation to protect his friend. Yet, the power inside him, the Raven, is ravenous, vengeful, calculated, and mortally dangerous — one might even term the entity bloodthirsty. Does this mean that either persona is either noble or savage? As mentioned, more investigation into the characters as the series continues will be needed to accurately evaluate this.

Despite this, *The Raven* offers no negative slant toward Native people in its thematic tone. While other comics may portray Native people with child-like intellects (*White Indian*) or as wizened sages with intrinsic knowledge of the spirit world (*Alpha Flight's* Shaman), The Raven simply presents a story with a Native protagonist.

This series succeeds in its portrayal of the humanity of Indigenous people. The lead character, Matthew, is not a perfect person and he is still discovering the power of the Raven inside him; yet, the character itself is believable for the most part. The series accomplishes this without drawing on tired stereotypes and does so without a Marvel budget. This commendable series deserves more support to encourage Indigenous creators, such as *The Raven's* Odjick, to continue attempting to tell our own stories. Odjick sums up *The Raven*: "if people are looking to see a Native character presented in a way we haven't in the past, I think these comics will give you a pretty decent chance at a read that doesn't do that. If you have ever felt that you didn't know as much about your background as you would have liked, if you have ever felt out of place, then I think there will be things you can identify with. Or at least, I hope so!"

CONCLUSION

The Raven is not without its imperfections, but we *are* talking about smaller presses here. I think Odjick would agree that there is some room for improvement with this character. Luckily (for Odjick), there is a chance for improvement now that the comic has been picked up by a somewhat larger publisher.

Still, despite the business and production side, *The Raven* makes some a very good attempt at Indigenous portrayal in comic books. As the new series begins, perhaps readers will get more information on Raven's origin. Until then, let's just be glad there is yet one *more* Native character out there who doesn't feel the need to sport the fringe and feathers.

Darkness Calls (Healthy Aboriginal Network, November 2006)

Another import from our Canadian neighbors to the North, *Darkness Calls* could be termed an educational comic book as it deals with teen suicide. Suicide is a serious issue for many young people, including members of Aboriginal groups in Canada. Produced by the Healthy Aboriginal Network, a "Non-profit promotion of Aboriginal health, literacy, and wellness," the comic is created, illustrated, and edited by Indigenous talent, making it all the more noteworthy.

Perhaps because Native people create this comic, it contains few stereotypes. *Darkness Calls* avoids language demeaning to Native people, at least not for ethnic or cultural reasons. In the comic, the central character is terrorized for his obesity, but it is other Indigenous kids who torment him because of his physical appearance, not because he is Native.

None of the Indigenous people talk like Tonto, not even the elder telling a traditional story. While this may be due to the level of Native interaction in the creation process, some of this probably has to do with the story's taking place in a modern setting. As we have seen with many other Native American characters set in contemporary settings, the Tonto-talk seems to fall away the farther the story gets from Old West times.

However, one critique is the appearance of feathers and a breastplate in the hero's costume. While modern accoutrements — armored boots, a suped-up motorcycle, and even a samurai sword — upgrade this costume, the feathers and breastplate seem to be a step backwards.

Steven Keewatin Sanderson, writer and artist for *Darkness Calls*, alluded at a 2007 panel discussion on Native Americans in comics that his main purpose was to present a character that an Aboriginal youth might mentally conjure when hearing a traditional story; yet, the youth imagines the hero with feathers. Perhaps because of the influence of stereotypic imagery in popular media, even Indigenous kids (who may, at times, have more direct interaction with Native culture) might have their imagination tainted with the notion of obligatory feathers. Having grown up around the same time as Sanderson (a youth during the 1980s) and seen similar comic book Natives, I can understand how this portrayal might come about.

There are no jokes about "firewater" or how stupid Indigenous people are in this comic. Mainly, the story serves to depict Aboriginal school-age children and does not rely on such comparisons for humor.

Similar to the *Educational Comic Book Series* from the Mille Lacs, *Darkness Calls* does not portray Native Americans as extinct historical artifacts. Both demonstrate the importance of continuance of Indigenous people.

While there is some play on the noble versus savage dichotomy with the use of the uber-good hero and ultra-evil bad guy, this is an expected element in many traditional Native stories. As in Morality Plays, this contrast serves more to support teaching young people ideas of good and bad behavior than it does ideas of Indigenous people themselves being inherently either good or bad. Indeed, the end of the story is all about choice between these two opposing forces.

The comic does not take a patronizing tone toward Native people and, most importantly, it illustrates the humanity of Native people complete with good and bad idiosyncrasies.

Does *Darkness Calls* contain all these positive aspects because Indigenous people create it? Most likely, but there are probably many other considerations as well, from its intent as a vehicle to reach Aboriginal youth to the creative freedom seemingly afforded to smaller independent presses to depict stories the way they want. Whatever the reason, *Darkness Calls* as well as the rest of the "Indie" comics deserve recognition for the strides they have made in avoiding certain stereotypes, especially those among these comics in which Native American creativity is present, which many of these comics possess. In order to combat the tired Indigenous stereotypes that plague comic books and other media, this trend must continue.

CONCLUSION

Unlike the majority of comic books with Native Americans in them, *Darkness Calls* is illustrated by an Indigenous artist (Sanderson). The comic is well drawn and written, and, most of all, very entertaining. It is my hope that we see *much* more material from Sanderson soon.

Summary

Many of the comics from smaller publishers contain fewer stereotypes overall. While these comics contribute to the destruction of Indigenous stereotypes, they do not have the large readership found with mainstream publishers such as Marvel or DC. We may look toward these larger publishers to gain a clearer idea of how popular culture views Indigenous people, but it is interesting that smaller titles such as these often depict our culture with more respect and humanity than those from the larger publishers.

If the innovation and accurate representations found in the "indie" comics were added to the commercial success of the larger publishers, the general audience would more readily accept and maybe even demand cultural accuracy in comics. It is a worthy goal, and we Indigenous people should continue developing such stories and refining them repeatedly to reach this commercial success. Only then, it seems, will we gain the attention needed to effect major changes in the industry.

CHAPTER ELEVEN

The Video Game Crossover:
Indigenous Comic Book Characters
Comin' Straight Atcha!

I ... am Turok! — *Turok: Dinosaur Hunter* (video game)

It is no secret that many of the different factions of popular media depend on one another for inspiration. *The Lone Ranger* started out as a popular radio show and then a comic strip. Because of the story's popularity — and because of penetration into several media — an examination of the Lone Ranger and Tonto's crossover seems important here.

Horn gives an excellent primer about the beginnings of *The Lone Ranger* in radio in *Comic of the American West*. With its thrilling soundtrack of the William Tell Overture, the radio show formed a personality of its own. Its popularity grew and extended its reach into daily printed media.

In the comic strip, the Lone Ranger and Tonto had many adventures. Of course, soon the strips were collected and packaged together in one comic book. From the comic books, we get to see one of the most famous Indian sidekicks in comic book history. Tonto has been the center of many topics within this discussion both because of his popularity and because of this stereotypic notion of Indian sidekick.

Leaping from the pages of comic books to the silver screen, the Lone Ranger and Tonto can be found continuing their battle against evil in the West. There were several film serials that carried the story into live action for audiences, including one of the most recent incarnations of the saga, released in the early 1980s with another cinematic attempt, The *Legend of the Lone Ranger* [William A. Fraker, 1981].

Yet, Tonto is not the only dime-store Indian translated into other media. There are many other stories of one medium bleeding over into another. Many of these continue to illustrate cultural misrepresentations and do little more than recast the same stereotypes repeatedly. However, within video games (a relative newcomer to media), there are some Indigenous characters who fare well in this transition.

Video Games

Comic books have long been present in another genre of popular culture: video games. While an entire study could be conducted (and perhaps, should be) about the representation of Native American culture within this particular medium, we shall but briefly touch upon this idea here.

It is no surprise that comic books have made this leap; both draw on a similar demographic audience. However, here our intent is to explore how Indigenous characters from one popular medium translate into another. Are these Native players mere stereotypes as well? Or does being in a relatively newer (and possibly three-dimensional) forum allow them some deeper sense of humanity?

Turok: Dinosaur Hunter (Valiant/Acclaim Comics, June 1993)

Dell Publishing Company released the first issue of *Turok: Son of Stone*. The story revolves around a Native American named Turok. One day, while searching for food, Turok and his friend, Andar, explore a cave and find themselves transported to a place called the Lost World. Once in the Lost World, which is a realm filled with dinosaurs and people of limited technological means, Turok has many adventures. There have been many incarnations of Turok, including a revamp of the original story through the late 1980s and early 1990s by Valiant (Acclaim) Comics.

Recently, Turok took a giant leap from the comics to the world of electronic gaming. During 1997, Acclaim Entertainment, Inc., turned the Turok character into a game for Nintendo's N64 System. *Turok: Dinosaur Hunter* was a big hit and several versions of the game have come out since.

Here the problem would be less pronounced if Acclaim had used the original Turok, a man taken directly from his pre–Columbian time period. Instead, the choice was made to change the Turok character. In this new mutation of the original, the position of Turok is now in the hands of Turok's grandson, Joshua Fireseed. There are three specific issues of misrepresentation that must be addressed.

First, this passing of the Turok title is another example of the lineage factor mentioned in the first section. This promotes the notion of mysticism by ancestry. The other problem lies with the way Joshua dresses when he becomes Turok. In his everyday life, Joshua is a college student (alleged to be a student at the University of Oklahoma) attending on an athletic scholarship. As such, he dresses as any other student would in modern times. However, when duty calls and he must battle otherworldly fiends as Turok, Joshua becomes clad in leather breeches, leggings and a breastplate. This brings up the second issue of misrepresentation.

While some Native Americans dress traditionally at specific times, there seems to be little point other than decor for Joshua Fireseed to be dressed as such. When we Indigenous people dress traditionally, it usually occurs in ceremony or in a type of honoring of our ancestral culture (in some cases a social dance, illustrating our history cultural ties). None of this occurs while Turok battles a big freaking dinosaur. It seems these elements serve to perpetuate conventions discussed earlier: the idea that if an Indian is to be an Indian, they must look and act a certain way.

Notice the wording the website utilizes. "You are now Turok — and your time has come." Players of the game not only get to save the world and hunt a bunch of killer dinosaurs, they get to share in the Turok lineage. While this is a savvy marketing strategy, it does not lessen the impact of cultural misrepresentation. For too long, media has not only allowed non–Natives to become Native within the story (think of Ricardo Montalban as an Indian), but now anyone with a game console can become Indigenous, namely, Turok.

In earlier renditions of this notion of becoming Native, such as *White Indian*, readers could only imagine themselves within the particular storyline and, therefore, only imagine that they were Indian. With video games such as Turok, participants get to live out this fantasy and interact with other storyline elements, as if they were indeed Indigenous. There is no guessing here; even the website tells its readers they are "now Turok." This notion goes further than just video games — it seems that *anyone*, despite heritage or upbringing, can now become Indigenous by simply going to the local bookstore.

Forge (*X-Men Legends*, Activision Inc., 2004)

While Forge never seemed to be an official part of the X-Men team (i.e., he was not one of Xavier's students), he is an integral part of the console game from Activision. Within, one can easily view Forge (whose voice is provided by actor Lou Diamond Phillips) by accessing the save menu. Here, Forge is the one you can buy and sell equipment to and from, in the hopes of obtaining better technology. Thus, here in this new milieu, Forge is the Maker, just as he is in the comic books.

Sadly, there is little interaction with Forge, save going to "visit" him for spare parts and one short level where he talks in your ear, to gain more information about his character.

There is nothing, including vocabulary, debasing about Forge's character. Essentially, he is the backbone of the entire gaming experience. Without him, one may not advance far in the game. The language reflects this; there are no racial slurs or verbal slips about his heritage.

Just like the comic book version, this Forge speaks in a highly intelligent manner. In fact, given his propensity for hi-tech gadgets, he holds a better grasp of the language than many other characters.

While sporting a Ramboesque bandana may qualify him for arrest by the mutant fashion police, Forge is not burdened with buckskin fringe and feathers. In the game, Forge wears a high-tech battle jumpsuit, similar to the other characters.

However, while his garb exhibits no generic stereotype, there is perhaps another element that may lend itself to this idea of the "feather-bonnet" tribe. In the video game, there are several special items that give anyone that wears them special additive powers. One such item is Forge's beaded necklace. This item alone, while not necessarily misrepresentative (Native Americans are known for beadwork) aligns Forge with generic ideas of what is Indian (beads).

In the game, comic interludes come from Forge's broad intellect, rather than from the lack of it. Indeed, only a few characters (Beast and Xavier, for instance) within the game seem as brainy as Forge. This representation contrasts sharply with characters such as Little Beaver, who seem destined to remain dumb.

Forge and the culture he represents are alive and well and living in modern times. While other Indigenous characters, such as Red Wolf, are trapped *only* within historical settings, Forge resides in a time not too distant from the present.

In the game, Forge conforms to neither of these generalizations. He is portrayed in human terms. While he is highly intelligent (thus not savage), he is not overly regal (nor noble): he gets frustrated like any other human being.

The overall tone of the video game is highly respectful of both Forge and his special ability as "maker." Forge even gets to serve as guide through a particular section; thus, his leadership role is well demonstrated.

While we may have a bit more information about Forge's character (and the subsequent emotional makeup of said character) within the comic book, there are specific items that reveal to us Forge's innate humanity. In the game, one can explore the various rooms of Xavier's mansion and find various tidbits. One such item in Storm's room is a note from Forge inviting her to dinner.

Building upon the storyline in *The Uncanny X-Men*, viewers-in-the-know understand the tender and genuine feelings Forge has for Storm. Given this evidence, we can definitely say that Forge is human, complete with all the emotions and defaults to which human beings are prone.

Wyatt Wingfoot (*Marvel Ultimate Alliance* 2006, Activision)

Honorable mention goes to Wyatt Wingfoot, Fantastic Four's friend and sometime unofficial team member. In *Marvel Ultimate Alliance*, there is even less interaction than with Forge in *X-Men Legends*. However, Wyatt does play an important role as official Avenger Quinjet pilot. He is completely free of fringe or feathers and he does not speak in Tontoese; thus, there are some good points to his being included.

So what does this tell us about video games in general? Unfortunately, the evidence is not substantial enough to garner much more than a fleeting glimpse of Forge and Wyatt's characters. While we are able to glean some idea of the character traits and subsequent representation within the game, it is mainly due to knowledge a priori of the storyline found in the comics.

However, what *is* clear is that the Indigenous characters have not been overly saddled with the stereotypes most familiar to Native Americans in comic books. While very little is revealed about Forge and Wyatt Wingfoot in the video games, what is *not* revealed, namely, the absence of those grossly overused stereotypes discussed in this book, becomes just as important in evaluating whether misrepresentation occurs. Here, very little of it occurs within Activision's video games.

CHAPTER TWELVE

Native Warriors: Indigenous Representation in the Military

*I'll hold off the guards — or I'll **die trying!***— Private Jay Little Bear, Captain
Savage's Leatherneck Raiders

While perhaps not a specifically *negative* stereotype, it is interesting that Native
American comic book characters, especially the male ones, are oftentimes cast into militaristic roles. Perhaps this idea stems from the idea of Native as warrior. Native American males have been portrayed as bloodthirsty savages in almost every medium. Has
this portrayal lent itself to the idea that Indigenous men — even so-called civilized
ones — might be more ferocious on the battlefield?

History itself may have contributed to this idea of the Indian soldier. Well before,
and certainly since, any Europeans set foot in modern-day North (or South) America,
Indigenous people have been intimately involved in battles, skirmishes, and all-out
warfare. In almost every Indigenous culture there is a distinct group (usually males,
but females, at times) that, since prehistoric times, sets itself apart by military valor.
Add to this, Indigenous "civil war" factions in the French and Indian War; various
allies (to both the British crown and the colonies) in the American Revolution; Army
scouts in the 1800s; Choctaw code-talkers in World War I; Navajo code-talkers
in World War II; and even the great many Native Americans that enlisted in the Vietnam conflict. Suddenly, the idea of Indigenous people in the military seems rather
obvious.

Of course, this idea of Native American military men may represent nothing more
than comic book creators tapping into their readers' standard demographics, which historically is dominated by males. Whatever the case, this depiction is a prevalent one in
comic books.

Bradford W. Wright sites several examples in which Native American comic book
characters serve as symbolic metaphors within the context of war. In one example (*Tomahawk*), Native Americans are used to make a statement on the Cold War: "At the end,
instead of going to war, the two sides [white and Native] agree to share the land, decid-
ing that cooperation is preferable to risking a military confrontation that could destroy
them all" [Wright 127].

In another example, this time in Kurtzman's "Custer's Last Stand," Native Americans are used to illustrate "a view of history which minimized social conflict and emphasized the "Great Americans" who had forged the proud nation" [Wright 145]. This is, in short, an antiwar message.

Given these examples, do the majority of Indigenous comic book characters serve as symbolic metaphors during these periods of military conflict and/or during the Cold War years? Do any other examples come to mind during these times in which the Native Americans seemed truly human or well-rounded characters? Wright responds:

> Yes, I certainly think that was the case during World War II and the early Cold War. The hearts and minds of indigenous peoples were contested during wartime, and this was portrayed in comic books. I cited a number of examples of this in my book. I also found some examples where Native Americans were shown in a sympathetic light, serving as a metaphor for criticism of or cautionary warnings about U.S. policies during the Cold War. The most memorable examples of those, I cited in [Comic Book Nation] and you just mentioned them. The implications of these were subtle, but based on what is known about the political views of Harvey Kurtzman and some of the DC staff (Jack Schiff, Alvin Schwartz), it seems safe to conclude that the intent of the stories were indeed to warn against the arrogance of U.S. military power [Wright interview].

Wright also reminds us: "Still, it's important to note that the overwhelming number of nonwhite characters during the 1940s and 1950s still fell into one of those three stereotypes that I discussed earlier" in the introduction chapter. (Wright interview)

Many Native characters discussed elsewhere in this text have their origins in military duty. Johnny Wakely, also known as the Red Wolf, originally tried his hand at uniting Indigenous and Anglo culture as a U.S. Army scout in the late 1800s. The X-Men's Forge lost his leg in Vietnam, where he was a sergeant in the U.S. Army. DC's John Butcher received much of his specialized training from the CIA during his time as U.S. Army Ranger extraordinaire. Even John Proudstar, X-Men's Thunderbird, first notices that his mutant powers manifest themselves during his enlistment.

While participation in armed activity is peppered throughout various comic books, a military vocation was not the main thrust of their stories. There are some Indigenous comic book characters, however, whose pages are filled with this idea of Native Warrior. Within these depictions, generalized stereotypes seem more prevalent than in others, as we shall soon explore.

Little Sure Shot (DC *Our Army at War*, no. 127, February 1963)

Louis Kiyahani, a member of the Apache people, is an army scout in Sgt. Rock's Easy Company, noted for his jungle tracking skills and called "Little Sure Shot" for his specialization as a sniper and sharpshooter. Originally part of the *Our Army at War* lineup, the *Sgt. Rock* series focuses on Easy Company's cultural and ethnic diversity, similar to Marvel's *X-Men* title.

Yet, this diversity seems coupled with generic stereotypes as indicators of this diversity. Take Little Sure Shot, for instance. Little Sure Shot is an example of this heavy-handed treatment of culture, though not the only one. Certainly, one does not have to look at the Jackie Johnson character very hard to find some similarities. It seems rather telling that, as he is one of the only African American members of Easy Company, Jackie is good at sports (he is a former championship boxer).

To start on a positive note, *Sgt. Rock* does not offer any disparagement in its description of Native Americans. While his particular specialties may be stereotypic, Little Sure Shot is revered and respected for his prowess on the battlefield. Perhaps given the historical setting, during World War II, there is more emphasis given to fighting common enemies (usually Germans or Japanese) than to the cultural differences that these Americans have.

In addition, Little Sure Shot does not speak in broken English like the Tonto character. He is able to effectively communicate with his partners in Easy Company. Despite this, his speech seems to generically reference his culture at every turn. For example, in response to Sgt. Rock's curiosity at Easy Company's sneaky behavior in issue no. 217 (they have a secret), Little Sure Shot gently teases, "You're getting jumpy as a papoose with his first **bow and arrow**, Sarge ... Relax." There are many other examples of this unfortunate dialogue.

While he may not sport a full bonnet or fringed buckskin, the "brave" feathers stuck to Little Sure Shot's helmet suggest a more generic "Pan-Indian" identification rather than a specific cultural identity. Certainly many Indigenous soldiers in World War II may have adorned their helmets with icons similar to his feathers, but without a fuller explanation, which would be easy to do in the comic book medium, as to their personal relevance to Little Sure Shot (i.e., explaining why he wears them and what they mean to him personally), they do little more than support the Hollywood-type notion that all Native people wear feathers.

Another positive aspect: his character does not provide the comic relief for the overlying story. Additionally, Little Sure Shot is not portrayed as the generic "stupid" or "drunk" Indian seen many times in other media, as in the aforementioned film industry. Thus, his character does not serve as the butt of continual jokes based on his ethnicity; the Little Sure Shot character shows signs of humanity.

Another positive aspect of the character: Little Sure Shot is not trapped in an historical-only context. Well, perhaps he is, given that the *Our Army at War* and *Sgt. Rock* series take place *only* in a specific historical setting (World War II). Yet, even this setting is a relatively modern one and not the usual temporal setting of the Old West. This supports depiction of Native Americans as a people living in the modern era, rather than only in the past.

Little Sure Shot does not fall into either of the typical fashion of many stories featuring Native people for Indigenous character roles: noble or savage. His character is portrayed as not only cool-headed but also calm and stealthy enough to be Easy Company's resident sniper. With another stereotype-laden comment, Little Sure Shot supports this, when volunteering to scout out some enemy territory in issue no. 413: "An Indian scout's as noisy as a shadow, sir!"

Using this quote as a springboard, the issue of patronizing tone must be addressed. As mentioned, while the Sgt. Rock series focuses on diversity, there is some level of disparity in the comic's tone toward Indigenous people. Yet, this negativity comes directly from Little Sure Shot's mouth. While other characters in the series do not convey any patronizing tone, much of what Little Sure Shot says has a generic element to it, making the tone somewhat negative. Even seemingly simple statements, such as the following in issue no. 217, seem rather culturally demeaning to Native people: "Yeah ... [Sgt. Rock] sure looks like he's on the **warpath!**"

Thus the question remains: does this series demonstrate Indigenous humanity in its character? Little Sure Shot certainly commands respect from the other characters in the series and he does not speak in Tontoese. Yet, while he does not wear a full bonnet, his helmet-feathers detract from these good points, somewhat. He is not the comic-relief-of-color, his character is not portrayed in an ancient setting, and he is not portrayed as either noble or savage. Yet, his speech, which announces his ethnicity in every phrase, makes the Little Sure Shot seem limited and one-dimensional. Overall, there are many positives about this character, which should be celebrated, but given his limited dialogue and lack of character development, there is little actual humanity in the Little Sure Shot character.

CONCLUSION

Part of me is proud that there is a Native American among Sgt. Rock's ranks, as they are an elite team that gets the job done. Yet, given how poorly the character comes off, it is hard for me to revel in this pride.

Little Sure Shot is respected by other members of the team for his prowess. Yet, this prowess is based on stereotypic generalizations of Native American people. He is a great "shot" because *all* Indians are good hunters; he can find the enemy because *all* Indians are good trackers (despite the fact that Asian jungles are nothing like American forests); and he is silent and stealthy because *all* Indians are thus. (Actually, that last one may be true; or at least my wife thinks so, as she accuses me of silently sneaking up on her when I'm doing nothing of the sort.)

Yet the truth is Native Americans are as varied and have special skills as varied as any other group of people. *Sgt. Rock* does not demonstrate this variety as it pushes the message that Little Sure Shot's skills are based on genetics and not developed skill.

Private Jay Little Bear (DC *Captain Savage & His Leatherneck Raiders*, no. 1, January 1968)

Private Jay Little Bear is a former professional wrestler in his civilian life and is drafted into the U.S. Marines during World War II. He carried standard issue U.S. military weapons, but he also utilizes a tomahawk and even bow and arrows.

Little Bear is well respected by his fellow men and often serves as the epitome of bravery, courage, and forthrightness. Yet, despite this respect, the character itself is poorly constructed, consisting mostly of generalizations and stereotypes. While not mentioned at length in this discussion, Native Americans are many times associated with a high level of athleticism (perhaps thanks to real life super–athletes such as Jim Thorpe). Given this assumption, naturally Jay Little Bear is a professional wrestler and not, say, a nuclear physicist.

As for the comic itself, there is no language demeaning Indigenous people used in this series. However, given the constant use of generalized statements toward Native Americans, one could possibly see them as demeaning vocabulary.

Little Bear speaks the English language as well as the rest of the characters (or better, in the case of the Frenchman). This mastery of language elevates his mental status above a character such as Tonto, who seems less human because of limited language skills. While readers may be unsure of Little Bear's exact academic level of achievement, he is at least as smart as the rest of the team, based on language skills alone.

While Jay Little Bear does not wear fringed buckskin or adorn himself with a full-feathered headdress — both of which might qualify him for a court-martial, since he was in the military — he does utilize a very pan-Indian accoutrement, namely, a Native-style bow with arrows. Little Bear uses this weapon at any opportunity. Thus, he does not dress in a stereotypic manner, but his use of the bow weapon demonstrates a generality that all Native people use bows and arrows exclusively in modern times (even during wartime?), despite the availability of more effective weapons.

Yet, despite this generality, the comic series does not poke fun at Native Americans by depicting them as drunkards or as simply being stupid. Little Bear is respected by his peers as well as by his enemies (in the short time just before he extinguishes their lives).

Also, given that Little Bear is engaged in campaigns in World War II, the idea of cultural continuance is supported. Little Bear is not depicted as just a part of the dying Old West nor is he the last of his tribe. In this comic book, Native people are not extinct and live in the modern times.

Yet, not everything about Little Bear is complimentary. Are the Indians either noble or savage? Little Bear walks a fine line between noble efforts and savagery. His intentions are noble enough: save the guys (his team), save the girl, win the war for America, and so forth. However, Little Bear sometimes goes overboard in his physical interaction, such as in issue no. 1 in which he performs the "Sitting Bull Swing" (twirling his enemy by his hair and then throwing him down), which leads to the notion of savagery. Still, perhaps we can assume that this savagery is due in major part to the wartime setting (not to mentioned the fact that, as a civilian, he is a wrestler, which can be a very 'hands-on' vocation), but it still smacks of generalization.

With phrases such as, "Sitting Bull Swing" and "Chief" (one of his aliases), there does seem to be some patronizing tonality to the comic book. It would be nice to be able to excuse this as just the vernacular of the specific timeframe (1940s), but, in truth, this type of verbiage is generalizing and demeaning, no matter the time period.

Despite all of this, Jay Little Bear is allowed to fall in love, which, among many other features, demonstrates his humanity. Yes, there is some detraction from this idea of humanity in Indigenous characters and these must not be ignored or excused. Yet, his ability to think beyond himself (and getting back home to make more money by wrestling), to think beyond warfare and killing, to think beyond merely the attractions of flesh toward ideals of true love, makes this character very human and very respectable, despite these other negative stereotypes.

CONCLUSION

Little Bear is a hard character to like. In the first issue, all he does is demonstrate his materialistic drive by constantly griping about how much money he makes as a professional wrestler versus how little he makes as a soldier.

As mentioned, there are some redemptive qualities to this character, evident as the series continues. However, getting to that point is a matter of perseverance and frankly not worth the wait. We can take pride in Native Americans in the military, but let's do it without the generalizations and pan–Indianism (such as calling him "Chief" or him using a bow and arrows). The series could be improved if Native American people were behind the creative wheel. They could add some cultural-specificity to the character, rather than perpetuating these misrepresentations.

Johnny Cloud (DC *All-American Men of War*, no. 82, December 1960)

Before you ask, Johnny Cloud is *not* some brand of soft paper tissue. To fans of this series, that is not even funny. Johnny is a member of the U.S. Army Air Corps during World War II. His real name (allegedly) translates as "Flying Cloud" and he was the son of a Navajo chief. He led an air patrol called "Happy Braves" ["DC Encyclopedia" 74]. The series lasted from issue no. 82 to no. 114 [Overstreet 262].

At first glance, *All-American Men of War* appears to both celebrate a Native American character and demonstrate the important role of Indigenous people during wartime. Respected by his fellows, Johnny also demonstrates his prowess as a pilot (he *is* the "Navajo Ace," after all). Yet, while this series centers on a Native character, it is not without some cultural blemishes.

Slight racial tension exists within the pages and there is some small level of demeaning vocabulary toward Native Americans in *All-American Men of War* (*AAMOW*). While the overall language seems to be used in a seemingly positive manner, some residue of uneasiness resides just under the surface of the words.

For instance, to demonstrate their eagerness to accept Johnny as their military leader, his men eventually referred to themselves as the "Happy Braves." Certainly, one can view this as an homage of sorts, citing the men's willing to identify, culturally, with Johnny. But why "Braves"? Why not just "Johnny's Men" or "Cloud's Killers"? Any other combination of names might suffice, but one was chosen that seems to identify Johnny (and his men) more by race than by fighting skills.

To go further, there are certain off-the-cuff remarks about Native culture that leave one scratching one's head as to their implied meaning. When one airman advises Johnny to fly a different airplane, one in which as many pilots have been killed, Johnny replies, "I thought **Indians** are supposed to be **superstitious!** Relax! I'll be back!" [*All-American Men of War*, no. 105].

Are Native people thought to be any more superstitious than Roman Catholics that wear St. Christopher medals for safe travel? This racially biased sentiment is later echoed in the comic as Johnny returns safely to his group. "This is one for the book! It took an Indian to teach us not to be jinxed by superstition" [issue no. 105].

"Best of Both Worlds?" Johnny Cloud demonstrates his modernity by combat in World War II while paying homage to the stereotype about all Native Americans being able to ride horses. *All-American Men of War.* "Killer Horse — Killer Ship!" no. 105, September–October 1964 (© DC Comics).

Comments like these do not celebrate Indigenous character; instead, at best they serve to confuse readers about issues of cultural identity and personal spirituality.

Despite these unsavory language bits, Johnny demonstrates a rather positive feature, as he does not speak like Tonto. He is fluent in English, having a firm grammatical grasp of the language. Johnny is even bold enough to use contractions in sentences, unlike Tonto. Thus, the reader is saved from a tired and overused verbal stereotype.

While Johnny dresses like all the other military men, the reader is privy to his civilian Navajo garments — at least during the flashback scenes. During these glimpses of Johnny's home life, one might expect fringe and feathers or other accoutrements more associated with Plains Indian culture. However, these moments show Johnny dressed in southwestern styles that more accurately represent Navajo people rather than the generic pan–Indian look.

While it seems hard to tell what Johnny's sense of humor is like, there do not seem to be any comedic elements constructed around the idea of the drunken or stupid Indian. The only clue the reader is given about humor comes from a description of Johnny's victory: "As we headed home, I smiled from the inside as only an Indian can" (issue no. 105).

By placing the Johnny Cloud character during World War II, the comic book is effective in portraying Indigenous people as living beings and not as people who existed only in the Old West. He is skilled enough in the use of modern technology (fighter planes and machine guns) to employ them to win his battles.

Neither is Johnny's character portrayed as simply noble or savage. He is a human being like everyone else in his company and, like others, he tries to do the best he can, and he sometimes fails. While he may be a "good" character, he is not inherently so just because he is Native American.

While the overall tone of the AAMOW is not patronizing, there is a certain uneasiness as well as confusion to the comic book's attitude toward Native American religious beliefs. Yet, this is offset somewhat by the humanity of the Native character that shines though the series. Johnny Cloud is a hero and receives respect from his peers and enemies.

Overall, this is a worthwhile character, despite some confusing stereotypes and descriptive language. Not only do readers get to see some Navajo-style clothing (a change from the typical fringe and feathers look) on occasion, but the fact that this character is set in modern times (outside the Old West setting) makes AAMOW and Johnny Cloud worthy of continued reading and celebration.

Conclusion

Cloud is an interesting character. Given the timeframe (the 1960s), it is laudable that a Native American could serve as the central protagonist and still remain popular enough to sustain publication. Cloud is (eventually) respected by all those around him; deservedly so, as he is made victorious by perseverance, dedication, and skill.

Yet, there is a sense of pan-Indian generalizations prevalent throughout this series. Much like Marvel's Jay Little Bear character, DC's Johnny Cloud could greatly benefit from the presence of Indigenous writers and artists to add real-life cultural perspectives.

Spirit (Marvel *G.I. JOE*, no. 31, January 1985)

Charlie Iron-Knife, called "Spirit" for his roots in mysticism, is a member of G.I. Joe — an elite paramilitary group consisting of specialists from many walks of life. Spirit's ability lies in his tracking skills and he is also portrayed in the comics as a shaman or healer, who possesses a very close relationship with nature and innate spirituality.

G.I. Joe: Order of Battle, no. 2 (which appears to pull its information directly from the side of the box containing the G.I. Joe action figure) officially describes Spirit as follows:

> Spirit comes from a family so far below the poverty line that they never realized they were poor. Was a hunting guide through high school. Served in Southeast Asia, then as a civilian completed his education. Returned to the service for reasons inexplicable to anyone but a native American mystic warrior.

His file concludes with this quote from an unidentified source: "Charlie is a Shaman, a medicine man. He's not a healer or a priest or a witch-doctor. There isn't any equivalent in our culture for what he is unless we had shrinks that could actually help people."

In the early issues of his appearance in Marvel's *G.I. Joe*, Spirit seems more like a caricature of a Native American rather than a "Real American Hero." He speaks in flowery metaphors such as, "You have the hand that heals ... and the eye that sees!... The eye that sees the hidden world!" Spirit also communicates with members of the animal kingdom, especially "Brother Eagle!" [Issue no. 32].

Interestingly, one very threadbare stereotype is stretched concerning his use of healing, herbal remedies. Since Spirit is not only a product of modern society, but also a member of an elite and resourceful group, he makes use of a local florist shop to obtain his particular herbal needs [Issue no. 33]. This modern "take" on an old stereotype is a subtle change from the idea that healers have some sort of special sacred herbal remedy, which can be obtained only within the confines of "nature" (i.e., the wilderness, desert, or other remote location).

Okay, so he has braids, is an expert tracker, speaks to animals, and uses florists like a holy drug store. Yet, for all his seeming characters flaws, Charlie "Spirit" Iron-Knife is an identifiable Native American character within the G.I. Joe team.

This ethnocultural identification is an important concept to understand. From a personal perspective, as a Native youth, it was very important to be able to identify Indigenous characters in order to feel some connection to them. Spirit is certainly an easily identified Native American. While this identification is important, it does not excuse any misrepresentation that may occur within the confines of the character. Yet, without identification, Indigenous characters can get lost in the shuffle, which is perhaps the case with Spirit's fellow "Joe" member, Airborne (codename), who is also Native American.

Franklin E. Talltree, known to the Joe team as "Airborne" based on his skills as a paratrooper, is a member of the Navajo people. *G.I. Joe: Order of Battle* no. 1 sums up his character thus: "Airborne jokes around and gets loose, but he's serious too ... dead serious. You look at him and sometimes he's looking right through you. Must be the Indian in him. The Navahos [sp] call it 'the far-seeing look.' Spooky."

Yet, other than this somewhat narrow description of him, Airborne's cultural identity is hardly mentioned. There is little chance to identify him as Native and little chance to identify *with* him, as his ethnic identity is not usually specified. Even in the issue above (no. 32), where Spirit makes Native-sounding spiritual comments and communicates with the local wildlife, Airborne does none of these things. Yet, in the subsequent issue (no. 33), Airborne does make one single reference to his cultural affinity with Spirit, "<Ahem> That sounds like a cue for me and my fellow Native Americans to make ourselves scarce around here.... Let's go, big fella!"

So what am I suggesting here? Would it be better for Airborne to have braids and speak in flowery metaphors, like a *real* Indian? Certainly not. Nor is the answer to make a character fraught with tired stereotypes, such as Spirit.

The real solution is to have Native American characters *celebrate* their ethnicity and culture rather than either exploit it or simply ignore it to the point that it becomes invisible. To do this, a balance must be struck between blatant generalizations of the Indigenous character (Spirit) and the furtive concealment of the character's "Indianness" (Airborne). Until such a balance is struck, the only Native American characters that one can be identified with are those that, like Spirit, fall into the generalized category. While there may be other Native characters, we may never get to know how great they are because their culture has not been celebrated.

One positive note about the *G.I. Joe* series: no one was put down for their ethnicity or culture. Similar to the *X-men* title, *G.I. Joe* tends to focus on the *melting pot* ideal of cultural inclusion rather than exclusion. The vocabulary, which is positive toward diversification and especially toward Spirit's culture, supports this.

Spirit does not speak in broken English. Yet, he does feel the need to fill his word balloons with metaphysical spiritualism (as in issue no. 32, mentioned above) and sometimes he offers his own brand of verbal disparagement: "Looks like Cobra squaws are fighters too..." [issue no. 33].

There are, of course, exceptions to both of these misrepresentations, especially in the revamped *G.I. Joe* series (by Image Comics), where Spirit conveys some dry wit to another *Joe* about his robot tracking skills: "After many years of honing my meditation skills and experiencing a number of visions, I have learned to consult the Great Spirit for guidance." When asked if he is serious, Spirit replies, "That ... and I spotted a fresh, distinctive oil trail near the manhole entrance, which I've been following ever since."

Also, while Spirit chooses a headband, fringed-leather pants (complete with loin-cloth / breechcloth covering), and twin hair braids, Indigenous readers can take *some* comfort from the character's distinct lack of feather in his apparel. Having a headdress or single "brave" feather would serve only to complete his stereotypic, Hollywood *Indian* look. In the Image series, Spirit tones down the clothing choices to basic black and long hair — much better choice!

There are no comedic plotlines contrived on the idea of *firewater* or the *stupid Indian* theme. Another positive aspect of Spirit, in both the original and subsequent series, is his representation of cultural continuance. The G.I. Joe team exists in modern times, thus demonstrating that Spirit, and thereby Native American people in general, have survived to this time period as well. Indigenous people are not just extinct artifacts of history in this series.

Spirit's character also does a fairly good job of avoiding the noble or savage dichotomy. Despite superficial appearances of being a goody-goody, there is some small level of complexity in his character: when another Joe complains of some offending cigarette smoke from a passerby (issue no. 33), Spirit comments, "It's a free country. If people want to poison themselves, they have the right." A more *noble* Indigenous character may have even confronted the smoker about harming Mother Earth or explained how tobacco is actually meant for spiritual purposes only. Thus, there is some small level of character complexity present.

That said, the overall tone of all the *G.I. Joe* titles shows much respect toward Spirit and his ethnicity. Again, the Joe team is highly diversified in its membership.

In all, Spirit's character shows much humanity in both the older and newer series. Certainly, some of his cultural representation is presented a bit heavy-handedly; yet, many times, Spirit alone shows elements of true humanity (compassion, intelligence, insight, etc.). With so many characters (all of the G.I. Joe team and all of the Cobra baddies) present and so few pages on which to tell the stories, individuals having blatant one-sided character traits come across more readily and seem more *real* than the others, who seem more complex and two-dimensional by comparison. To sum up: yes, there are some unsavory elements that come to mind (being a tracker based on biology, a shaman, and speaking in mystical gibberish), but overall Spirit is a strong, respectable character. Add to this fact that many of the elements mentioned above are remedied in the Image remake of G.I. Joe and he becomes an even more palatable — and more human — Indigenous character.

CONCLUSION

What Native American can honestly say Spirit is a bad character, altogether? He was one of the few choices for Native American characters Indigenous youth had when I was growing up. All of the other *Joe* members looked up to and respected him, so why couldn't we?

He is also easily identifiable as Native (perhaps too much so, as mentioned above). What other G.I. Joe team member got to wear *buckskin* as part of their uniform? In addition, Spirit is the only one tough enough to go toe-to-toe with Cobra's ultimate ninja, Storm Shadow (in the *G.I. Joe* television series). Again, what's not to like?

Summary

As we have seen, Native American characters are sometimes thrust into militaristic plots perhaps because of notions of the great Native warrior. Whatever the case, many times these characters are freighted with generalities and stereotypes to define their characters. The majority of these warrior characters are males. What of the female characters? What roles do they most often play? In the next section we will explore Native American female characters and their place in comic books.

CHAPTER THIRTEEN

The Power of Indigenous Women: PIW in Action!

*My first priority is a long, hot **bath**. I'll be out in a couple of **days**.* —Danielle Moonstar

Female characters in general — and more specifically, Native American female characters — seem underrepresented in comic books. Perhaps this is due to the mostly male readership or maybe it is due to the comic writers, who are usually men as well.

Native American comic book females are subject to not only the same stereotypes as other female characters, but also they face even further denigration, based on ethnicity and race. *Commies, Cowboys, and Jungle Queens* offers up the general *raison d'être* for female comic characters, especially the "jungle queens": "the jungle queens were there primarily for cheesecake, as were many other women [characters].... They reflected male criteria for the ideal woman: long hair, long legs, large breasts, physical agility, and proclivities rather more emotional than intellectual" [Savage, 78].

It seems little has changed from the jungle queen character even with the introduction of more modern and (hopefully) less stereotypic female comic book heroes. Compared to the 1940s and 1950s (when jungle queens ruled the pages), modern comic book women seem even *more* like Savage's "cheesecake," but, now they are on uber-steroids! Take (the new) Wonder Woman, She-Hulk, Super Girl, Invisible Woman, Zatanna Zatara, Jean Grey, (the new) Captain Marvel, or even (sometimes) villains like Catwoman and Elektra — each is a testament to male-defined anatomical perfection, not to mention being given gravity-and-physics-defying abilities at times.

Yet, as mentioned, Indigenous female characters face far more adversity than just serving as eye-candy for male readers. The representation of the Native female gender has long been far baser in nature than just one founded in physical perfection. It has reached further into overt sexual icons.

Stedman discusses the reasons for the sexual energy of *la belle Sauvage*: "No one can tell, of course, exactly when the portrait of an unspoiled benefactress in feathers was first conceived, or, perhaps, transferred to the Indian. That the ages-old theme of bounty from a virgin goddess (or earthly representative) had simply found a rich growing medium in the untouched New World could well be argued" [Stedman, 21].

This treatment is echoed within the film industry. Perhaps this Indian princess-as-sexpot ideal is supported by Hollywood, which has, for many years and countless films, portrayed Indigenous peoples as wanton children of nature, endowed with little intellectual capability. "The presumed lack of mental prowess may have something to do with the images of the Native American as intensely sexual — more creature than human, more bestial than celestial. Sexuality has historically constituted an important dimension of Hollywood Indians, both male and female" [Kilpatrick, xvii].

The point? Not only are Native female heroes sometimes portrayed simply as jungle queen "cheesecake" — representations that fit male readers' and male creators' idea of the perfect woman — but also the characters have been carrying with them this latent sexual iconography associated with Indigenous females perhaps since John Smith penned his fanciful memoirs, *A Description of New England*, in 1616.

While only limited space can be given to a discussion here, the subject — especially that of *la belle Sauvage* in comic books — merits further exploration and perhaps even its own book. For now, let us examine the actual characters and their particular significance.

Many of these Native women face the same misrepresentations and stereotypes that their male counterparts do. Unfortunately, there are few that warrant actual praise. Even so, we must celebrate the fact that they exist at all, given the underrepresentation of Native American female characters in comic books.

It is peculiar, but not surprising, given the inherent nature of the genre that, while these characters represent strong heroic traits, many do not warrant their own comic book series. Perhaps this is a comment about the audience or, more likely, the authorship. Nevertheless, the following characters are noteworthy for their demonstrated continuance.

Danielle "Dani" Moonstar (Marvel, *The New Mutants* 1982)

Dani Moonstar is Cheyenne and a member of Marvel's *X-Force*. Dani has the mutant ability to turn her innermost fears into reality. While she can initially launch an attack within close range, when Dani shoots with her "psychic arrow" she can accomplish this feat from a distance. To accommodate the stereotype of the Indian-at-one-with-nature shtick, Dani can communicate with most any animal. To add to her mysticism, in recent editions Dani has been given the ability to heal others as another of her powers.

On a positive note: Dani has never spoken like Tonto. She has always been articulate. Even though she has never been subject to the broken–English syndrome, her clothing is another story. Initially Dani's look was somewhat stereotypic; during her debut in *The New Mutants*, Dani wore leather-wrapped braids — similar to the way so many other Indigenous female characters are portrayed in comics. Later, of course, Dani was able to let her hair down.

The important element that Indigenous people are alive in the world today is present. Dani exists in current (modern) times. Thus, her character is not constrained by having to exist only in history in order to move the story along. This is a very positive element of her character.

"The Braided Story." Similar to her Indigenous contemporary mutant, James Proudstar (Warpath), Danielle Moonstar has had her share of stereotypic fashions, as noted in her early "braided" days in *New Mutants*. *The New Mutants*, "Away Game," vol. 1, no. 16, June 1984 (© 2008 Marvel Characters, Inc. Used with permission).

Dani is not generally portrayed as either noble or savage — she is simply another (mutant) character trying to do what is right. She is not stuck in either of these polarized positions of totally good or totally evil.

Overall, Dani's character may have some flaws, but it has evolved over the years into a realistic, believable, and very likeable Indigenous female figure. Those looking to find strong women characters would do well to look at some of Dani's elements — *after* she evolved and got rid of the braids.

CONCLUSION

Dani has always held a special place for me. She is both a strong female and a capable figure on the battlefield. Her character started out as somewhat stereotypic in a visual sense (braids and the use of the bow), yet her character has evolved and grown as the series has continued.

Given that not only is she tough as nails (she worked for S.H.I.E.L.D. for a while!), but also that her powers are culturally independent (for the most part), she is a Native American character whom readers can admire. There is some criticism about the explicit sexual nature of her character, but she is also surrounded by other females equally endowed, so this sexual symbolism is not based on her ethnicity but upon the way in which female characters are generally depicted in comics.

Talisman (Marvel's *Alpha Flight*)

Elizabeth Twoyoungmen (known as the Talisman) is the daughter of *Alpha Flight's* Shaman. As the Talisman, Elizabeth has complete control over the spiritual realm. She also receives this special endowment as part of a "prophecy of three hundred generations" (*Alpha Flight*, no. 19). In other words, she receives this power thanks to her Indigenous lineage. Similar to her father (Michael Twoyoungmen, aka "Shaman"), Talisman's powers demonstrate the stereotypical idea of *instant shaman*; namely, the notion that an Indigenous person can become a holy person without the lifetime of training that real shamans go through. She seems more a sorcerer than a holy person (at least from an Indigenous perspective).

Fortunately, the descriptive language used for Talisman's ethnicity is positive and not demeaning. In fact Elizabeth's transformation into her Talisman alter ego is heralded by some very positive descriptors. Upon seeing Elizabeth in issue no. 19, Snowbird (a descendent of Nelvanna, the Eskimo God of the Northern Lights) prostrates herself at Elizabeth's feet exclaiming, "Hail to thee, O Promised one. Thy unworthy servant bids thee welcome and awaits thy least command!"

Talisman's use of verbal speech is free and clear of Tonto-like garbles. She is a well-educated Native American woman; while contemplating her father's heroic identity, Elizabeth reminisces about her education and the recent changes in her life: "I mean ... a week ago I was an art college student with no more interest in the occult than reading my horoscope in the **Calgary Herald**." (*Alpha Flight*, no. 19)

Talisman's costume should also be commended. In the early years of the character's inception, it was free of the fringe-and-feathers syndrome that so many Native superheroes fall victim to. Her clothing, which might be best described as a sexy

"Nothing Personal ... Just Business." Dani Moonstar would do away with the generic style and opt for more personal attire, as seen here in her best mafia-like business suit. *X-Force*, "Lies and Deception," vol. 1, no. 72, December 1997 (© 2008 Marvel Characters, Inc. Used with permission).

"Kicking Up Her Heels." From this cover image, at first glance it is hard to decide whether Talisman's costume falls into the stereotypic style of many Indigenous characters (are those moccasins?); yet, on closer examination, she does not have the fringe and feathers normally associated with Native characters. *Alpha Flight*, "Turn Again, Turn Again, Time in Thy Flight," vol. 1, no. 19 (© 2008 Marvel Characters, Inc. Used with permission).

"Sunday Best." Elizabeth Twoyoungmen is transformed into the Talisman, fulfilling an age-old prophecy. While still a nearly all-powerful being, the Talisman character derives her power from her ethnic lineage and not from years of study and training. *Alpha Flight*, "Turn Again, Turn Again, Time in Thy Flight," vol. 1, no. 19 (© 2008 Marvel Characters, Inc. Used with permission).

sorceress's gown with tiara and tiny boots, avoids this common clothing stereotype rather well. Sadly, stereotypic fringe would be added to this character's costume in later years for dramatic effect.

Elizabeth does not drink and, as noted above, she has a college education. Thus, her character does not fit either the drunken or the stupid Indian category.

Also, despite the fact that Talisman and members of the *Alpha Flight* team travel back in time during her inaugural adventure, she is not a product of historical times. Talisman exists in the modern age, which demonstrates that Native people survived the days of Old West and are not an extinct species.

Neither she nor her father, Shaman, can be described in terms such as, noble or savage. Both are complex characters who fight on the side of good, but they do so with reservations at times. Talisman spouts the following venom regarding her transformation at her father (*Alpha Flight*, no. 37): "Am I not what my beloved father here has **made** me?... Too bad you didn't prepare me for the fact that fulfilling my destiny would cost me my humanity!" Talisman is a complex hero, indeed.

Add to her character's portrayal of humanity that Talisman is endowed with no patronizing tone and you have an Indigenous character relatively free of stereotypes. Thus, while her status of instant shaman remains problematic, Talisman constitutes a somewhat positive representation of not only Indigenous characters, but also strong female characters.

Conclusion

Talisman is not a strong character — or at least, she is not portrayed that way. Her character has always seemed too immensely powerful for the small role she plays within the *Alpha Flight* series.

Certainly, Talisman has many positive traits: college education, immeasurable powers, and physical attractiveness (with very little overt sexuality). There are few stereotypes (besides the obvious, *instant* shaman routine) that plague her character. Yet, Talisman's characterization never seems to live up to its potential from a storyline point-of-view.

That said, I must concede her importance to the overall genre of comic books: Talisman is a female Indigenous comic book character from a mainstream publisher (Marvel). This alone makes her worthy of mention and admissible for positive identification from Native readers.

Risque (*X-Force*, no. 51, February 1996)

Gloria Dolores Muñoz, otherwise known as Risque, is another mutant with the ability to implode inorganic matter and make it collapse on itself. Risque has brief associations with the X-Force team, specifically in her romantic (and tumultuous) relationship with James Proudstar (Warpath). Similar to Echo (another Indigenous character from Marvel), her ethnicity includes Native American (Seminole mother) and Latin American (Cuban father) roots; thus she is not only a female comic book hero, she is also a multiethnic one as well.

Risque is a hell-raiser and respected by those around her. There is no disparaging language used to describe Risque.

"Strong Enough for a Man." During first outings, Talisman has no idea the extent of her powers and must learn how to best utilize her new abilities. *Alpha Flight*, "Turn Again, Turn Again, Time in Thy Flight," vol. 1, no. 19 (© 2008 Marvel Characters, Inc. Used with permission).

Risque is a modern Native female and does not speak like Tonto does; she uses modern English, similar to any other character within the *X-Force* comic.

She is also one of the few Native American comic book characters who does not wear any vestiges of pan–Indian clothing to mark her heritage. While she dresses in modern clothing, she is most often seen in black.

Despite having intimate ties to a club in her home stomping-grounds (Florida), where she and the bartender are friends, Risque does not appear to be an alcoholic. No mention of Indigenous people as drunkards or as being stupid occur.

Risque is a modern character and effectively represents cultural continuance. She is not seen against an Old West backdrop and is not portrayed as a historical artifact. Risque, and by inference Native American people, are represented as having a living and thriving existence.

Despite betraying Warpath early in their relationships, she is not portrayed as either noble or savage. Risque is a complex character who has the potential for making both good and bad choices.

The overall tone used to portray Risque is one that celebrates her ethnicity, but the main emphasis is given to her powers and her relationship with X-Force. There is nothing patronizing in her representation.

Given her modernity, her lack of pan-Indian clothing, and her complexity, Risque represents Indigenous humanity rather well. Add to this, being an underrepresented female *and* multiethnic character, and you get a surprisingly well-devised and well-represented Indigenous comic book character.

Conclusion

Risque is a great character. Not only does she have acceptably cool powers but she is as mysterious and rebellious as her name implies. The lack of generic stereotypes she represents helps with this level of coolness, as well. Characters such as Risque, who accurately represent and celebrate Indigenous culture, multiethnicity, and the female character, should not only be noted by Native readers, but should also be granted their own individual comic book title to continue the effective storytelling.

Sarah Rainmaker (Image's *GEN13*)

Sarah Rainmaker is a fictional character from the comic book series *Gen13*. Sarah is a member of the Apache tribe from the fictional San Carlos reservation. Her powers seem to be limited to the natural, environmental elements: she can control the weather, launch lightning from her hands, utilize wind currents to fly, and redirect moving water to new locations.

Yet, these powers seem very specifically connected to Mother Nature. Akin to the instant shaman stereotype, her connection with nature, based on cultural heritage, is not surprising.

Jeff Mariotte, one of the many writers for *Gen13*, offers this reaction when asked if her powers might be somewhat stereotypic:

You're definitely right about that. Certainly, there are characters whose powers are connected to their racial/ethnic backgrounds — or stereotyped versions of those backgrounds — but there's no law that says they have to be. It would be interesting to see a Native character whose powers came from European or Asian traditions, for example, but that didn't happen in this case. I think there's a creative rut that she unhappily fell into — like, "it's cool that we've created this character with Apache roots, so we [the writers] don't have to put any thought into it beyond that" [Mariotte interview].

In addition to being an Indigenous female character, Sarah does triple duty for underrepresented groups. Sarah is one of the few lesbians of note in the comic book world and possibly the only Native American lesbian comic book character to date. Her sexual orientation would change to "bisexual" before the end of the *Gen13* series.

A plus to her character, Sarah never speaks in broken Tonto-like English. This demonstrates her intelligence and modernity.

Also, with a few feather exceptions here and there, Sarah eludes the stereotype of wearing fringe and feathers. While she occasionally wears accessories that allude to her cultural heritage, her costume does not contain these elements.

Is this because the *Gen13* creators were sensitive to this stereotype? Mariotte offers some insight to this: "I suspect it's because, as I outlined above, the creative process was about creating characters who were modern and exciting to contemporary readers. The tradition being paid homage to there was the tradition of spandex-clad superhero babes, not the tradition of Sarah's Native heritage, and to go back to the beads-and-feathers look we've seen on a lot of other comic characters would have made her seem old-fashioned." Thus, the lack of stereotypic clothing was more or less a side effect of trying to make the characters more modern and not about accurately portraying the characters — just blind luck, in this case, but effective, nonetheless.

Like many other Indigenous comic book heroes, Sarah is not an alcoholic nor is she portrayed as stupid because of her ethnicity. Mariotte says: "The tone of *Gen13* was always light — full of pop culture references and humor. Alcoholism and the perils of life on the 'rez' were touched on only occasionally, but as a steady diet those stereotypes would have been contrary to the book's intent. The main stereotype that applied in her case were the nature-based powers (and of course the stereotype of the young, hot bisexual babe)."

Given the thematic modernity of the comic and Sarah's existence within the super-powered team, Native characters are depicted as living beings existing in modern times, not as extinct species, within the *Gen13* title. Mariotte shares the following:

When I wrote *Gen* stuff, though, the most important thing to me was that the kids were modern, contemporary kids who were about the same age as their readers. The people who created them, especially artist J. Scott Campbell, weren't much older, and I think that's where their popularity came from. The Teen Titans had already been around for decades, and were probably created by guys in their 30s or 40s to begin with, so a new teen superhero team that spoke directly to their readers, with characters who listened to the same music and watched the same movies, was a big deal.

As an added bonus, Sarah is not portrayed as either noble or savage. She is a young woman with human complexities, not a polarized caricature of either good or evil.

The overall tone of *Gen* is respectful of Sarah's heritage, but it does not overly focus on it. While one *Gen13* trade paperback (TPB), "Spirit Song," focuses on her heritage exclusively, the series seems to center on other characters more often. Mariotte supports this: "I always thought Sarah was a fun character, but she was always kind of a second-tier *Gen* character. There was a time in the 1990s when *Gen* was the hottest comic around, so even a second-tier character got a lot of exposure, but she was never used to her full advantage. I think most people considered the main team to be Fairchild, Freefall, Burnout and Grunge, and then Rainmaker."

More importantly, Sarah's character is very human and believable. Like other comic book characters, she has flaws, but she remains a very readable character. While her powers may seem somewhat stereotypic, she represents a positive female Indigenous comic book character. To sum up, Mariotte explains his focus when writing for *Gen13* "So when writing those characters, I wasn't focusing on their race or heritage. I've had a couple of part–Cherokee girlfriends, and I wrote Sarah more like them — strong, modern women who happen to have that background, not as characters who had to stand for some idea of what Native women should be like."

CONCLUSION

Rainmaker is a milestone, but she is a short-lived character. The *Gen13* series does a good job of celebrating her Native American heritage while not exploiting it beyond recognition. She is intelligent, powerful, and physically attractive; yet, her sexuality is a main focus of her character at times. However, the tables are turned somewhat on this sexuality, by the choice of lesbianism (at least before she changed to bisexual).

In all, I agree with Mariotte: Rainmaker does not live up to her full potential, at least in the *Gen13* series. Still, her character is worth noting for the lack of general stereotypes and her character's demonstration of modernity and cultural continuance.

Echo (*Daredevil*, Vol. 2, no. 9, December 1999, Marvel Comics)

Maya Lopez, aka "Echo" (also later known as Ronin), is a fictional character created by David Mack and Joe Quesada, a Marvel Comics super heroine and a supporting character in the Daredevil title. In addition to being a Latina Native American, she is one of the few deaf comic superheroes.

Her metahuman power lies in mimicry: Echo can imitate to perfection anything she sees. Thus, she can become an expert piano player or dancer simply by seeing someone do it once. Her abilities stand out as atypical for an Indigenous character: they are not based on her ethnicity (i.e., shaman, tracker, one with nature, etc.). Creator David Mack gives further details on her power:

> I just write the character based on who they are as a person. Their history and upbringing and their psychology. Echo's unique abilities come from her experience of growing up deaf. She had to piece together the visual clues of the world to help her make up for the language of the 'audible world' that she did not have access to...so she learned to see all visual movement as language. And she became fluent in the language of physical movement [Mack interview].

"Devil's Advocate." Despite a physical disability (total deafness), Maya Lopez ("Echo"), seen in this dramatic Daredevil cover, derives her power from imitating instantly and perfectly anything she sees. *Daredevil*, "An Object in Motion," vol. 2, no. 14, March 2001 (© 2008 Marvel Characters, Inc. Used with permission).

Her biological father, William "Crazy Horse" Lincoln is killed by Wilson Fisk (the Kingpin), who later became Echo's adoptive father at the request of Lincoln. Mack talks about Echo's father, saying she:

> grew up with her father telling her stories, and the meaning of these stories has played a part in the stories I've written with Echo. She is a sort of storyteller in her own way. Like her father, and like the Chief on the Rez that taught her stories from Indian Sign Language. Through the imagery that corresponds to this Indian Sign Language, and the imagery and mythology of many Native American stories, I saw an overlap between the mythologies of those cultures and the mythologies of our modern comic book heroes that I enjoyed bridging together in the story.

In addition to being a storyteller, or perhaps because of this, Echo does not use Tonto-talk. She is not only eloquent, but she also has no speech impediment despite her hearing impairment. Of course, this also demonstrates both her power of mimicry as well as her mastery of storytelling, as Mack relates above.

When she dons her "Echo" guise, she is recognizable by a white hand stain, which covers most of her face (more on this in a moment). Her costume is actually pretty cool: tightly fitting black body suit with elegant combat boots and tape-wrapped hands and arms. However, like so many other Native characters, Echo sports a few feathers to complete her look.

While these accoutrements are seemingly done in good taste (making one wonder if perhaps this stereotype can pass), feathers on an Indigenous character still seem obligatory and only add to the notion that in order to be *Indian*, one only has to grab some feathers before walking out the door. The truth is, we are Native *all* the time, whether we have feathers or not.

Still, they look good on her — and I can imagine several Native people affirming that certain feathers are symbols of power and personal resilience. So, while this element can pass, it must still be noted as a common stereotype.

Mack offers insight as to the handprint: "That initial look of Echo was from the visual story she was telling in her theatrical performance called 'Echoes.' She was retelling one of her father's stories in the play and dressed to invoke the archetypes of that story. The hand paint on her face is from her personal story of her father touching her face when he died, and leaving his handprint, his 'echo' on her."

Mack goes on to explain the tape-wraps on her hands:

> She was a boxer, so when she sought to confront Daredevil, she wore her boxer boots, and when taping up her hands boxer style, just continued to tape up her arm, and included some of the iconography from her story which played the major part in her motivation to confront Daredevil. On that personal vendetta she dressed herself in personal imagery and the artifacts that made up her psychology and the practical gear that she had personal access too. When she became a part of the Avengers, and had access to their larger resources, and team motivations, she wore a large suit of protective armor.

There are no comic interludes built on the notion of the drunken or stupid Indian. Both Echo and her father are very serious and do not use alcohol or drugs. Mack talks about this lack of negative stereotyping, saying, "I just don't think in those terms. When writing, I think of the character as a real person, with personal motivations and identity based on her personal history."

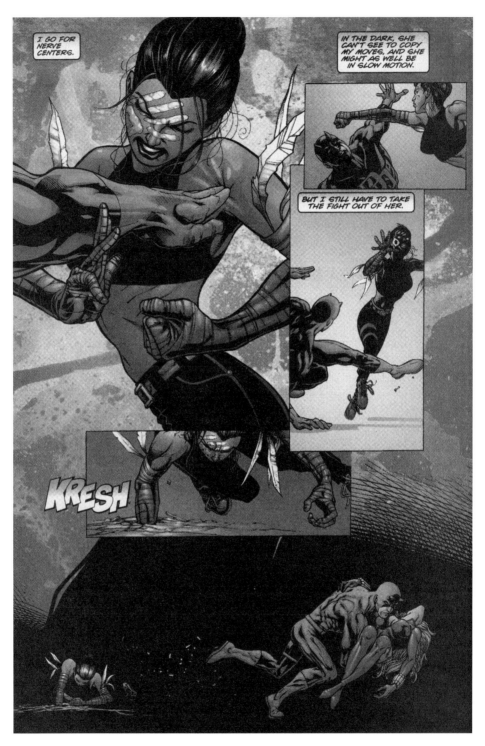

"Give the Lady a Hand." Why the painted handprint on Echo's face? Is it illustrative of her Native heritage, iconography similar to the painted palm prints on Indigenous ponies? The symbolism is based on heritage, but not ethnicity. *Daredevil*, "An Object in Motion," vol. 2, no. 14, March 2001 (© 2008 Marvel Characters, Inc. Used with permission).

Echo's character exists in modern times, thus representing Indigenous people as indeed existing past the cowboy days of the Wild West. Continuance, modernity, and healing through story are all important themes to Mack's character.

> For example, there is a man named Matt Atkinson (also called Smoking Hawk) who is a therapist to abused and troubled teenagers in Oklahoma City. He is Ojibway, and he uses story and imagery including the Echo story to help with his patients. He owns a lot of the original artwork from the Echo story, which he displays in his office as a means of communication and healing with his patients. He uses the art and the story of Echo to communicate with his patients and to help them communicate and discuss their issues.... This kind of the cycle from the stories reveal that the power of stories to help and heal and communicate is infinite, and a continuous cycle, in the same way that is described in the Echo story. I believe this concept of passing on ideas that are helpful and practical and even healing through the means of storytelling and imagery is one of the integral concepts encrypted into the practice and culture of Native American Storytelling [Mack interview].

While it is not extensive, there seems to be a touch of savagery about Echo's attacks, especially when attacking Daredevil, whom she believes killed her father. However, she is an intelligent person with whom one can reason; thus, she is neither noble nor savage.

Overall, the tone of Echo's character is handled with much care, and the humanity of her character is highly evident. Mack shares his thoughts on the Echo character as well as on her cultural and spiritual significance:

> [A] lot of the story of Echo, and her relationship to her father and the older storyteller character, came from my uncle telling me stories as a child. What he liked to do, was tell me stories and describe these ideas to me, and he asked me to draw for him the stories and concepts that he told me. So at a young age, these stories became integrated with imagery for me. I learned to see this imagery as a kind of language and communication of the stories and ideas.... From these stories with Echo, I've received a lot of wonderful feedback and insightful response to the story from readers who are of Native American descent.... That kind of response is so encouraging and rewarding and validating to the effort and intentions that I put into the story.
>
> So I didn't want the Echo story to just be about *some* of these ideas. I wanted it to actually serve the same function and be the idea itself...the story itself is constructed with the same structure that I find many of the Native American stories have in common. [More information on Echo available from creator, David Mack's website: http://www.davidmackguide.com.]

Conclusion

Anyone who has read Mack's *Echo: Vision Quest* knows what an amazingly cool graphic novel it is. This only adds to the fact that Echo is a well-developed Native American female character whose culture is treated with much respect by the creative team.

While Echo does have her share of cultural generalizations — she practices a vision quest without the aid of an Indigenous spiritual leader and she has a slight proclivity for feathers — overall, her character is one that Native readers can be happy to identify with.

Soothsayer (*Canyon Comics presents Eco Squad*, no. 2, Summer 1996.)

Mary Bearclaw is a Native American female from an undisclosed tribe. She is a member of the Guardians (later called the Eco Squad) team, which serves to protect the environment, specifically, the Grand Canyon. When she and other members of the Guardians were granted special powers to protect the environment by the Mother Earth, Mary Bearclaw is transformed into Soothsayer: "Mary Bearclaw, you whose people have not forgotten me, I charge **you** with protecting the past, keeping safe the cultures of those whole before so that we may **learn** from them" (*Eco Squad*, no. 2).

Soothsayer's powers are mostly elemental in nature: she can control the weather. While this particular power is very useful, she also seems to have the unexplained ability to fly (perhaps similar to how the X-Men's Storm flies, she flies by controlling wind currents, but it is not explained).

Soothsayer does not speak in broken English, as Tonto does. However, her form of verbal communication — seemingly over-flowery sentences — is almost as unbearable as Tonto's "ughs" and "get 'em ups." To help put out a potentially dangerous wilderness fire (issue no. 2), Soothsayer descriptively asks for help from the spirit world. "Oh, **Spirits** of the sky and storm, **heed** your sister's call. Let the heavens split asunder, and let the rains pour forth. Let the cleansing waters of the sky trample these raging flames, O' Might Spirits. **Let it rain!**" The use of this superfluous language is commonly found in various popular media and suggests that *all* Indigenous people speak in such a manner.

On a positive note, neither Mary Bearclaw nor her alter ego, Soothsayer, dress in pan–Indian style clothing. While her costume does contain a certain amount of feathers — as she has feathered wings during flight — she does not wear a headdress or fringe, as seen in a multitude of other comic books. To add relevance to this, stylistically-speaking, Soothsayer looks like any other superhero, more so than just an "Indian" superhero. This depiction is definitely a plus for this comic.

Yet, other representations are not as generous in this comic book. Despite being set in modern times, the only Native American people seen (other than Soothsayer) are those in a small village back in the middle of the sixteenth century (issue no. 3). Portraying Indigenous people only in the historical setting, as in this time-traveling story, only serves to reinforce the notion that Native Americans are an extinct species. Perhaps this might have been avoided by providing readers with information on Soothsayer's people and their *current* whereabouts and/or status, thus commenting on Native continuance. However, this information is not provided in *Eco Squad*.

Soothsayer's character seems to fall into the *noble Indian* stereotype. While readers know that she is both Native American (showing, perhaps, her cultural affinity for other Indigenous people) and an anthropologist (thus, demonstrating her knowledge of ancient cultures), it is not known why she chooses to fight for Mother Earth. Readers must accept that she fights for good because...well, just *because*. In reply to a young Native boy, who mistakes her for a Kachina — a representative from the spiritual realm — Soothsayer explains (in issue no. 3): "No, small one, I am no Kachina Spirit. But I have come to **help** you."

Despite these setbacks, the overall tone of the comic books is rather complimentary and reverent, at least in its depictions both Soothsayer and of ancient Native life. However, the respect shown does not negate the manner in which Soothsayer is presented to the reader.

Overall, the Soothsayer character is unremarkable and one-dimensional. Certainly, she is "good" and fights alongside the *Eco Squad* to protect Mother Earth. Yet, readers have no insight to any of the complexities or nuances of the character. Her character's ethnicity seems a simply ploy to advance the plot at times and offer some connection between the Grand Canyon and the people that originally resided in the area. Without this sense of character depth, Soothsayer seems more like a caricature based on simple stereotypes rather than a fully developed character.

CONCLUSION

While I am sure — well, I *hope* that I am sure — that EcoSquad and, subsequently, Soothsayer are written with the utmost respect for not only the environment but also the Native American people within it, this is no way makes up for the limited plot and character development found within its pages. Soothsayer represents the kind of Indigenous character that should be avoided at all costs: the truly underdeveloped and one-dimensional generalization of what outsiders believe Native Americans are like.

This character could be improved with some simple additions; namely, tribal identification, use of modern English (like the other characters), or endowing her with even better execution of her powers. However, as the character is presented, the reader is left with a shallow representation of what Native American female comic book characters are and, as such, she is a character worthy of identification from Indigenous readers.

"Ties that Bind." Kako, seen here protecting a young Aquaman, later becomes Corona, a fire elemental. *Aquaman: Time and Tide*, "Part 3: Snowball in Hell," no. 3, February 1994 (© DC Comics).

Honorable Mention

There are many other Native female characters worth mentioning. Acrata (DC *Superman* [2 series] Annual, no. 12, August 2000) is of Latina, possibly Mayan ancestry, adorns herself with Mayan symbols, and operates in Mexico City. Although her powers, which may stem from ancient Mayan mystics, make her character somewhat susceptible to misrepresentation, she is a strong character with outspoken political beliefs.

Corona (DC *Aquaman: Time and Tide*, no. 3, February 1994), an Inuit named Kako and Aquaman's former wife, becomes the superbeing, Corona, after Gaea (earth spirit) revives her (from death) and gives her powers. As Kako, the character exhibits few stereotypes, however when she becomes Corona, her powers (controlling fire) could possibly be misconstrued as making her just another Native person who is close to nature.

Wenonah Littlebird (DC *Super Friends*, no. 7, October 1977), aka "Owlwoman," is a full-blooded Native American from the Cherokee tribe in Oklahoma. She became Owlwoman and is first seen assisting Hawkman and his wife, Hawkwoman, in dismantling a bomb. She

Above, left: "Birds of Feather." Owlwoman, seen here helping Hawkman and Hawkwoman, invokes the Trail of Tears as a reason not to lose. *Superfriends*, "The Warning of the Wonder Twins," no. 7, October 1977 (© DC Comics). *Above, right:* "Why the Long Face, Buddy?" Characters like Super Chief are seen only in the placement of times long gone by ... almost as if Native people did not exist into the modern day. *Superman*, vol. 33, no. 245, December 1971–June 1972 (© DC Comics).

has the power of flight and enhanced senses, which prove useful on occasion. She also retains the ability to transform her claws into talons, which can rip through steel. Owlwoman lives in modern times and thus demonstrates that Native people can exist outside and beyond the Old West timeframe.

Dawnstar (*Superboy* Vol. 1, no. 226, April 1977, DC) represents quite a puzzle: she is from the far-distant future, but she is still seen wearing fringe and feathers. She was originally a bounty hunter from the thirtieth-century Native American colony world "Starhaven" and joined the Legion Academy, where she helped Superboy out at age 16, and later joined the Legion of SuperHeroes. She is later known briefly as "Bounty."

Manitou Dawn (DC *Justice League Elite*) is the former wife of Manitou Raven (deceased). They both existed in the prehistoric Obsidian Age of the DC universe and traveled forward into the future to become members of the Justice League of America team but later joined the offshoot, Justice League Elite, where Dawn began having an affair with Green Arrow. After Manitou Raven's death, Dawn inherited his powers as Manitou. She is from the ancient past, thus supporting the idea that Indigenous people existed only long ago, but she fights alongside modern heroes thanks to time travel. As in other cases, her character received mystic power based on Native ancestry.

In all, these Indigenous female characters have various levels of both positive and negative representation. However, given the sheer amount of male protagonists found in comic books, it is important to identify these characters and note their powerful roles within the genre. With time, perhaps these heroines will not only shed some of the misrepresentations that still trouble some of them, but also become more plentiful.

Conclusion: Knowing Is
Half the Battle

"But wait," you say, "what about *White Boy*, the comic strip from the 1930s? Why didn't you mention the Marvel Scalphunter character in comparison to the DC one? Where is the information about Charles Little Sky, aka Portal? Shouldn't you mention Chief Man-of-Bats somewhere in here? Why don't I see *Red Prophet* listed anywhere? What about the newer *Lone Ranger* series from Dynamite Entertainment? Hey, isn't there a Native American character in Marvel's *Vampire Hunter* series? You never mentioned anything about (Green Arrow's sidekick) Speedy's Indigenous mentor, Brave Bow!"

Of course, a book of this size is not able to cover every Native American comic book character in existence; nor should it, as this book's main purpose is to give readers the tools to identify stereotypes and misrepresentations themselves. As with all media forms (descriptive texts from plays, books, and film), comic books are replete with stereotypical Native American characters, even within the modern and progressive pseudo- and semi-politically correct world in which we live.

Despite the emergence of new media forms, including those begotten from and inspired directly by comic books (cartoons, video games, movies, and an unnamed host of other forms of entertainment), the existence of stereotypes seems to remain unchanged. The recurrences seem not to have lessened by many degrees. Stereotypes that exist with the newer comic books seem to be newer versions of many of the old ones.

Older characters such as Tomahawk and White Indian support the ago-old idea that white people can become better at being Native than the Indigenous people are able (stemming partly from the "Mohican Syndrome" found in James Fenimore Cooper's *Leatherstocking* stories). Worse, these pretenders usually portray the people they revere and emulate so much with such poor generalizations that their whole act seems pan-Indian, at best. Characters such as DC's Scalphunter demonstrate this latter point best.

Conversely, while there are characters that pretend to be part of two (or more) cultures, some come by it honestly, such as Johnny Wakely (Red Wolf), Joshua Brand (Stalking Wolf), and Maya Lopez (Echo). Because multiethnic heroes are not able to disguise themselves as well or easily as the wannabes can, they endure various levels of misfortunes for the sake of their heritage. Despite the step in the right direction (making the characters at least somewhat biologically identifiable to the culture they represent), there is much focus on their tribulations from both peoples. Similar to cinema, multiethnic characters many times find little acceptance from either group.

Yet some Indigenous characters find limited acceptance from white culture by becoming the token sidekick to the dominant white character, for one reason or another. Sure, characters such as Little Beaver, Tipi, and Tonto have their share of adventures, but they do so at the direction of a white protagonist. Moreover, even later, when some of these characters were popular enough to merit their own comic book series at times, they are best known for simply being good subservient helpers and not heroes in their own right.

Eventually, Native characters earned their own sidekicks as they set out on their own adventures. While this is a noteworthy milestone, it is unfortunate that the sidekicks of Indians turned out, in many cases, to be nonhuman animals. Tonto had Scout, his faithful horse; (Tim Truman's) Scout cavorted with Gahn, a chipmunk, as his sprit guide; Red Wolf has his devoted canine companion, Lobo; and Weasel, a totemic weasel apparition, is the jelly to Muktuk Wolfsbreath's peanut butter. We can be thankful that Turok finally broke this pitiful chain by getting a real human as a sidekick (twice!). This feat, however, has not been reproduced since.

One stereotype that *has* been reproduced time and time again over the years is the idea of Indigenous people as instant shamans. Shaman (*Alpha Flight*), Joshua Brand (*Shaman's Tears*), DC's Manitou Raven, and even Forge (*X-Men*) have all fallen victim to the idea of Native people being naturally spiritual or mystic in some way. Elements of the mystic Red Man shine through in his relationship to the natural world and often he is able to communicate with animals.

In a similar vein, Native characters such as American Eagle and Charlie "Spirit" Iron-Knife (*G.I. Joe*) are naturally skilled trackers simply because of their Native American lineage. However, upon closer look, comic book heroes such as DC's Butcher are good trackers because of their intensive combat training. On a positive note, at least these specific characters appear in stories set in modern times, unlike so many other Indigenous characters.

Too many Native characters become stuck in the past, usually set around the time of the Old West. Though too numerous to mention, Tonto — perhaps one of the most well-known Native American comic book characters of all — is trapped in a fringe-filled, sepia-colored historical setting. Other Indigenous temporal prisoners include Tipi, Little Beaver, Powwow Smith, Red Wolf, Super Chief ("Flying Stagg"), and even the original Turok: Son of Stone (who was stuck so far back in the past that he dealt with dinosaurs, I mean, "honkers," on a daily basis).

This is why we must celebrate the *modern* Native American comic hero. Because casting an Indigenous character in the past is the norm, characters placed in modern times sometimes seem a rarity. Such modern Natives include Forge, Street Wolf, Dani Moonstar, Turok (Dinosaur Hunter), Thunderbird, Warpath, Shaman, Stalking Wolf, and Echo. Extra points are awarded to Native superheroes set in the future: Dawnstar and Scout. Futuristic characters do much to demonstrate cultural continuance beyond the era of the Old West.

Other comic book creators choose to demonstrate Native continuance by rewriting tired stereotypes and accepted histories. Revisionist versions of Indigenous comic books are ones that strive to present stories in a different light. Topps Comics's *The Lone Ranger and Tonto* as well as Jon Proudstar's *Tribal Force* are prime examples of revisionism. *The Lone Ranger* serves to rewrite the familiar tale of the Masked Man and his Faithful Indian companion and *Tribal Force* sets out to reconfigure Native American comic book characters altogether.

Of course, *Tribal Force* could also fall into the independent, small-press category, as it had a limited publication run and readership. There are many other Native American comics that do a good job dispelling stereotypes, accurately representing Indigenous continuance, and providing Native human characters, but that do so on a much smaller scale than Marvel or DC releases. Some of these even intricately engage the Native community during the creation process. Examples of these include *Educational Comic Book Series* from the Mille Lacs Band of Ojibwe, *Chickasaw Adventures*, *Peace Party*, *Darkness Calls* from the Healthy Aboriginal Network and *The Raven*, both from Canadian presses.

While these smaller "indie" comics have attained a measure of success, they deal with mostly male Indigenous characters. What about the Native female characters? Both major comic houses, Marvel and DC have produced their fair share of the fairer gender. Marvel gives us Dani Moonstar, Talisman, Echo, and Risque, to mention a few, while DC has produced such memorable heroines as Dawnstar, Manitou Dawn, and Owlwoman. While we must celebrate the existence of these Indigenous female characters, many still carry with them no small measure of stereotypic accoutrements.

We even see the influence of Native American comic books reaching into other media. While Indigenous imagery breaks new ground — especially in Role Playing Games and more recently, video games — problems of negative stereotypes and misrepresentation remain despite these changes in media forms.

With the *Turok* video game, the idea continues of spiritual power attained through ethnic lineage, that is, Instant Shaman. In RPGs like *Shadowrun* (now an Xbox 360 game at the time of this writing), stereotypes found within not only preserve notions of Indian mysticism but also serve to allow the Mohican to take new form: they allow non–Native participants the luxury of becoming the "white Indian" themselves.

Cultural problems of representation remain constant over the years even with the change from the inanimate comic book page to animated and other forms of media. Even as American pop culture may seem, on the surface, to cater to more educated tastes, and demonstrate an attention to more politically correct sensibilities, the continued cultural stereotypes demonstrate otherwise.

The topic of Native American representation in comic books is a complex one, to say the least. It is not an easy one to unravel, in part because many of the elements needed for examination are constantly shifting, as is our interpretation of them. We are investigating not only *just* comic books or *just* the Indian characters in them, but also the understated meaning of the negotiated relationship of these two elements to each other.

Such elements can include timeframe and context. Attention must be given to the collective meanings associated with a particular era, as comics many times constitute detailed *snapshots* of popular culture's history. Similarly, the very manner of the Indigenous character and how the individual is portrayed within the comic must be explored to assess what the contexts mean to a reader.

In addition to an examination of the elements, there are many texts that offer valuable information about comic books, which can often assist in decoding a comic book's meaning. Specifically, these texts serve to describe the importance of the genre in relationship to the outside world. While source material on comic books in general is illuminating, such material provides little specific information about Native American comic book characters.

Thus, a survey of the comic books themselves is imperative for this study. By examining several different titles that include Indigenous characters, common connections and patterns begin to emerge in the way we (Indigenous people) are represented. Upon examination, there are some very specific patterns of generality that most Native American comic books characters fit, which are outlined in this book. By contrast, there are some comics that do not follow this *gestalt*, that in fact establish new precedence for Native characters, which shall also be celebrated here in this text.

Additional insight comes from the very creators of these comic books. It is interesting to see not only what views the authors have about their character but it is also amazing to see how much the characters are changed by the time of publication in order to meet commercial success.

Separately, none of these sources would do much to answer the question of how Native Americans are represented in comic books. However, when used in combination, they become extremely useful in understanding both the presence of Indigenous misrepresentation and what that means for readers. In addition, as an Indigenous comic reader, I draw on all these sources to analyze and explain my interpretation of the depiction.

This multitextural examination has been employed by others who have already produced studies of Indigenous people in various media forms. Stedman's *Shadows of the Indian* extrapolates from many sources, including theatrical plays and harlequin romance novels to examine Native stereotypes. Similarly, Kilpatrick's *Celluloid Indians* finds source material in James Fenimore Cooper's work as well as Sherman Alexie's *Lone Ranger and Tonto Fistfight in Heaven*. While these (and many others listed in the Literature Review section) offer considerable information to Native American characters, none target comic books exclusively. Thus, when examining Indigenous representation in the comic books, we must be flexible in our sources.

Most importantly, aside from all the critical examinations of this topic, it is imperative to gain perspective from a member of the group being misrepresented. I am a member of the Caddo Nation, which allows me to provide a sense of how *one* Native American might view such portrayals. Yet it would be too easy to say that interpretation of this research represents the viewpoint of *all* Native American people, which is absolutely not the case.

Just like any other group of people, no two Native people see eye to eye on a given issue. While I can make an attempt to give a serious and unbiased opinion from a Native American standpoint, in the end, the statements made are my take on the issue and mine alone. In short, while I am Indigenous, I do not speak for *all* Native People on this issue; nor would I want to. Thus, the information and discussion encompasses the data gathered from published discourses, the creators of comic books, and my personal view of the treatment of Native Americans in comic books.

What are solutions to these problems of misrepresentation and stereotyping in comics and other popular media? Perhaps one method to combat ignorance and irreverence for a particular culture is to place control of popular media in the hands of the very peoples being victimized by it. Put simply, it is time for Indigenous people to begin authorship of media that portray us, notably in becoming authors and creators of our own comic books.

Jon Proudstar gives us his opinion about the most important elements about Indigenous comic book characters and the change that is needed. He states that comic creators need to remember:

> That we are a people not a decoration. That we love, hate, live and die. That we are plagued by the by product of sins and atrocities committed by the American forefathers. That the blood of our people stripe the American flag. These facts are constants to our people. And true that some of us are not the best representations of what has survived. But survive we did. The country scorns our existence because we are a constant reminder of a terrible act that was committed by the Americans. And until that sin and or atrocity is acknowledged and the treaties are honored this country will never know solace. We are not a race of illiterate beggars with our hands put forward begging. We are the care takers of God's Earth. It was our responsibility and that sacred promise was ignored by the Americans. Now it is up to their children to write the wrongs of their blood line. Return our right to protect and watch over the sacred lands. Let us walk the way our Ancestors walked and live in a good way.
>
> The best advice that was ever given to me was, "Write what you know." To comic book writers I say this: If you don't know about us then don't write about us [Proudstar interview].

Mayhap it is time to wrest creative control from the hands of those who do not or cannot understand the true meaning of being Indigenous. In the film industry, recent trends have allowed Indians to represent ourselves in ways that we see fit. Take the movie *Smoke Signals* (Chris Eyre, 1998), for instance, which is written, directed, and coproduced by Native Americans. Perhaps a similar revolution must take place within the comic book industry, a change that would allow us as a real people to be represented with distinction and integrity. Maybe.

Until then, comics remain as a useful tool to gauge the world in which we must live. As one author states, "comic books ... [offer] a world-view to a large segment of the American population ... that did not as yet have one [of their own]" [Savage *ix*].

Jon Proudstar believes comic books reflect the overall attitude of the general populace. He aptly states that this "is pretty sad if you think about it. Not only is their portrayals of us off but it sets a standard for youth who know nothing at all of the indigenous culture. If someone at least dips the character in some cultural aspects and slight accuracy that would be great. But writers don't want to do the homework or the time to disseminate tribe from tribe. Why do that when you can just create one or smash a bunch of them together with pictures from history books and dialogue from b-movies?" [Proudstar interview].

With some artistic control from Indigenous writers and artists, comic books may offer a less narrow view of Native Americans. It is my hope that this occurs more and more in the comic industry; if not, then individuals such as I and others may have failed in our attempt to terminate such ignorance. Comics will continue to leave their mark on popular culture and its audience. The choice rests with us as just what mark they leave in the future.

Appendix A:
Major Native American
Comic Book Characters

Indigenous Character/Alter Ego	First Appearance or Series	Publisher	Tribal Affiliation
Acrata	*Superman* (2nd series) Annual no. 12 August 2000	DC	Mexican Indian
American Eagle / Jason Strongbow	*Marvel Two-for-One Annual* no. 6	Marvel	Navajo
Arak, Son of Thunder	*Warlord* no. 48 August 1981	DC	Quontauka tribe
Arrowhead	*Arrowhead* no. 1 April 1954	Atlas	Pawnee
Black Bison / John Ravenhair (occasional villain)	*The Fury of Firestorm* no. 1 June 1982	DC	Bison Cult
Black Condor / John Trujillo	*Uncle Sam and the Freedom Fighters* no. 3 November 2006	DC	Navajo
Jesse Black Crow	*Captain America* no. 292 April 1984	Marvel	Navajo
John Butcher	*Butcher* no. 1 May 1990	DC	Lakota
Captain Fear	*Adventure Comics* no. 425 January 1973	DC	Carib tribe
Chief Man-of-Bats / Great Eagle	*Batman* no. 86 September 1954	DC	Sioux
Johnny Cloud/ "Flying Cloud"	*All-American Men of War* no. 82 December 1960	DC	Navajo
Corona / Kako	*Aquaman: Time and Tide* no. 3 February 1994	DC	Inuit
Coyote / Sylvester Santangelo	*Coyote*	Epic	Paiute
Dawn / Manitou Dawn	*Justice League of America* no. 75 January 2003	DC	Prehistoric North American Native
Dawnstar / Bounty	*Superboy* (1st series) no. 225 March 1977	DC	30th-century Native American planet, *Starhaven*
Duran (villain)	*Superman* (2nd series) Annual no. 12 August 2000	DC	Mexican Indian
Echo / Maya Lopez	*Daredevil* Vol. 2, no. 9 December 1999	Marvel	Cheyenne

Indigenous Character/Alter Ego	First Appearance or Series	Publisher	Tribal Affiliation
Flying Fox	Young All-Stars no. 1 June 1987	DC	
Forge	X-Men no. 184	Marvel	
Gan	Tribal Force no. 1 2002	Mystic Comics	Apache
Hawk, Son of Tomahawk	Tomahawk no. 131 December 1970	DC	
Tom Kalmaku (sidekick; no powers)	Green Lantern / 2nd series no. 2 September 1960	DC	Eskimo
Koda	Koda the Warrior no. 1 2003	Pony Gulch Publishing	Dakota
Little Beaver	Red Ryder no. 1 September 1940	Hawley/Dell	Navajo
Little Raven / Red Raven	Batman no. 86 September 1954	DC	Sioux
Little Sure Shot / Louis Kiyahani	Our Army at War no. 127 February 1963	DC	Apache
Jay Littlebear	Captain Savage & His Leatherneck Raiders no. 1 January 1968	Marvel	Unknown
Manitou Raven	Justice League of America no. 66 July 2002	DC	Prehistoric North American Native
Gabriel Medicine God	Tribal Force no. 1 2002	Mystic Comics	Lakota
Danielle Moonstar "Dani"	The New Mutants / X-Force	Marvel	Cheyenne
Muktuk Wolfsbreath	Muktuk Wolfsbreath: Hard-Boiled Shaman no. 1 August 1998	DC/Vertigo	Siberian Native
Nanabozho / Coyote	Doctor Strange III no. 25 January 1991	Marvel	Native American God
Night Eagle	The Adventures of Superman no. 586 December 2000	DC	Unknown
Ian Nottingham	Witchblade no. 1 1995	Image Comics	
Owlwoman / Wenonah Littlebird	Superfriends no. 7 October 1977	DC	Cherokee
Portal / Charles Little Sky	Avengers no. 304 (1989)	Marvel	New Mexico tribe
Pow-Wow Smith / "Ohiyesa"	Western Comics no. 44 April 1954	DC	Lakota
Psi-Hawk / Michael Proudhawk	Untold Tales of the New Universe: Psi Force no. 1 March 2006	Marvel	
Puma /Thomas Fireheart	Amazing Spider-Man Vol. 1 no. 256 (1984)	Marvel	
Rain Falling	Peace Party no. 1	Blue Corn	Hopi

Indigenous Character/Alter Ego	First Appearance or Series	Publisher	Tribal Affiliation
Sarah Rainmaker	*Stormwatch* no. 8 March 1994	DC/Wildstorm	Apache
Red Warrior	*Red Warrior* no. 1 January 1951	Marvel/Atlas	
Red Wolf / Johnny Wakely	*Avengers* no. 80 September 1970	Marvel	Cheyenne
Michael Redstone	*Squadron Supreme* no. 9 May 1986	Marvel	
Ripclaw / Robert Bearclaw	*Cyberforce* no. 1 October 1992	Top Cow Productions	
Risque /Gloria Dolores Muñoz	*X-Force*, Marvel Comics, no. 51 February 1996	Marvel	Seminole/Latina
Scalphunter / John Greycrow	*Uncanny X-Men* no. 210 October 1986	Marvel	
Scalphunter / Brian Savage	*Weird Western Tales* no. 39 March/April 1977	DC	White, raised by Kiowas
Scout	*Scout: War Shaman*	Eclipse	Apache
Sequoia	*The Adventures of Browser and Sequoia*		Unknown
Shaman /Michael Twoyoungman	*Alpha Flight*	Marvel	Sarcee
Silver Deer / Chanka	*Fury of Firestorm* no. 25, July 1984	DC	
Silver Fox	*Wolverine* no. 10 August 1989	Marvel	Blackfoot
Snake Standing	*Peace Party* no. 1	Blue Corn	Hopi
Snowbird / Narya / Anne McKenzie	*Uncanny X-Men* no. 120 April 1979	Marvel	Inuit
Soothsayer	Chasm, Guardian of Grand Canyon/EcoSqaud	Canyon Comics	Unknown
Spirit / Charlie Iron-Knife	*G.I. JOE* no. 31 January 1985	Marvel	
Straight Arrow / Steve Adams	*Straight Arrow* February-March 1950	Magazine Enterprises	Comanche
Street Wolf / Nathan Horse	*Street Wolf*	Blackthorne Publishing	possibly Nayago
Strong Bow	*All-Star Western* no. 58 May 1951	DC	
Super Chief / "Flying Stagg"	*All-Star Western* no. 117 March 1961	DC	Wolf Clan
Talisman / Elizabeth Twoyoungmen	*Alpha Flight*	Marvel	Sarcee
Lucas Telling-Stone	*Tomb of Dracula* (3rd series) no. 1 December 2004	Marvel	

Indigenous Character/Alter Ego	First Appearance or Series	Publisher	Tribal Affiliation
Victor Ten Eagles	*X-Men 2099 no. 6* March 1994	Marvel	
Tezumak	Justice League of America no. 66 July 2002	DC	South American Native
Thunder Eagle	*Tribal Force* no. 1 2002	Mystic Comics	Lakota
Thunderbird / John Proudstar	*Giant-Size X-Men* no. 1, May 1975	Marvel	Apache
Tipi	*The Durango Kid,* October/November 1949	Magazine Enterprises	Catawba
Tomahawk / Thomas Hawk	*Tomahawk*	DC	White
Tonto	*The Lone Ranger,* no. 1 January/February 1948	Dell	Apache or Potawatomi
Turok: Son of Stone (later Turok: Dinosaur Hunter)	*Four Color Comics* no. 596 December 1954	Gold Key Acclaim	Kiowa
Warpath / James Proudstar	*The New Mutants / X-Force*	Marvel	Apache
Werehawk / Matthew Blackfeather	*Marvel Graphic Novel no. 9: The Futurians* 1983	Marvel	Dakota
Wicasa Wakan / Joshua Brand	*Shaman's Tears* no. 1 May 1993	Image	Lakota
Willpower / William Twotrees	*Primal Force* no. 2 December 1994	DC	Jicarilla Apache
Wyatt Wingfoot	*Fantastic Four* no. 50 May 1966	Marvel	Keewazi Indian Reservation, Oklahoma
Basho Yazza	*Tribal Force* no. 1 2002	Mystic Comics	Navajo

Appendix B:
Literature Review and Resources

The examination of Indigenous people within comic books covers much theoretical ground. While many critical studies of the genre of comic books exist, literary examination of the topic of treatment of Native American characters in comic books is sparse. Much of the information found in this book was derived from an extensive look at the comic books themselves, with supporting evidence from the few critical sources that shed light on this topic. The following works and resources are some of the most important or informative for those interested in the history of the representation of Indigenous peoples, whether in comics or in other media.

Pewewardy's Superheroes

One specific text dedicated to the idea of Natives in comic books is Cornell Pewewardy's chapter "From Subhuman to Superhero," in *American Indian Stereotypes in the World of Children*, edited by Arlene Hirschfelder, et al. (Lanham, MD: Scarecrow Press, 1999). In this chapter, Pewewardy discusses the cultural evolution of Native American characters over the years. As the title suggests, Indigenous people have grown from serving simply as colorful background pieces to become full-fledged heroes.

"Despite the mixed results, there is an encouraging trend toward the increasingly sensitive portrayal of ethnic characters in the comics," says Pewewardy. In many ways this is a true statement, yet not completely accurate, as the *same* stereotypes and generalizations continue to appear in modern comics. Pewewardy cites *Tribal Force* as one of the comics that illustrates this trend toward accurate portrayal of Indigenous people. However, at the time of Pewewardy's writing and at the time of this writing, *Tribal Force* fails to capture the attention of a mainstream audience.

Nevertheless, despite this observation, Pewewardy brings a very important element to the reader's attention. In the text, Pewewardy includes an article featuring information on *Tribal Force* written by Bill Jones in a 1997 edition of *News from Indian Country*. One of the comic's artistic creators, Ryan Huna Smith (Navajo/Chemehuevi), comments on the prevailing stereotypes found in American comic books. He states that

Indigenous characters are more often than not "trackers, or they wear bone necklaces and lots of fringe, or have a cloud of mysticism and an eagle hanging around them." This single statement, in many ways, sums up much of this book's revelations. In addition to the synthesis provided by Pewewardy, his observations prove to be true over and over again with respect to Indigenous characters, and they are discussed at length within this text.

Conversely, Pewewardy provides much research into the imagery found in comic *strips* rather than in comic *books*. Only in the latter portion of the chapter does Pewewardy investigate Indigenous characterizations in comic books. At that, only a brief mention of *Tribal Force* and Dani Moonstar of Marvel's *The New Mutants* is given. This is as far as Pewewardy's cataloging of Indigenous comic characters goes.

While his text is brief, it speaks volumes regarding cultural representation of Indigenous people in mainstream media through the years. Indeed, while it constitutes only a chapter, it is an important work. It stands alone as a serious critique of Indigenous culture in comic books.

More important than all of this, the critique and analysis comes from an Indigenous author (Pewewardy) and thus provides an insider's viewpoint to Native American representation as we see it. For this reason, much respect must be given to his work.

Anyone with a serious interest in ethnic or cultural representation in comic strips would benefit from Pewewardy's text. The author examines the portrayal of many ethnic minorities in comic strips, and he provides commentary on their relevance. While this work focuses on comic books, there is still much research to be done on Indigenous imagery in comic strips, and researchers interested in the latter would do well to begin their investigative efforts starting with Pewewardy's text.

Stedman's Instrument

Raymond William Stedman's exploration of Indigenous stereotypes found in *Shadows of the Indian: Stereotypes in American Culture* (Norman: University of Oklahoma Press, 1982) has been invaluable to this research. While there is only a very brief, specific mention of comic books, Stedman addresses the origins of Indigenous people in popular literature. His analysis of James Fenimore Cooper's work serves as a wonderful primer for those wanting more information on how Cooper has influenced comic books — and the Indigenous people in them — over the years.

Stedman touches upon establishing criteria by which one can evaluate whether a particular medium has negative stereotypes for Indigenous people. These criteria are indispensable for evaluation of both comic books and comic strips, and they are especially important because they stem from the viewpoint of an Indigenous reader. Stedman gives eight guidelines by which to judge media that contain Native content.

(1) *Is the vocabulary demeaning?* Does the media use terms such as *redskin, savage, squaw, brave,* and so forth when describing Indigenous people? People who would normally never speak or write words like "darky" or "mulatto" or "mammy" or "pickaninny" take no notice at all of "redskin" or "half-breed" or "squaw" or "papoose." There is little disagreement today that such terms carry negative connotations. There-

fore, when evaluating comic books, if such descriptions are used, it will be noted that the media employs demeaning terminology.

(2) *Do the Indians talk like Tonto?* Stedman devotes an entire section to this problem. We will see that this comes up time and time again in our examination of comic books. "[No] approximation of Indian conversation in English which smacks even remotely of *Robinson Crusoe* and *The Lone Ranger* can be acceptable until time has made the stereotyping disappear." "The old-time Indian talk is wrong, dead wrong. Someday even writers for the popular media will realize that fact. Someday." Thankfully, there are some exceptions to this Tonto-talk rule in the world of comic books. This work examines several comic book creators who have taken great strides to ensure that this negative stereotype is not perpetuated.

(3) *Do the Indians belong to the feather-bonnet tribe?* Indigenous people thrive on cultural diversity. Much popular media have adopted a pan–Indian approach when portraying Native people. Mass media have "long fostered the idea that Indians have one ethnic, national, and linguistic identity, that said, perhaps, from minor differences in dress or mode of transportation, all Indians look, think, and talk alike." Indigenous people in North America are much more diverse than they are similar. Put another way, while we may share *some* cultural similarities, no two tribal nations are exactly the same. Nor do we all dress alike, though it would seem that way to someone reading comic books. Popular media, however, seem to think that we all should look a certain way or that we should look "Indian" enough. Sadly, many comic books fall into this visual trap.

(4) *Are comic interludes built upon "firewater" and stupidity?* Too many times, the media portray Indigenous people as drunkards, stupid people, or just stupid drunks. "It is the special misfortune of the Indian that in comedy situations of fiction he is either the drunken fool or the sober dolt." In many ways, this type of humor illustrates cultural superiority of one ethnicity over another. Many readers will liken this mentality to media dealing with "jungle" themes, where the natives may be restless and waiting for their white savior. Many comic books of earlier years extensively used this "stupid Indian" device. Some examples of Native characters portrayed with limited mental resources include *Red Ryder's* Little Beaver and *The Lone Ranger's* Tonto.

(5) *Are the Indians portrayed as an extinct species?* This is one of the biggest concerns in examining characters in comic books. This presentation of Natives as existing in the past *exclusively* is a recurrent element. "In popular fiction and drama the settings of Indians stories are almost always the past, a situation that can cause even adults to forget that [at the time of Stedman's writing] more than 1.3 million Indians are living varied lives within the boundaries of the United States. Unfortunately, literature and educational materials for children tend to encourage the focus on the past with hundreds of items telling what Indians *did* or *knew* or *were* like. Many of these materials handle the past intelligently, but leave the Indian there."

(6) *Are the Indians either noble or savage?* This dichotomy has pervaded much popular media over the years. This misrepresentation carries over into comic books as well. "An Indian too good to be true or too bad to be believed? Suspect shallow research and narrow viewpoint — especially if those feather bonnets are in view." In comic books, an Indigenous character can seem ill-developed when they are too noble or too savage.

Typically, these characters are only stereotypes of human traits. Many comic books suffer from this shortcoming even today (thankfully less frequently than in times past).

(7) *Is the tone patronizing?* While it should be self–explanatory, this theme is a bit harder to define within the comic book realm, given that many of the early works were written for a younger audience. When examining patronizing tone in comic books, generally speaking, references are made that utilize the above stereotypes. While these negative characteristics may manifest themselves explicitly (through actions or imagery), perhaps they only make reference to these stereotypes (through words). A patronizing tone can be just as harmful as an overtly negative imagery.

(8) *Is Indian humanness recognized?* While this should be a no-brainer, it is one of the most important elements of the criteria and it is a recurring problem in comic books. This also serves as a main focus for this book: evaluating a medium for its ability to recognize that Indigenous people are human and real. "In sum, are [Indigenous people] seen in something resembling full dimension?" It is important that Indigenous people are seen as "real" people and not just caricatures.

Comic Book Culture

One cannot accurately discuss comic books and their cultural significance without referring to William J. Savage, Jr.'s examination of comic books. Often cited in many sources on the analysis of comic books, this text offers a snapshot of America's attitude as reflected in comic books. Thus, this text's relevance is immeasurable.

In *Commies, Cowboys, and Jungle Queens* (Boston: Wesleyan University Press, 1998), Savage illustrates the idea that comic books serve as indicators of culture as he comments on the mental attitudes of Americans from 1945 to 1954. Comics serve as an insight to the American psyche and, therefore, they reflect America's attitude toward Indigenous people during this time. In fact popular media seem to be illustrative of a dominant American culture — one that portrays Indigenous people in a slanted way.

While there are few references to Native Americans in Savage's work, it is important to note the cultural ideas reflected in this book. As noted, this text offers a snapshot of the nation's attitudes toward ethnic minorities and others. Savage's examination serves this study well in exploring comics from that era (1945–1954), such as *Tomahawk*, *Red Ryder*, *Turok: Son of Stone*, and *Tonto*.

Maurice Horn's definitive *Comics of the American West* (New York: Winchester Press, 1976) provides much in the way of illuminating studies in this area. This text offers a clear definition of Red Wolf and his role as hero. Thus, Red Wolf's cultural identity is presented in specific terms.

Red Wolf, who was also "Army scout Johnny Wakely, working out of Fort Rango," was, in actuality, the last descendant in a long line of Cheyenne justice-fighters, the *Owayodata*" (emphasis Horn's). While the series was canceled after only nine issues, Horn tells us that "*Red Wolf* was original enough to be remembered with respect." It is important to note here that Horn does an excellent job of illustrating why this particular character's representation is important for Indigenous people. This text provides background information on Red Wolf's multiethnic identity and also provides the reader with pertinent information concerning tribal affiliation.

Horn relates more about the series cultural importance: "*Red Wolf* marked the first time that an American Indian had assumed the role [of mysterious avenger], and it certainly should be remembered at least for breaking ground in a new direction, even if it proved temporarily unsuccessful." Therefore, when investigating Indigenous characters, especially superheroes, one must understand Red Wolf's role as progenitor of sorts (of course, there are other Native heroes that came before and after him, but Marvel is fairly happy with itself for *saying* he was the first).

Also, Horn points out another feature of *Red Wolf* that lends itself to many other comic book Natives, namely, the presence of a sidekick from the animal kingdom. There was the ever-present "Lobo ... the wolfhead warrior's lupine companion." This became a stereotypic character that would be featured time and again throughout many other comic books peopled with Indigenous characters. In some cases, the animal companions would also take the form of spirit animal.

While Red Wolf is limited to an animal sidekick, other non–Native western heroes were afforded a faithful Indian sidekick. Horn's text serves as an indispensable reference source for these Indigenous sidekicks. Red Ryder's Little Beaver and (of course) the Lone Ranger's Tonto come to mind.

In addition to this information, Horn discusses issues surrounding the interaction of Native Americans within the western comic book. As the author dissects the role of Indian in this genre, it becomes clear that early Indigenous characters were never detailed individuals, whether portrayed as menace or as savior. "The Indian menace was always portrayed as collective: the Apaches, Navahos, Comanches and Cheyennes seen ambushing wagon trains, attacking white settlers, and raiding isolated army outposts did so en masse in a vast display of primitive, demonic and blind destructiveness.... Indians were for a long time depicted as the legions of doom, the modern embodiments of the horsemen of the Apocalypse." This analysis is consistent with Pewewardy's critique of Indigenous characters as being subhuman that existed in comics from earlier years.

Adding to this, Horn's *The World Encyclopedia of Comics* (New York: Chelsea House, 1976) is an extraordinarily wonderful resource for information about the history and players involved in the creation of early comic books. However, it lacks a cultural commentary, especially a Native voice. While this in no way lessens its relevance to our exploration of comics and their place in history, it limits our understanding of cultural relevance within comic books. Horn's texts prove to be excellent sources about comic books in general, yet they require much synthesis of the information to obtain an in-depth examination of Indigenous comic books.

Wright and Philosophy

One source that does take into account both historical and cultural relevance is Bradford Wright's *Comic Book Nation* (Baltimore: Johns Hopkins University Press, 2001). This text illustrates how comic creators attempt to change with the times in order to remain in business over the years. With some of these changes, comic books began altering the way they dealt with and portrayed both the idea of culture and the existence of ethnic minorities.

Comic Book Nation contains relatively few references to Indigenous people within its text. However, even this number is far above the amount found in most other texts. While brief, Wright investigates some key issues in comic books that contain Indigenous characters.

One chapter examines comic books from the World War II era (1939–1945). In this segment, Wright illustrates the message of unity found in comic books. "A recurring theme found superheroes urging American Indians to abandon their traditional hostility towards the United States for the sake of the national war effort." In one such example cited in Wright's notes on *Spy-Smasher,* no. 1, a group of Native Americans are incited to revolt by a Japanese spy pretending to be one of them.

Wright's notes indicate that this representation of Indigenous people as easily duped — and therefore of a lower intelligence — is an all-too-common stereotype found in other comics as well. An example includes *All Star Comics,* no. 12, "wherein Japanese agents incite Southwestern American Indians to attack a U.S. Army base." However, this stereotype of the stupid Indian is lifted in *Green Lantern,* no. 6, "in which various tribes throughout North and South America pledge to fight for their respective governments against the Axis" and appear "intelligent and cosmopolitan."

In the 1950s, not even Indigenous people in comic books were safe from Cold War mentality. "DC's comic books consistently emphasized cooperation and understanding over accusation and confrontation." In one DC comic, *Tomahawk,* no. 11, Indigenous people and whites settle their differences and work together. In lieu of "military confrontation that could destroy them all," this is a notion that mirrored the fears of many individuals at this time. In Wright's estimate, one missing element (thankfully) is any mention of Indigenous stereotypes.

Of course, not all Indigenous comic book stories offered so creditworthy a scenario. In Wright's description of revisionist writer and comic book creator Harvey Kurtzman, we are given a less positive outlook. In *Two Fisted Tales,* no. 27, General George Armstrong Custer is portrayed as a bloodthirsty warmonger. While the non–Native is cast in a villainous light, the comic did point out some mistreatments Indigenous peoples had suffered at the hands of the American government. Yet, in doing so, this comic book made Native Americans into perpetual "victims." While these wrongdoings are indeed true, portraying Indigenous people as victims lends itself to a certain degree of stereotypes as well.

Indeed, this idea of the Indigenous victim was portrayed in other comics as well. Wright discusses the *Green Lantern/Green Arrow* series in the chapter "Questioning Authority." During the Vietnam War era, this comic book attempted to revamp its image by questioning outlooks that reflected blind optimism in the government's policies. In doing so, the series "immersed its superheroes in the social and political issues of the times" including "the plight of Native Americans." Most assuredly, this "plight" was similar in tone to the Kurtzman comic book (above) and also, most assuredly, cast Indigenous people as helpless victims with no free will of their own. While many transgressions occurred to Native Americans, they are still human and not just victims.

Wright's text includes a discussion of the roles Indigenous people have played in

American comic books over the years. The presence of Indigenous people in comic books could at times serve to illustrate changing ideals in America. The text points out that these changing ideals have led to changes in the identity of superheroes, allowing more minorities to become metahuman champions. Of course, several of these were Native American superheroes.

Wright points out how comic book publishers "took some inspiration from the awakening of multiculturalism and the transformation of popular assumptions about race." Because of this awakening, creators began to explore superheroes of ethnic minority. Wright describes Marvel Comics "first Native American superhero, Red Wolf, [which] lasted only nine issues" by stating that the "Red Wolf adventures were set in the Old West and transpired outside the Marvel universe."

Initially, while this may not seem to offer an in-depth amount of information, the text does contain much that is noteworthy. The description of Red Wolf is short yet highly informative. It was written at a time when publishers were exploring ideas of multiculturalism, and it is useful to notice that the series was killed off after only nine issues. Therefore, while the Red Wolf character might have represented an attempt by the publishers to broaden the comic's cultural content, the purchasing public seemed to care very little.

Also note the temporal setting of *Red Wolf*. This superhero is found "in the *Old West*" (emphasis mine). This is not a contemporary Indigenous champion of modern times. Red Wolf, like so many other Indigenous comic books characters, is forced to remain locked in historical times only. This gives credence to the stereotypic notion that Indigenous people existed only in the past and do not live today.

As Wright continues, Marvel's next attempt at a Native American superhero was even less successful than the first. Thunderbird was a member of the new X-Men. Wright describes him "as an angry young man that was deeply hostile towards white society." Because of this he was in constant quarrel with his new teammates. Wright describes the success of this Indigenous character by stating, "the series' creators killed him off after only three appearances." Ouch.

While Wright and Savage discuss the mentality of white America mirrored in comic books, we must also understand the Indigenous worldview. To do this, some key concepts must be explored, namely, the uniqueness of Native philosophy and the diversity found among every tribal nation and it respective worldview.

Tedlock and Tedlock's exploration of philosophical ideals within Native American life found in their *Teachings from the American Earth: Indian Religion and Philosophy* provides an interesting foil to preconceived notions of how Indigenous people act and think within the world of comic books. By contrasting stereotypes with real-life situations and worldviews, the reader is able to see how far from cultural reality some comic book characters fall. While this source does not comment on comic books directly, it does provide a lucid picture of a real worldview by members of specific tribal nations.

Kilpatrick's Insight

From her work, *Celluloid Indians: Native Americans and Film* (Lincoln: University of Nebraska Press, 1999), Jacquelyn Kilpatrick offers much illumination on the notion of misrepresented Native American culture in media. Despite offering commentary exclusively with respect to film, much of the same thematic elements can be applied to comic books, as the two media (many times) share common origins.

Indeed, some Native American comic book characters made it to the silver screen in one incarnation or another. Kilpatrick's work strikes a similar thematic vein and should not be ignored. Also, many stereotypes inherent in both genres stem from similar literary and cultural sources, which Kilpatrick explores and explains. Thus, Kilpatrick's work comprises a healthy companion to this work, as it covers many of the same stereotypic pitfalls that comic books fall into.

Overstreet's Unearthly Knowledge of Comic Books

Robert M. Overstreet's *The Overstreet Comic Book Price Guide* (Gem Stone Publishing, 2000), when used properly, can serve as an invaluable map to a particular comic's history. Bits of knowledge such as publication date, length of run, and publisher can prove immensely valuable in this investigation, especially when so many titles appear with similar names (i.e., *Indians*, *Red*, *Shaman*, *Savage*, or any combination thereof). In addition, Overstreet provides valuable commentary about the current state of collecting comic books in the first few pages of every edition of the book.

Indigenous Humor Explained: Vine Deloria

Despite the name, comic books do not necessarily contain a great deal of humorous material. In fact, there are very few Indigenous people portrayed with a Native sense of humor in comic books. In *Custer Died for Your Sins: An Indian Manifesto* (Norman: University of Oklahoma Press, 1988), Vine Deloria gives an excellent tour of what Indian humor really consists of.

This work serves well as a thematic foil to many of the one-dimensional Indigenous characters found within comic pages. Thus, Deloria serves to provide a template for those individuals developing and creating Native American characters and a sharp contrast for many of the characters examined here.

Coyote Tricks from Dorsey

To better understand how Indigenous culture views Coyote, George A. Dorsey's *Traditions of the Caddo* (Lincoln: University of Nebraska Press, 1997) gives a tribal-specific look at the trickster figure. In addition, since I share this tribal affinity, I am better able to provide synthesis where needed. This text allows for a better identification with the trickster character, Coyote, as found in the comic book with the same title from Epic Comics.

The DC and Marvel Encyclopedias

Information from *The DC Comics Encyclopedia* and *The Marvel Encyclopedia* has no parallel. Both offered from DK Adult Books, these references provide a brief but detailed look at nearly every character within these comic book powerhouses.

Certainly, not all characters can be covered, which can be somewhat limiting, given the (sometimes) obscure popularity of some Native American characters. However, much relevant materials and background information can be found simply by looking through the encyclopedias in their entirety. Many times, while an Indigenous character may not warrant their own succinct entry in the books, they are sometimes at least referenced within other characters' biographies. Thus, the books offer information about Native American comic book characters even when they do not warrant they own individual entries.

The Web

I would be an outright liar if I downplayed the invaluable information on the Internet to research on popular culture, such as this one. The Internet offers thousands (millions?) of websites, each replete with various opinions on comic books (as well as other popular media), some good and some not so good. Along with a wealth of information, there is much useless material to sift through. Despite this, once one removes the nonessentials, much data can be gleaned about comic books.

In addition, the Internet offers amateur comic collectors, the author included, a greater chance to obtain those issues that can be hard to find. (Overstreet comments on this relatively recent phenomenon in his price guide.) With this in mind, here are some websites that offer insight into the world of Native Americans in comics.

Blue Corn Comics

http://www.bluecorncomics.com/

Robert Schmidt may be white, but he and his website offer a wealth of information, views, news, reviews, and opinion on Native American representation in *all* forms of popular media. Using his comic book, *Peace Party* ("A multicultural comic book featuring Native Americans") as a focal point, Schmidt and others ferret out as much information on Indigenous stereotypes as they can find (which is a lot, actually). Recently Schmidt (an avid comic collector himself) expanded the website to include a blog, which offers even more information on stereotypes and in a very timely manner.

The Grand Comic Book Data Base

http://www.comics.org/

The GCD, while not extensive in its information, is an invaluable tool for those researching comic books. Supported more or less by a community of comic book readers, fans, and collectors, the website offers clean, high-resolution scanned images of comic book covers.

These images provide a great deal of information, allowing researchers to view the comic with just a click of the mouse. In addition, GCD offers other bits of information about creative credits, publishers, and publication years, which also greatly assist the researcher of comic books. GCD states as their goal: "We are building a simple database that will be easy to use and understand, easy to add to, and easy for people to contribute to. We will include information on creator credits, story details, and other information useful to the comic book reader and fan. If we are able to take this to its ultimate conclusion, this database will contain data for every comic book ever published."

Michigan State University Libraries — Comic Art Collection, Special Collections Division

http://www.lib.msu.edu/comics/

MSU's online comic book resources, which lists the materials held in the libraries, is a great place to start for those individuals looking to get their digital feet wet or even to expand their collection of Native American characters in comic books. While (at the time of this writing) the information is available only in text, perhaps the online experience can be expanded someday by allowing Internet participants to view a digital copy of the comic books listed here. Until that time, the library's collections of notes, the organization of information, and bibliographic credits serve as important components of research into Indigenous representation.

The Unofficial Guide to the DC Universe

http://www.dcuguide.com/

While this website may not be officially sanctioned by the good folks at DC comics, the information it provides is largely accurate and expansive, at least within the scope of Native American characters.

While the website's search engine works well enough, as an added bonus, the website provides both a biography and a chronology of comics in which the character has appeared. This makes trips to the local comic book shop (or even trips to eBay) more efficient, using an entire list to search for comics with specific Native American characters. The website sums up its position by stating, "This site is not used to make a profit, rather its purpose is to attract more people to the greatness that is DC COMICS."

eBay

http://www.ebay.com

While on the subject of shopping, eBay should be noted. Think what you will about the shopping website, but know that it can indeed benefit those individuals, this author included, looking for very specific comic books, ones that are usually either out of circulation, obscure in popularity, or a combination of both.

Beyond this convenience, the website also has other real benefits. Similar to the Grand Comic Book Database, eBay offers rich and detailed images digitally captured by the sellers. Along with the potential to obtain these particular comic books, this makes eBay an important resource for this subject of study.

Wikipedia

http://www.wikipedia.org/

More and more, wiki sites, like Wikipedia, are becoming a mainstay of individuals looking for particular information. Maintained by and submitted by users, the information is sometimes skewed or inaccurate; however, wikis are a great place to start to begin amassing information, as they provide countless links to internal and external references. Even better are the specialized wikis, which are tailor-made for a particular subject or subtopic only, such as the Official Marvel Wiki below.

Comic Book Resources (CBR)

http://www.comicbookresources.com/

CBR has been around for awhile and they are a great resource for anyone wanting more information on comic books. They have a bevy of contributors and a large online community of people that all share a common interest in the medium. Plus, CBR gets into the heads of many of the big and important names in the creative aspect of comic books, thus the site offers much insider information from the pros themselves.

Marvel Universe: The Official Marvel Wiki

http://www.marvel.com/universe/

"The Marvel Universe is a dynamic, community-fueled online encyclopedia of all things Marvel. It's **THE** definitive place online to find biographies of the 5000+ characters, places, and things that inhabit the Marvel Universe!" This resource, which any comic book reader can contribute to ("subject to moderation, of course!"), is the officially sanctioned wiki for Marvel Comics.

While searching and navigating the website is fairly user-friendly, the real gem is the plethora of official information provided in the character biographies. In addition, similar to the Unofficial Guide to The DC Universe, Marvel's wiki provides an expansive list of comic books where those characters make an appearance. Had such websites such as Marvel Universe existed when I first started this research, this book would have been in print many years ago.

Works Cited

Black Elk (through Joseph Epes Brown). "Hanbleeheyapi: Crying for a Vision." In *Teachings from the American Earth: Indian Religion and Philosophy*. Edited by Dennis Tedlock and Barbara Tedlock. New York: Liveright, 1975.

Deloria, Vine. *Custer Died for Your Sins: An Indian Manifesto*. Norman: University of Oklahoma Press, 1988.

Dorsey, George A. *Traditions of the Caddo*. Lincoln: University of Nebraska Press, 1997.

Edwards, Jen Murvin. Personal Interview. June 3, 2006.

French, Jack. "Straight Arrow: Nabisco's Comanche Warrior." 1996. Online at: http://otrsite.com/articles/artjf003.html.

Grell, Mike. Personal Interview. June 7, 2004.

Horn, Maurice. *Comics of the American West*. New York: Winchester Press, 1977.

_____. *The World Encyclopedia of Comics*. New York: Chelsea House, 1976.

Jimenez, Phil, Daniel Wallace, and Scott Beatty. *The DC Comics Encyclopedia*. New York: DK Adult, 2004.

Kilpatrick, Jacquelyn. *Celluloid Indians: Native Americans and Film*. Lincoln: University of Nebraska Press, 1999.

Mack, David. Personal Interview. Monday, May 21, 2007.

"Marvel Comics Apologize to Hopi." (Reno) *Native Nevadan*, April 30, 1992.

Melmer, David. "American Indian Comic Book Wins Award." *Indian Country Today* (online). Posted: May 24, 2000. http://www.indiancountry.com/content.cfm?id=2555.

Metcalf, Greg. "If You Read It, I Wrote It: The Anonymous Career of Comic Book Writer Paul S. Newman." *Journal of Popular Culture* 29, no. 1 (Summer 1995): 152.

"Native American Portrayals in Comics." Special Program. Eiteljorg Museum of American Indians and Western Art, March 10, 2007.

Odjick, Jay. Personal Interview. April 23, 2007.

Ostrander, John. Personal Interview. April 27, 2004.

Overstreet, Robert M. *The Overstreet Comic Book Price Guide*. New York: Gemstone Publishing, 2000.

Pollack, Rachel. Personal Interview. April 27, 2004.

Pewewardy, Cornell. "From Subhuman to Superhero." In *American Indian Stereotypes in the World of Children*, ed. Arlene Hirschfelder et al. Lanham, MD: Scarecrow Press, 1999.

Rasmussen, Knud. "A Shaman's Journey to the Sea Spirit Takanakapsaluk." In *Teachings from the American Earth: Indian Religion and Philosophy*, ed. Dennis Tedlock and Barbara Tedlock. New York: Liveright, 1975.

Ridington, Robin, and Tonia Ridington. "The Inner Eye of Shamanism and Totemism." In *Teachings from the American Earth: Indian Religion and Philosophy*, ed. Dennis Tedlock and Barbara Tedlock. New York: Liveright, 1975.

Savage, William W. Jr. *Commies, Cowboys, and Jungle Queens: Comic Books and America, 1945–1954*. Boston: Wesleyan University Press, 1998.

Schmidt, Rob. Author's forum. *Peace Party*. Vol. 1, no. 1, "Beginnings," 1999. Blue Corn Comics.

_____. Author's forum. *Peace Party*. Vol. 1, no. 2, "A Prayer of a Chance," 1999. Blue Corn Comics.

Schwartz, Alvin. Personal Interview. April 19, 2004.
Slotkin, J. S. "The Peyote Way." In *Teachings from the American Earth: Indian Religion and Philoso-phy*, ed. Dennis Tedlock and Barbara Tedlock. New York: Liveright, 1975.
Stedman, Raymond William. *Shadows of the Indian: Stereotypes in American Culture.* Norman: Uni-versity of Oklahoma Press, 1982.
Truman, Tim. Personal Interview. February 22, 2004; June 4, 2004.
Wallace, Daniel, et al. *The Marvel Encyclopedia.* New York: DK Adult, 2006.
Wright, Bradford W. *Comic Book Nation: The Transformation of Youth Culture in America.* Baltimore: Johns Hopkins University Press, 2001.

Major Comics Cited

All-American Men of War. "Killer Horse — Killer Ship!" No. 105, September–October 1964.
Alpha Flight. "Turn Again, Turn Again, Time in Thy Flight." Vol. 1, no. 19, February 1985.
Alpha Flight. "Death Birth." Vol. 1, no. 37, August 1986.
Blaze of Glory, no. 1, Marvel Comics.
The Butcher, no. 3, July 1990. DC Comics.
Canyon Comics presents Eco Squad, no. 2, Summer 1996. Grand Canyon Association.
Canyon Comics presents Eco Squad, no. 3, 1999.
Dreams of Looking Up. Published by the Mille Lacs Band of Objibwe, 1999.
Giant X-Men, no. 1, "Second Genesis," 1975.
A Hero's Voice. Published by the Mille Lacs Band of Objibwe, 1996.
The Lone Ranger and Tonto, no. 1, August 1994. "It Crawls! Part One of Four." Topps Comics.
The Lone Ranger and Tonto, no. 2, September 1994. "It Crawls! Part Two of Four." Topps Comics.
The Lone Ranger and Tonto, no. 4, November 1994. "The Last Battle." Topps Comics.
Marvel Two-in-One Annual! The Thing and Introducing ... American Eagle. "An Eagle from America." Vol. 1, no. 6, 1981.
The Official Handbook of the Marvel Universe. Vol. 1, no. 1, January 1983.
Peace Party. "Beginnings." Vol. 1, no. 1, 1999. Blue Corn Comics.
Red Wolf. Vol. 1, no. 1, May 1972. Marvel Comics.
Scout, no. 17. March 1987. Eclipse Comics.
Scout, no. 3, January 1986. Eclipse Comics.
Shaman's Tears, no. 1, May 1993. Image Comics.
Street Wolf, no. 1, 1986. Blackthorne Publishing.
Tribal Force, no. 1. Special Edition. August 1996. Mystic Comics.
Turok: Dinosaur Hunter, no. 13. Valiant/Acclaim Comics.
Turok: Dinosaur Hunter, no. 4. Valiant/Acclaim Comics.
Turok: Dinosaur Hunter, no. 9. "Almost Heaven: New River, Part 3." Valiant/Acclaim Comics.
The Uncanny X-Men. "Lifedeath: A Love Story." Vol. 1, no. 186, October 1984. Marvel Comics.
The Uncanny X-Men. "The Dark before the Dawn." Vol. 1, no. 224, December 1987. Marvel Comics.
Weird Western Tales, no. 39, March–April 1977. "Scalphunter." DC Comics.
Weird Western Tales, no. 62. DC Comics.
Weird Western Tales Starring ... Scalphunter. Vol. 9, no. 47, July–August 1978. DC Comics.
Weird Western Tales Starring ... Scalphunter. Vol. 9, no. 49. DC Comics.
White Indian, no. 12. "Sleep of Death." A-1, no. 101. Magazine Enterprises, New York, 1954.
White Indian, no. 12. "Trees of Doom." A-1, no. 101. Magazine Enterprises, New York, 1954.
X-Force. "Lower East Side Story." Vol. 1, no. 65, April 1997.
X-Force. "The Proudstar Brothers — Together Again for the First Time." Vol. 1, no. 1, July 1997. Mar-vel Comics.

Index